The Payroll Tax
for Social Security

# Studies of Government Finance
## TITLES PUBLISHED

# The Payroll Tax
# for Social Security

## JOHN A. BRITTAIN

*Studies of Government Finance*

THE BROOKINGS INSTITUTION

WASHINGTON, D.C.

*Copyright* © *1972 by*
THE BROOKINGS INSTITUTION
*1775 Massachusetts Avenue, N.W., Washington, D.C. 20036*

THE BROOKINGS INSTITUTION is an independent organization devoted to nonpartisan research, education, and publication in economics, government, foreign policy, and the social sciences generally. Its principal purposes are to aid in the development of sound public policies and to promote public understanding of issues of national importance.

The Institution was founded on December 8, 1927, to merge the activities of the Institute for Government Research, founded in 1916, the Institute of Economics, founded in 1922, and the Robert Brookings Graduate School of Economics and Government, founded in 1924.

The general administration of the Institution is the responsibility of a Board of Trustees charged with maintaining the independence of the staff and fostering the most favorable conditions for creative research and education. The immediate direction of the policies, program, and staff of the Institution is vested in the President, assisted by an advisory committee of the officers and staff.

In publishing a study, the Institution presents it as a competent treatment of a subject worthy of public consideration. The interpretations and conclusions in such publications are those of the author or authors and do not necessarily reflect the views of the other staff members, officers, or trustees of the Brookings Institution.

# Foreword

THE PAYROLL TAX that finances the social security program has increased faster than any other tax since the Second World War, climbing from 4 percent of federal revenue in 1949 to 23 percent in 1971. By 1971 the combined yield of all payroll taxes substantially exceeded that of the corporation income tax and was more than half the yield of the individual income tax. Less important taxes have received detailed scholarly examination, but the payroll tax has grown to its present level with little critical evaluation. Since it has a major effect on income distribution and on aggregate economic activity, a searching analysis is overdue.

In this study John A. Brittain, a senior fellow in the Brookings Economic Studies program, examines and evaluates the economic effects of the federal payroll tax. He argues that the half of the tax nominally paid by employers is actually borne by employees and that the tax is regressive, since no exemptions are allowed and the effective rate of taxation falls as earnings increase. Thus, he maintains, it works not only against antipoverty policy but also against the progressivity of the individual income tax. Moreover, he says, the payroll tax has often been increased, with perverse effect, in times of substantial slack in the economy, and it is ineffective as an automatic economic stabilizer.

Although the regressive effect of the tax on present earners will ultimately be offset by a progressive retirement benefit structure, Mr. Brittain believes that this does not justify the current social security tax rate of more than 10 percent on wage earners in poverty today. He suggests that the introduction of personal exemptions could largely eliminate the burden of the tax on the working poor with only a small loss in revenue. He also presents a case for gradually eliminating the payroll tax and meeting the cost of social security through the personal income tax.

This is the thirty-third volume in the Brookings series of Studies of Government Finance. This study was supported in part with funds provided by the Ford Foundation.

The author is grateful to Charles E. McLure, Jr., Ida C. Merriam, Arthur M. Okun, Joseph A. Pechman, George L. Perry, Carl S. Shoup, Nancy H. Teeters, and others who offered comments and criticism on the manuscript. Capable research assistance was provided by Julia Clones and Sheau-eng Lau; Joan A. O'Brien and Karen Wattel programmed additional computations. The manuscript was thoroughly checked for accuracy and consistency by Brookings staff members under the direction of Evelyn P. Fisher; it was edited by Ella H. Wright; the index was prepared by Joan C. Culver.

The views expressed in this study are the author's and should not be ascribed to the Ford Foundation or to the staff members, officers, or trustees of the Brookings Institution.

KERMIT GORDON
*President*

*July 1972*
*Washington, D.C.*

# Contents

## Appendixes

## Index 281

## Text Tables

## Text Figures

## Appendix Tables

## Appendix Figure

The Payroll Tax
for Social Security

CHAPTER I

# Scope and Significance
# of the Issues

THE PAYROLL TAX earmarked for the financing of social security easily
qualifies as the leading growth tax of the era following World War II.
In 1971 tax collections to finance only the federal old-age, survivors,
disability, and health insurance program (OASDHI, commonly
called social security[1]) reached $44 billion—27 times the level of
1949. This increase represents a compound annual growth rate of
more than 16 percent—enough to raise the share of this tax in the
federal revenue total from about 4 percent to 23 percent. Although
designated a "contribution" in the social security law, it is in fact an
involuntary tax levied without exemptions. In view of further large
tax increases already scheduled, it seems surprising that little critical
or analytical attention has been given to this form of taxation, while
every other type of tax of significant magnitude has been the subject
of detailed analysis in one or more studies. Like Topsy, the payroll
tax just grows while no one is looking.

It is also ironical that, although there is a declared war against

---

[1] Referred to as OASDI before 1966, when health insurance was added, making it
OASDHI.

1

poverty, the fastest-growing tax should be levied on labor income, without exemptions for families in poverty. This absence of exemptions, combined with the ceiling on taxable earnings, results in effective payroll tax rates for the working poor that are far higher than those for upper-income groups. Thus this expanding tax not only tends to thwart antipoverty policy in general, but also works more specifically against the long-overdue relief for the working poor provided under the 1969 income tax legislation (and proposed under the family assistance plan of 1969). These contradictions have escaped the attention of many citizens, presumably because some properties of the payroll tax are not clearly perceived.

A seventeenth-century fiscal maxim concerning the choice among alternative taxes cynically advises "plucking the goose . . . while provoking the smallest possible amount of hissing."[2] Although it is doubtful whether this guideline has been consciously followed, the virtually unchallenged and rapidly increasing reliance on the payroll tax is certainly consistent with such a policy. The main reasons for the lack of resistance to payroll tax increases are: (1) many taxpayers have the impression that their payments are vested in them individually, or at least assume prospective benefits to be worth the cost; (2) the tax rates *seem* low in comparison with income tax rates, and most earners probably do not realize just how much they are actually paying in this form of taxation; they do not consider the employer portion of the tax as a possible burden on themselves, and even the employee portion is subjected to no annual scrutiny such as that given by taxpayers to the income tax at "settling up" time. It will be suggested in this study that several misconceptions have been (and no longer need be) responsible for public acquiescence in this extraordinary expansion of a tax that bears most heavily on the working poor.

The case for the social security program has been skillfully presented. Because the benefit side of the program has probably made a greater contribution than any other public institution to the prevention and alleviation of poverty in the United States, social security has attained the status of a virtually invulnerable political institution. Criticism of the financing of the program has traditionally aroused fears among its veteran advocates that the critics are trying to undermine the entire system. In this setting it may be in order to enter a

---

[2] Jean Baptiste Colbert (1619–83), as quoted in *Forbes*, Vol. 109 (Feb. 15, 1972), p. 22.

preemptive "not guilty" plea at the outset. A negative evaluation of major features of the payroll tax does not necessarily imply a desire to "throw out the baby with the bathwater," as is sometimes suggested. Furthermore, no general critique of social security is implied or intended. However, it will be suggested that the social security tax can be evaluated independently of benefits and that there are more acceptable means of financing this major social program.[3]

The view that "more acceptable" means of financing social security programs are available implies a value judgment on the relative merits of different taxes. This should be made explicit. It is taken for granted in this study that the rate of taxation on income recipients should be based on their "ability to pay," as deduced somehow from their receipts and responsibilities. While no measure of ability to pay commands universal acceptance, it is assumed that high-income groups should be taxed at relatively high rates and that the rate on a given income should be relatively low for large families. Although these principles are not without their critics, they appear to represent a social consensus symbolized in practice by the progressive individual income tax. The payroll tax will be evaluated on this basis and, to repeat, independently of the use made of the tax proceeds.

Although this study seeks to establish some general propositions about any special tax on earnings, it concentrates for illustrative and empirical purposes on actual payroll tax structures in the United States and abroad. Its primary focus is on aggregate payroll taxation, exemplified in this country mainly by the OASDHI tax, including the tax on self-employed persons, and secondarily by the unemployment insurance (UI) tax. Together, these two taxes amount to over 90 percent of all contributions to federal social insurance funds. The UI tax, though small, is included as a part of this total because of special properties discussed in Chapter IX.

The separate retirement compensation taxes on railroad earnings, though levied at higher rates, contain no significant features not illustrated by OASDHI. Federal, state, and local retirement contributions by government employees were also excluded from explicit consideration, because such contributions are more akin to premiums for individual annuities than are other payroll taxes. In the general

---

[3] From the program's inception the possibility of some measure of general revenue financing has been under official consideration, but no substantial proposals along these lines have yet been submitted to Congress.

international analysis of incidence, payroll taxes for family allowances, workmen's compensation, and sickness and maternity are also included in the total.

The scope of this study is limited in two important respects. First, the main emphasis is on the payroll tax itself, rather than on the characteristics or magnitude of associated benefit payments, although there is a digression in Chapter VI in which lifetime income redistribution under the social security program is considered. Since any kind of levy can be used to finance benefit payments, independent analysis of the payroll tax is quite appropriate. However, concentration on the tax precludes any extended discussion of the history and nature of various social security programs.[4] Second, with the exception of the analysis of income distribution effects, the primary concern is with the aggregate impact of payroll taxes, as distinct from allocative effects through a differential impact on industries, firms, and types of labor. This approach is pertinent to the U.S. experience with payroll taxes of uniform rates and very broad or near-universal coverage.[5]

The findings of Chapters II and III imply that allocative effects are of secondary importance in the case of any payroll tax with broad coverage. In recent years the appearance or consideration of discriminating levies, such as the British selective employment tax (SET) and earnings taxes on commuters, has led to interest in possible allocative effects. In the context of an analysis of incidence, the impact of a discriminatory tax of the SET type is considered briefly under simplified assumptions in the next chapter. The model indicates the determinants of the degree of reallocation of factors to the favored sector, but the primary objective is to show that such reallocation is

[4] For a recent analysis of the objectives, history, structure, and effects of the principal U.S. social security program (OASDHI), see Joseph A. Pechman, Henry J. Aaron, and Michael K. Taussig, *Social Security: Perspectives for Reform* (Brookings Institution, 1968). Also see, for example, earlier descriptions and analysis of this program by Seymour E. Harris, *Economics of Social Security: The Relation of the American Program to Consumption, Savings, Output, and Finance* (McGraw-Hill, 1941), and Robert J. Myers, *Social Insurance and Allied Government Programs* (Irwin, 1965).

[5] Even in the case of the UI tax, which has differential rates and falls considerably short of universal coverage, the coverage is broad enough to make little reallocation due to the tax seem feasible. The relatively small and structurally atypical excluded sector could not absorb much capital and labor from the predominant covered portion of the economy. Nor do the rate differentials seem large enough to cause movement of capital or labor between states. (This is not to say that such differentials are never important; possible effects are discussed in Chapters II and IX.)

not inconsistent with the hypothesis that labor bears the employer tax. Although largely beyond the scope of this study, allocative effects merit future consideration in their own right, even though SET, the most interesting and controversial case, appears near its end.[6]

Were it not for conceptual ambiguities concerning payroll taxation, its sheer magnitude would undoubtedly have been sufficient to attract considerable attention over the years. The broadest variant of this tax at the federal level is designated "contributions for social insurance" in the national income accounts and applies to wage, salary, and self-employed income. This tax on employment income reached about $56.0 billion in calendar year 1971, substantially exceeding the corporation income tax and bringing in over one-half the yield of the federal individual income tax. Contributions to state and local social insurance programs amounted to an additional $9.2 billion in 1971.

The maximum tax per employee for OASDHI alone rose from $60 in 1949 to $811 in 1971 and is due to reach $1,320 in 1974, by which time as much as $2,640 annually may be paid in the name of a two-earner family, even if no further tax increases have been enacted. The steady growth of this tax has at last stimulated grumbling: "After hearing for years that Social Security benefits are too low . . . Congressmen are now deluged with complaints that Social Security taxes are becoming burdensome."[7] This long-delayed reaction would undoubtedly have appeared earlier and been sharper if the public had had a better understanding of the function and burden of these taxes.

In addition to the quantitative importance of payroll taxation, its properties are highly significant for many policy questions. What marks may be given its rate structure in the context of antipoverty policy? How does the tax structure fare on other tests of equity? Does this tax on the use of labor affect employment, tending to encourage

[6] The only comprehensive and important study of the allocative effects of the SET is W. B. Reddaway, *Effects of the Selective Employment Tax: First Report on the Distributive Trades* (London: Her Majesty's Stationery Office, 1970). Although a careful study, it seems inconclusive because it cannot separate the effects of SET from the effects of "other abnormal new factors." The study was praised for raising the level of debate "by introducing much new material, by correcting misunderstandings and by setting an example of clinical objectivity" in the *Times* (London), March 5, 1970. However, an opposing view stated: "The report is academic speculation run riot, and a fearsome demonstration that economic analysis can blast off and soar into the empyrean beyond the range of human comprehension" (George Schwartz, *Sunday Times* [London], March 15, 1970).

[7] *New York Times* (March 20, 1967), p. 15.

automation and the replacement of labor by capital? How should the employer contribution be treated in the collective bargaining setting? What is the appropriate income tax treatment of that portion of employee compensation withheld for social security contributions? What role does payroll taxation play in economic stabilization and growth? What ultimate rate of return can employees expect to receive on their "saving" under this tax? What is the impact of payroll taxation on international economic relations, migration, and the relative labor costs of competing economies? The answers to these questions emerge from an analysis of the incidence and other key properties of the tax.

There is also evidence that issues surrounding the payroll tax will become even more important in the years ahead. The upward trend in this tax is spreading to the local level, where city governments are resorting to payroll taxes of various types, particularly as a means of taxing nonresidents employed in the city. The upper limit of this form of taxation has obviously not been reached in this country; it bulks far larger in Europe (about 30 percent of payrolls in France, for example) and in many less industrialized countries. In addition, Britain has endowed payroll taxation with a "functional" role, seeking to move labor from service industries to manufacturing by means of a selective payroll tax favoring the latter. Thus the payroll tax is sufficiently important to merit far more analysis than it has received to date.

## Misconceptions Shielding the Payroll Tax

Large increases in social security payroll taxes have sailed through Congress again and again with scarcely a ripple of opposition from congressmen and (until recently) from their constituents. To ask why repeated increases in a direct tax of this magnitude should arouse so little reaction could be instructive; certainly this acquiescence is in marked contrast to the fierce opposition generated by virtually any proposal to raise income tax rates. A "good press" and rising benefits have helped prevent the development of public criticism of the payroll tax. More specifically, there appear to be two major misconceptions that have enabled payroll tax increases to pass almost unnoticed through the political process. An initial understanding of these is essential to evaluation of this form of taxation.

## The Misleading Analogy to Private Insurance

The key misconception is the image of the payroll tax as a "contribution" to a "trust fund" analogous to private contributions under a private insurance program. This conception persists despite the facts that (1) the tax is involuntary, (2) the trust fund at a given moment could finance only about one year's benefits, and (3) individual benefits are only tenuously related to taxes paid.[8]

From the point of view of this study, a critique of the insurance "principle" is the first order of business; there is no logical justification for independent analysis of the tax unless this insurance analogy is challenged.

Social security experts have fostered the analogy between social security and private insurance since the inception of the program. For example, the Social Security Administration has told covered earners: "Your account number on your social security card identifies your old-age and survivors insurance account. Your card is the symbol of *your insurance policy* under the Federal social security law."[9] This language is not used currently; however, more recently Wilbur Cohen, then undersecretary of Health, Education, and Welfare, wrote:

Under Social Security the risk insured against is loss of earnings from work. When earnings stop because of disability, retirement, or death, insurance benefits are paid to partially replace the earned income that has been lost. The loss occasioned by the occurrence of the risks is actuarially evaluated, and contributions sufficient to cover these costs are provided for. Benefits are paid from those contributions on a predetermined basis when and if the risks covered eventuate. The right to these insurance benefits is a legal right enforceable in the courts. These are the characteristics that make Social Security "insurance."[10]

While social insurance and private insurance have elements in

---

[8] Under any given piece of social security legislation, prospective benefits are related to earnings experience. However, this relationship has generally changed under each new legislation, and no level of benefits either absolute or relative (among age cohorts) is guaranteed by law. For a contrary view stressing the significance of benefit–earnings relationships, see Carl S. Shoup, *Public Finance* (Aldine, 1969), pp. 164, 167.

[9] Social Security Administration, *Insurance for You and Your Family* (1952), p. 11, as cited by Ray M. Peterson, "The Coming Din of Inequity," *Journal of the American Medical Association*, Vol. 176 (April 8, 1961), p. 38. (Emphasis added.)

[10] Wilbur J. Cohen in a letter to the editor, *Washington Post* (Sept. 1, 1967), p. A 20.

common, the above statement is seriously misleading and in some respects inaccurate. First, the risks or expected costs cannot be "actuarially evaluated" in the usual sense because (1) the expected loss is not related to age, health, and other individual characteristics, and (2) even in the aggregate, demographic projections are not the sole basis for forecasting the cost of the program; this depends heavily also on future benefit legislation, which cannot be forecast by scientific means. Second, benefits are not on a "predetermined basis," since they are not vested in any individual and are changed repeatedly by legislation. Third, not only are individual benefits only loosely related to taxes paid, but "the right to these insurance benefits" has on occasion been denied by the courts on grounds that it is not a contractual interest and therefore not really analogous to the case of a private insurance or annuity program. Fourth, unlike a private program, participation and "contributions" are compulsory.[11]

Despite the weaknesses of the argument, this strenuously promoted insurance analogy has proved extremely powerful; it has been used explicitly to stave off criticism of the payroll tax and such suggested reforms as the introduction of exemptions. For example, over a decade ago, a high social security official stated: "The argument as used in the United States for [rejection of low-income exemptions] under Old-Age Insurance is that the contributions, though legally a tax, *are a premium* for social *insurance benefits.*"[12] Thus, the implication of the insurance analogy is that the poor must pay for their federal social security as they would under private insurance programs—if they could afford them. From this viewpoint the tax is to be charged without consideration of ability to pay. It should be added that under social security the working poor are given no choice: they are required to pay the tax now and go deeper into poverty. In the private sector they are at least free to take their chances on the future rather than to make themselves even worse off in the present. In contrast, the social security program has adopted a patronizing attitude; it appears to imply that the poor are profligate if they prefer to spend their income now and that they must not be allowed to do so. The

[11] This point should be qualified. Pension schemes collectively negotiated in the private sector, for example, are not voluntary for the person accepting a particular job. However, the collective agreement on pension plans is voluntary, unlike the requirement to pay a tax.

[12] Robert M. Ball, now commissioner of the Social Security Administration, cited in Peterson, "The Coming Din of Inequity," p. 38. (Emphasis added.)

issue this raises is not whether provision should be made for the future of the poor; the real issue is whether this should be accomplished by a tax on the poor themselves or by other means. Adherence to the ability-to-pay criterion obviously rules out the taxation of the poor and calls for an alternative pattern of financing.

The persistence of the conception of the "contribution" as an insurance premium is especially surprising in light of the obvious fact that individual benefits are not closely related to the tax paid. For example, groups first covered after World War II, such as older self-employed persons (including physicians), have received benefits far beyond anything remotely "justified" by their brief taxpaying experience.[13]

On the other hand, workers who will have paid into the system for nearly fifty years are not guaranteed any specific level of benefits. The Supreme Court has stressed that the taxpayer does not have a contractual interest in benefits; the court has also stated: "The noncontractual interest of an employee covered by the Act cannot be soundly analogized to that of the holder of an annuity, whose right to benefits are based on his contractual premium payments."[14]

The government has been selective in its invocation of the insurance principle. For example, the ruling in the case cited above involved a 1960 test of the constitutionality of a provision prohibiting payment of social security benefits to persons who had been deported for subversive activities. In this context the insurance principle became a logical liability to the government. In its brief, denying that a right to benefits was earned by paid contributions, the administration explicitly rejected the insurance concept: "The OASI is in no sense a federally-administered 'insurance program' under which each worker pays 'premiums' over the years and acquires at retirement an indefeasible right to receive for life a fixed monthly benefit, irrespective of the conditions which Congress has chosen to impose from time to time."[15]

Since the insurance principle has been officially endorsed in support of taxes and rejected in denial of benefits, it is not surprising

[13] Disparities of this type will tend to disappear with maturation of the system; however, as shown in Chapter VI, some earners fare much better than others for many other reasons.

[14] *Flemming v. Nestor*, 363 U.S. 603 (1960).

[15] *Ibid., Records and Briefs* 10.

that attempts have been made to lay it finally to rest. Barbara Wootton made a lucid effort to dispose of the insurance analogy as follows:

As things are, everybody now recognizes an increasing element of fiction in current insurance schemes. As Americans have cause to realize, the coverage of income-maintenance schemes tends almost irresistibly to expand. But as these schemes become more generalized, their insurance basis becomes more and more illusory; until in cases where, as in Britain, virtually universal coverage has been attained, fiction ousts fact altogether.

At this point, the simple facts of the situation are that benefits on a prescribed scale have been promised, and that funds must be provided to meet them; that is all. In these circumstances, the allocation of precise fractions of contributors' payments to cover particular risks becomes an academic, rather than a genuinely actuarial, exercise. The performance of this exercise in the sacred name of insurance demands, however, elaborate and expensive systems of recording the experience of millions of beneficiaries. These monumental systems are indeed a tribute to the skill and accuracy of the administrators who devise them, and to the ingenuity of the mechanical devices employed in their operation; but are they really necessary, and have they, indeed, any meaning? Is it, in fact, worth maintaining what has become no more than a facade?[16]

Mrs. Wootton's rhetorical concluding question is perfectly reasonable, but the answer is a simple one; the fact is that many believe maintenance of the insurance analogy is indeed essential for pragmatic reasons.[17] The facade and trappings of insurance encourage the conception among individual social security taxpayers that their "contributions" to a trust fund insure them against income loss before and after retirement age and that they get what they pay for, plus interest.[18] The insurance analogy constitutes a "preemptive strike" against potential taxpayer and legislative resistance to payroll tax increases; the budget-minded legislator in particular may be soothed by the concep-

[16] Barbara Wootton, "Impact of Income Security upon Individual Freedom," in James E. Russell (ed.), *National Policies for Education, Health, and Social Services* (Doubleday, 1955), pp. 386–87.

[17] It is commonly believed that Congress will approve substantial benefit increases only if they are financed by the payroll tax and viewed as insurance benefits. Even if this is true, it does not follow that further modest departures from the insurance model (sparing the poor, for example) would choke off benefit increases.

[18] In the developing stages of the system, participants with a short taxpaying experience have fared much better than this, but such results are not likely under a mature system; and no level of benefits is legally guaranteed, even in *current* dollars, as it is under private insurance. These issues are discussed in Chapter VI.

tion that each prospective recipient of benefits will pay his own way under the system instead of living off taxpayers in general.[19]

It would probably be generally agreed that the celebration of the "insurance principle" has been a key factor in the headlong growth of payroll taxation in the United States. It also seems unlikely that social security benefits would have reached even their present level (widely judged to be inadequate) had it not been for the conception of the tax as an insurance premium. However, even though the conception is strained, it is time to recognize that its perpetuation may also have had undesirable effects. It tends to shield the payroll tax from rational criticism. A general understanding that individual taxes and benefits are not tied together either legally or in practice would open the door to consideration of alternative financing of benefits. No longer would it be possible to assert convincingly that a heavy tax on poor families today is justified on the ground that they—like others more fortunate —are simply saving for their old age. The response to such an assertion could be threefold: (1) there is no contractual connection between what they are paying and what they will get; (2) even if there were, forcing the poor to save is a unilateral act denying them the opportunity to exercise their understandably high preference for present income over future income; and (3) there is no reason (other than possible pragmatic ones) for failing to discuss alternative mixes of taxation that would finance the same total level of benefits in a way less burdensome to the poor.

It is not the role of this study to document the degree of departure of social security programs from the pure pattern of private, individual "pay-for-yourself" insurance and pension plans. The compulsory "contribution," the lack of contractual commitment, and the absence of accumulation of payments in the name of the individual offer significant evidence of the discrepancy. The fact that the net impact of taxes and benefits over the lifetime of participants reduces the inequality of lifetime incomes can also be readily established. In fact, this lifetime redistribution assures that low-income groups do better under

---

[19] The insurance premium conception is only one variant of the "earmarked" tax. There are other examples of easy passage for such taxes—for instance, large payments into trust funds for highway programs. While these taxes are not strictly comparable, one reason for public tolerance of social security and highway tax increases is that they can be related to visible results.

social security than under most pay-for-yourself plans and shows clearly that social security is already a redistributive program.[20]

In short, the insurance analogy is a contrived one at best and is certainly not forced upon us by the facts. The essential point here is to make clear that the analogy has had unintended side effects. Most important, it has encouraged a virtually unchecked growth of the payroll tax while inhibiting examination of the features of the tax itself, such as its burden on the poor. It seems evident that the link between individual taxes and benefits is so weak that the tax can and should be examined independently and on its own merits.

## The Unperceived Burden on the Poor

The second major factor shielding the payroll tax from the criticism to which other taxes are usually subjected is a lack of perception of the burden it imposes. In the first place, in weighing the tax burden on individual earners there is a tendency to consider only the employee portion of the payroll tax and to ignore the employer portion. If, as economic theory suggests, the employee pays both parts, the burden on earners is twice as great as what is perceived by most observers.[21]

A second aspect of the tax burden, perhaps generally overlooked, is the failure to exempt the first bracket of income, to say nothing of the failure to take into account the family responsibility of the earner. With no payroll tax return to file, taxpayers are not likely to dwell on this. Even earners who note the absence of exemptions may not realize the extent to which this raises the payroll tax on low incomes. In the continued absence of exemptions, the total OASDHI and UI tax paid in the name of the working poor is scheduled to approach an effective rate of about 13 percent by 1973. In sharp contrast, even though the income tax rate for the first bracket is 14 percent, the exemptions

---

[20] The differential yields to various hypothetical participants are illustrated in Chapter VI. Far greater contrasts in yield could have been demonstrated if such cases had been considered as those of very-short-term contributors qualifying for the minimum and very-long-term contributors who worked after the age of sixty-five and lost benefits as a result.

[21] It should be reemphasized that assertions in this study about the burden of taxes do not imply that later (related) benefits are unlikely. Even current benefits are undoubtedly present in any social insurance program, since earners are spared some of the cost of supporting relatives. However, the issue considered (especially in Chapters II and III) is the real burden of the tax earmarked to finance social security benefits. Since part of the tax on earnings is nominally paid by employers, this question is especially important.

and standard deductions lead to an effective income tax rate of zero for most families in poverty. If a typical family of six earning a poverty-range income of $5,000 (and exempt from income tax) believed that it could retain about $650 more in take-home pay if there were no social security taxes, its resistance to the tax would probably be far greater than at present.

In sum, the image of the payroll tax as an insurance premium and the inadequate conception of its burden combine to insulate the tax from the kind of criticism likely to be engendered by a large levy that imposes its maximum rate (with respect to wages) on earners below the UI ceiling (generally $4,200) and therefore on many working poor.

## Issues concerning the Burden of the Tax

It was suggested above that the payroll tax probably places a heavier burden on earners than is generally realized.[22] Presumably most taxpayers assume that the employee tax reduces their take-home pay but that the employer tax does not, since it is not deducted from their stated wage. However, such an assumption may be questioned on two grounds. First, it conflicts with a generally accepted theorem of public finance (subject to minor qualifications) that the effects of a tax are the same whether it is imposed on one side of the market or the other —in this case, either the employer side or the employee side. Second, many economists dealing with the issue have taken the position that labor bears both taxes. The incidence analysis in Chapters II and III concentrates explicitly on the employer tax, because its incidence has been most explicitly debated in the literature. However, it should be borne in mind that, according to the theorem mentioned, any result established for this tax holds for the employee tax as well. (This methodological question is taken up in detail in the technical note at the end of Chapter II.)

The OASDHI employer tax is portrayed in some of the official literature as fundamentally different in both nature and effects from the employee tax, which is generally thought of as a premium on which the employee's ultimate benefits will depend (even if the rela-

---

[22] Some of the problems considered in this section and in Chapters II and III were discussed in the author's article, "The Incidence of Social Security Payroll Taxes," *American Economic Review*, Vol. 61 (March 1971), pp. 110–25 (Brookings Reprint 197).

tionship is not a close one). However, the insurance analogy is not always applied to the employer portion, even though this tax is also paid in the name of individual employees. While statements on this subject issued in the name of the Social Security Administration do not necessarily represent an official position, the individual expressions of opinion are instructive. According to Robert J. Myers, then chief actuary of the Social Security Administration, the employer contribution "must necessarily be considered to be pooled for the general benefit of all covered persons."[23] In particular, this part of the payroll tax is to be used to help cover "past service credits"—substantial benefits paid to late arrivals within the system and benefits to others whose lifetime contributions were meager.

Although conceding that the employer tax "is borne in considerable part by employees,"[24] this 1967 statement by the actuary rejects its imputation to individuals in whose name it is paid as inaccurate and inconsistent with the *assumed* pooling of the employer tax. Rejection of this imputation in the context of analysis of income distribution effects builds a bias into the analysis if, in fact, employees do bear the tax in aggregate. It does so by failing to take account of a tax that increases income inequality. How a tax borne by labor in the aggregate can be ignored in weighing the burden on individuals has never been explained. The effect of the assumption is to treat the tax as though it is a burden on everyone in general and at the same time a burden on no one in particular.

Obviously, the arbitrary assumption concerning the allocation of the employer portion of the tax among benefit recipients is irrelevant to an appraisal of the burden of the tax itself on individuals. It is a non sequitur to assert that the employer tax must be pooled in allocation of benefits and that *therefore* the burden of the tax itself cannot be assigned to individuals. Nevertheless, the selective application of the insurance concept has inhibited analysis of the tax and its incidence. Adherence to the concept with respect to the employee tax (despite substantial contradiction by the facts) discourages consideration of modifying the tax. Rejection of the concept with respect to the

---

[23] *President's Proposals for Revision in the Social Security System*, Hearings before the House Committee on Ways and Means, 90 Cong. 1 sess. (1967), p. 331. It should be repeated that this statement on behalf of the Social Security Administration represented the opinion of Mr. Myers, who has left the administration after many years as chief actuary.

[24] *Ibid.*

employer contribution has been used to exclude imputation of this tax to labor in studies of income distribution effects.[25]

The question whether there is any inherent difference between the two taxes is directly relevant to the incidence question. Many writers concerned with the social security tax have assumed that the employee tax is borne by labor;[26] if there were no difference between the two taxes it would follow that the employer tax is also borne by labor. It is difficult to conceive of any difference between employer and employee taxes other than their labels. From the point of view of the employer, his share of the tax is no less a part of his total labor costs than the portion of wages and salaries that he withholds for the employee tax. From the point of view of the employee, there should be no distinction between those parts of his total compensation (as officially defined in the national income accounts) that are withheld as employer and employee tax respectively. Each tax is withheld from his total compensation and sent to Washington, just as is his income tax. From that perspective, the employee is paying both parts of the payroll tax.

It should be added that a questionable conception by the employee that the taxes are fundamentally different would not, in any case, cast doubt on the hypothesis that labor bears both taxes. A defense of the latter assumes only that the employer makes no distinction between the two and regards each as a part of his total costs. The real amount of total compensation, including the withheld contributions, that can be extracted from him depends on fundamental factors such as productivity and product demand. (This does not rule out short-run deviations from this norm, such as those caused by lags between tax increases and wage adjustments.) There is no reason to suppose that an increase in either of these withheld payroll taxes would increase the total amount of employee compensation. Thus, it is to be expected that any tax increase will tend to result in an after-tax wage increase that is lower by about the same amount. If so, the tax is completely shifted to the employee through a direct trade-off between the tax and the after-tax wages.[27]

[25] Some studies mentioned in Chapter IV have nevertheless considered various imputations of this tax to individuals.

[26] For examples, see Chapter II.

[27] If employees do not view social security contributions as part of their income and react to tax increases by adjusting hours worked, the issue is more complicated (see Chapter II).

This reasoning is elaborated in Chapter II and tested empirically in Chapter III. The methodological approach relates the after-tax wage to productivity and tax per worker. One general finding is that, given the level of productivity, the higher the tax, the lower the after-tax wage by about the same amount. This offers empirical support to the plausible a priori proposition that labor bears the entire payroll tax. The finding has significant implications for the appraisal of the effects of the tax on employment, income distribution, stability, and growth. It is also essential to appropriate income tax policy, appraisal of the rate of return on "contributions," rational collective bargaining, and the impact on migration and relative labor costs of competing economies.

## Effect of the Tax on Current and Lifetime Income Inequality

The steady development of the progressive income tax into the nation's heaviest levy and the recent provisions for low-income relief indicate a strengthening of the earlier social consensus in favor of exemption of low incomes as well as a rate structure varying with income.[28] However, the more rapidly growing payroll tax, with high rates on low incomes and low rates on high incomes, is increasingly offsetting the egalitarian impact of the income tax. Although families in poverty are generally exempt from income taxes, the total (employer-employee) payroll tax rate on their earnings is higher than the rate for families well above the poverty range. Furthermore, with respect to earnings, the payroll tax is so regressive above the taxable maximum that the combined rate curve for these two direct taxes is actually regressive over a substantial earnings range. For example, in 1973 the combined rate curve applicable to the wages and salaries of a family of four will begin to fall above the scheduled $10,800 ceiling and will not pass its previous peak until the $19,700 earnings level (about $23,000 in the two-person family). With respect to total income, the payroll tax is even more regressive above the ceiling, since the higher the earnings bracket, the lower the share of earned income in the total. The large combined direct taxes on the poor and the

[28] Although the recent low-income relief worked mainly to restore the real value of exemptions, its impact was more progressive than general exemption increases that would also "relieve" higher-income groups.

discrimination against middle-income groups are not justifiable under any generally acceptable standards of equity.

The strong upward trends in this taxation of low-income families are also demonstrated in Chapter IV. For example, the payroll tax rate on wages and salaries only for a family of eight at the poverty borderline rose from about 3.3 percent in 1949 to 10.5 percent in 1969. On the other hand, such a family was completely shielded from the individual income tax throughout the twenty-year period. Before-tax measures of overall earnings inequality showed a slight upward trend over that entire period, but this upward trend was more pronounced in the inequality measures after payroll taxes.

Reforms designed to alleviate the burden of payroll taxes on the poor are considered in Chapter V. It is shown that an exemption scheme with benefits concentrated among low-income families could have removed most of the 1969 payroll tax burden on families in poverty, while the loss of revenue would have been only about $3.2 billion. This loss could have been recouped by a 4 percent rise in the income tax yield, or by other moderate adjustments. Thus the most undesirable feature of the payroll tax could be removed by a modest reform. A complete replacement of payroll taxes by the more equitable income tax would have entailed a 45 percent increase in the income tax yield in 1969. Although this may seem to require an enormous adjustment, it will be shown that an alternative income tax rate structure could accomplish this with a net tax saving to the great majority of taxpayers and without unrealistically high rates for upper-middle- and top-income groups. In sum, low-income relief is within easy reach, and even an end to the payroll tax appears feasible.

There has been considerable debate in recent years about how young earners fare over a lifetime under the social security system. Although this study concentrates on the tax side, Chapter VI digresses to appraise the likely yield on lifetime contributions to social security. Under various simple assumptions, three principal findings emerge: (1) most participants are likely to receive real yields much higher than those averaged on savings accounts over the last half-century and much lower than average yields on equity; (2) the combined tax and benefit system is generally progressive on a lifetime basis, with low-income earners receiving the highest yields, and it would, of course, be more so if the payroll tax were made less regressive or ended altogether; and (3) even though extreme cases are excluded, variations of potential yield from one class of participant to another are great enough to confirm the looseness of the insurance analogy and undermine it as a defense of the payroll tax.

## Effect on Stability, Growth, and Resource Allocation

In Chapters VII and VIII the payroll tax is shown to be a weak automatic stabilizer. Automatic offsetting changes in response to income changes are far less than those under the income tax for several reasons. The payroll tax is smaller, and it operates at a uniform rate up to the ceiling. The ceiling itself renders a large portion of the tax impervious to income changes. As a result, the payroll tax is an ineffectual damper on business cycles and can even become a destabilizer under certain circumstances. On the other hand, as a tax on labor, it cuts less into saving than would a tax on capital and therefore constitutes a lesser drag on growth.

One feature of the payroll tax causes variations in tax collections independently of earnings and rate changes. Because of the ceiling on taxable earnings, monthly collections tend to decline throughout most of the calendar year.[29] These changes may be stabilizing or destabilizing, depending on the phase of the cycle affected. In the case of the UI tax, one feature generally regarded as destabilizing is the "experience rating" system. Seeking to reward employers with stable employment experience, the program reduces (raises) the tax rate when unemployment goes down (up). However, no empirical evidence has been found that this procedure has seriously aggravated postwar cycles.

With respect to the frequent changes in the payroll tax structure, the tax has often proved destabilizing because of arbitrary timing of increases. The tax is revised upward ostensibly to finance benefit increases, rather than serving as a functional contracycle tool. On several occasions the tax increase has aggravated recessions by going into effect just before or during a recession. On the other hand, the 1972 social security legislation (Public Law 92-336) signed July 1, 1972, provides for automatic ceiling and benefit adjustments. The ceiling will move annually in proportion to changes in average taxable earnings in the first calendar quarter (when nearly all earnings are taxable). This holds the effective tax rate approximately constant so that the

---

[29] The decline is not continuous because of lags in collections, as well as of a seasonal low in the earnings base early in the year.

average tax per worker will keep pace with average earnings. At the same time average benefits are to be adjusted only as fast as the consumer price index. Since earnings usually grow faster than this price index, the system will tend to generate surpluses, imposing a "fiscal drag" on the economy, if not offset by higher benefits, other spending increases, or tax cuts.

As indicated earlier, no intensive examination of allocative effects has been undertaken in this study. However, a few points made in Chapter IX concerning this problem may be summarized here. A nearly universal payroll tax borne by labor should have virtually no allocative effects by industry. Differential aspects of some payroll taxes may produce some allocative effects, however. In the case of the British selective employment tax of 1966, nominally paid by employers, the Reddaway report[30] indicates (though not conclusively) that the tax has probably achieved one of its objectives; it appears to have been associated with a shift of labor from services to manufacturing, and an increase in productivity in the former sector sufficient to recoup a substantial portion of the tax. (It will be shown in Chapter II that such an allocative effect is not inconsistent with the proposition that labor bears the payroll tax.)

Regional differences in the employer tax rate for UI and differences among employers may have some allocative effects even though the tax is borne by labor. These should be analogous to SET, with labor tending to move to areas or employers that have low tax rates. However, in the absence of substantial labor mobility, the differentials are probably too small to produce a significant reaction. Finally, a selective payroll tax on commuters could also be expected to have some behavioral effects. In particular, it could slow down the flight to the suburbs of earners with central city jobs; on the other hand, employers would be encouraged to move jobs to the suburbs in order to compete successfully for suburban labor.

## Policy Implications

Policy issues are discussed in some detail in Chapter X; however, it may be noted here that the findings of the study are not unanimously for or against the payroll tax. There is no reason to believe that the tax aggravates unemployment or places a drag on growth,

[30] Reddaway, *Effects of the Selective Employment Tax*.

except insofar as its proceeds are not fully spent. Although the tax is a weak stabilizer, this seems a minor consideration. It is in the area of equity that the tax merits its most severe criticism. Behind the facade of the insurance principle a very large, growing, and regressive tax has come to place a substantial burden on millions of working poor. The finding that the tax rests on labor alone shows that the tax on earners is heavier and more regressive than is generally realized. While low-income earners have recently been granted relief from the income tax, the payroll tax bears on them more heavily than ever and without exemptions.

As the tax rate on the working poor nears 13 percent (11 percent for OASDHI plus about 2 percent for UI), it would seem especially patronizing for their more affluent fellows to assert that it is good for the poor to be forced to save for their old age. It is not for lack of puritan virtue that they want that 13 percent now and would prefer to take their chances on the economic future. Estimates in Chapter VI indicate that some low-income participants will earn real rates of return in excess of 7 percent over a lifetime. Still, it is scarcely justifiable to force the impoverished to save at that yield when they may be forced to borrow at much higher rates to recoup the tax in order to pay current expenses.

Significant additional inequities arise from the ceiling on taxable earnings and the exemption of property income. In short, the case against the payroll tax on equity grounds is very strong. It remains to be seen whether the equity principle can overcome the expediency of the payroll tax as a virtually unchallenged source of revenue.

# CHAPTER II

# Payroll Tax Incidence: Preliminary and Theoretical

THE FUNDAMENTAL PROBLEM in the analysis of payroll taxation is the question of which economic group is *actually* (not nominally) bearing the burden of the employer and employee taxes.[1] The effects of the payroll tax on income inequality and other measures of the performance of the economy depend heavily on the incidence of this tax. Although payroll taxation is based on employment income, part or all of it is designated as an employer "contribution," and the most intense controversy has centered on the incidence of this portion of the tax. Many economists, including the writer, assume that the effects of the two portions of the tax must be essentially the same, but this view does not predominate in the literature on social security. For that reason it was decided to concentrate first in this study on the highly debated employer tax and to reserve inferences about the employee portion until later. This should not disturb the reader who assumes

---

[1] The concept of tax burden applied here and the methodological problems associated with it are discussed in detail in the technical note at the end of this chapter. In broad terms the incidence of the tax is interpreted as its impact on the distribution of income available for private use, with special emphasis on its effect on relative factor shares and real rates of return to factors.

that the effects of both taxes are the same, since for him any acceptable finding concerning one tax is equally applicable to the other.[2]

## Earlier Views and Evidence

Although there has been little written analysis in recent years of the burden of the employer tax, some economists believe that it is virtually axiomatic that the employer contribution is borne by labor in the long run. For example, Milton Friedman has written:

[The total tax for social security] includes what is euphemistically called "a contribution by the employer." Again, this is mislabeling. It is no contribution by the employer; it is a compulsory tax and it isn't paid by the employer; it is, in effect, paid by the wage earner. It is part of his wages that is sent to Washington instead of going to him. The form, the name, doesn't change the substance.[3]

Informal comment by some economists reveals a remarkable confidence in their opinion that labor bears the tax. For example, in a letter of January 17, 1967, Friedman welcomed preliminary statistical confirmation of his view by the author but added: "Indeed, I may say that if your statistical analysis had shown any other result, I would be inclined to regard that as a criticism of your statistical analysis, not as evidence against this particular proposition."

Before World War II considerable analysis of payroll tax incidence appeared in the economic journals. The early literature on the incidence of the employer tax was summed up in 1941:

Economists who, in the years preceding the introduction of the Social Security Act, had given the problem of incidence careful consideration seem to have been in general agreement that a pay-roll tax, whether levied on the worker or the employer, would be paid ultimately by the worker. . . .

In the years that have passed since the Social Security Act became law, the weight of informed opinion still seems to be that the pay-roll tax is borne largely by the workers.[4]

---

[2] Reasons for emphasis on the employer tax are discussed further in the technical note at the end of this chapter.

[3] "Transfer Payments and the Social Security System," *Conference Board Record*, Vol. 2 (September 1965), p. 8. For more detailed analysis by Friedman, see Wilbur J. Cohen, *Social Security: Universal or Selective?* (Washington: American Enterprise Institute, 1972).

[4] Seymour E. Harris, *Economics of Social Security: The Relation of the American Program to Consumption, Savings, Output, and Finance* (McGraw-Hill, 1941), pp. 285–86.

The postwar opinion of economists has been less one-sided. Among government and labor officials who face the issue at the practical level, an agnostic view of the proposition that labor bears the employer tax also appears prevalent. The tax is thus seen by some as mitigating the regressive impact of the tax on employees;[5] similarly, a statement by the Social Security Administration has taken the position that the employer tax should not be imputed to employees in comparing lifetime taxes and benefits under the social security system:

First, it is necessary to make it clear that any such comparison should not include the employer contribution, because that contribution must necessarily be considered to be pooled for the general benefit of all covered persons.[6]

This reason for excluding the payroll tax is unacceptable, since the distribution of *benefits* payable out of the receipts from the employer tax is irrelevant to the question of the incidence of the tax itself. It certainly does not justify treating the tax as a burden on no one. However, acceptance of the premise that the employer tax should not be imputed to labor would have major implications for the analysis of the tax.

The prewar consensus among economists on payroll tax incidence appears to have broken down. For example, George Jaszi has concluded: "The shifting of social security taxes is a matter about which little is actually known."[7] A well-known textbook repeats this view in a very cautious summary of the state of knowledge:

The incidence of these taxes cannot be predicted with any great degree of assurance. On the whole, the safe conclusion would seem to be that it is

[5] The employee tax, if it is not shifted, is generally regressive because the marginal tax rate is usually proportional below some earnings ceiling, and zero above it, and because the tax does not apply to property income, which is concentrated in the higher brackets; a tax truly borne by employers would tend to offset this. On the same incidence assumption, it has been argued that the employer tax can be used to finance the very high return achieved by pensioners with short payment experience in the system, thereby relieving less fortunate workers taxed from an early age.

[6] *President's Proposals for Revision in the Social Security System*, Hearings before the House Committee on Ways and Means, 90 Cong. 1 sess. (1967), p. 331.

[7] "The Conceptual Basis of the Accounts," in Conference on Research in Income and Wealth, *A Critique of the United States Income and Product Accounts*, Studies in Income and Wealth, Vol. 22 (Princeton University Press for the National Bureau of Economic Research, 1958), p. 53.

divided among employers, labor and consumer; but in what proportion cannot definitely be said.[8]

A more recent study suggests: "The popular assumption is that (a) the employee share of the payroll tax is borne by the wage earner and (b) the employer share is shifted forward to the consumer in the form of higher prices."[9] Among laymen, skepticism regarding the classic conclusion that labor bears the entire tax is undoubtedly widespread.

The cited divergence of opinion about the incidence of the employer payroll tax does not appear to be due to differing concepts of incidence. In the past there has sometimes been confusion. Most writers stress the effect of the tax on factor shares, but others have regarded any economic effect as part of its incidence. Still others have stressed the net effect on income distribution of the tax and the benefit sides considered as a whole. However, the writers cited above have generally agreed in emphasis on the shares of labor and capital or rates of return to these factors, although sometimes the effect on "the consumer" is also mentioned.

The concepts of "incidence" and "shifting" to be adopted here are discussed in the technical note at the end of this chapter. However, the criteria of factor share and rate of return do not permit distinction between "forward" shifting through price increases and "backward" shifting through wage restraint. If the relative importance of these mechanisms could be determined, this would shed further light on the effects of the tax on the relative position of economic groups, such as fixed-income recipients on the one hand and earners on the other. It is argued in the technical note at the end of this chapter that it is not possible to separate the effects of the tax from those of other macroeconomic policies. In any case, an analysis of the impact of the tax on the share of labor tells the major part of the story.

### Significance of the Incidence Question

As payroll taxation bulks large, the unresolved question of its incidence becomes important for a number of reasons. First, to de-

[8] Harold M. Groves, *Financing Government* (6th ed., Holt, Rinehart and Winston, 1964), p. 157.

[9] Joseph A. Pechman, Henry J. Aaron, and Michael K. Taussig, *Social Security: Perspectives for Reform* (Brookings Institution, 1968), p. 175. The authors themselves make a strong case for the proposition that labor bears the entire payroll tax (pp. 175–78).

termine whether the employer contribution alleviates the generally regressive impact of the employee tax (if the latter is borne by the employee), as well as certain inequities within the social security tax structure, it is necessary to know whether or not the employer can shift his tax. Second, it is essential to know whether each tax falls on capital or on labor in order to appraise its role as an automatic stabilizer and its impact on growth. Third, it is necessary to understand the incidence of both employer and employee contributions in order to decide their appropriate treatment under the income tax. Fourth, knowledge of incidence is essential to clarification of the expected rate of return on contributions under social security. Fifth, it is necessary to know the incidence if collective bargaining is to be conducted in a rational manner. And finally, postwar efforts at international economic cooperation have intensified interest abroad in the possible impact of these employer taxes on migration and relative labor costs.[10] For such questions the location of the tax burden is essential.[11]

## *Opinion and Practice in the Labor Market*

Although interpretation of their own behavior by participants on the economic scene is not notably reliable, it is worthwhile to ask how the parties in the labor market view the impact of the employer payroll tax. The issue could be expected to surface explicitly and fre-

[10] For example, a recent attempt to show that capital was relatively heavily taxed in Western Europe rested entirely on an a priori assumption that payroll taxes are borne by capital. See Vito Tanzi, "Tax Systems and Balance of Payments: An Alternative Analysis," *National Tax Journal*, Vol. 20 (March 1967), pp. 39–44. For a useful and thoughtful presentation of an opposing view, see Bela A. Balassa, *The Theory of Economic Integration* (Irwin, 1961), pp. 216–24. The author concludes (subject to a few exceptions) that all payroll taxes are borne by labor and that intercountry "harmonization" of these taxes is therefore unnecessary for integration and would cause allocative distortions. If the tax is borne by labor, its effect on migration would depend on the extent to which labor expects to get benefits from the tax proceeds.

[11] One other issue raised in the literature is the possibility that if the employer bears part of the payroll tax, so that it increases the cost of labor, this could aggravate the unemployment problem by promoting the substitution of capital goods for labor. This fear appears groundless, since in the long run the cost of capital goods will tend to rise along with the cost of labor, unless the interest rate falls. See, for example, "A New Theorem on Nonsubstitution," in Joseph E. Stiglitz (ed.), *The Collected Scientific Papers of Paul A. Samuelson* (M.I.T. Press, 1966), Vol. 1, pp. 520–36. For a brief exposition of the argument denying incentives for substitution, see Carl S. Shoup, *Public Finance* (Aldine, 1969), pp. 412–13.

quently in those European countries having a much heavier tax than the United States. The strong redistributive impact of family allowances financed by the tax has also caused heated discussion. For example, a French union official clearly implied in a graphic opinion that the employer "contribution," in large part earmarked for family allowances, is in reality paid by labor. "We are getting paid less and less for our work, and more and more for being 'Father Rabbit,' " he complained.[12] It is clear that he was taking for granted that the tax on employers used to finance family allowances was paid at the expense of the basic wage. A similar French union opinion has been reported: "The real incidence of social and indirect wage charges made 'the working class function as a vast mutual aid association in which . . . it was the poor who were helping out the poorer.' "[13]

There is some evidence that the conception of the employer tax as a substitute for basic wages enters the collective bargaining session. According to Lorwin, "French employers frequently argue in collective bargaining that the imposition of social charges precludes their granting of wage increases."[14] The French case is not necessarily typical. Not only is the employer payroll tax high (on the order of 35 percent of the nominal wage), but the family allowance scheme was originally introduced in the private sector during World War I as an explicit substitute for and defense against general wage increases. When a compulsory public family allowance system was introduced in 1932, many employers plainly demonstrated that they viewed their "contribution" as a substitute for basic wages; they undertook to cut wages in an explicit attempt to recoup the tax from labor, ultimately provoking legislation seeking to prohibit this. Such shifting by outright wage cutting is probably uncommon, and restraint of wage increases in the face of rising payroll taxes is probably much more prevalent. For example, even in Sweden, where the tax is much smaller than in France, it appears to have forestalled wage increases in 1959:

The duration of this year's agreement will be 1 year instead of the customary 2 years. One reason for this was the employers' desire for an early review of the wage scale to take account of their contributions to the Gov-

---

[12] Val R. Lorwin, "France," in Walter Galenson (ed.), *Comparative Labor Movements* (Prentice-Hall, 1952), p. 362.

[13] *Ibid.*

[14] Cited in James C. Vadakin, *Family Allowances: An Analysis of Their Development and Implications* (University of Miami Press, 1958), p. 131.

ernment's pension fund, beginning in January 1960. . . . Swedish workers attached immense importance, during the wage talks, to the pension plan which the Government was expected to adopt. . . . The unions felt, however, during the wage negotiations, that they could not get both a pension law and a substantial contractual wage increase this year, since the pension bill called for sizable employers' contributions to the pension fund, amounting to 1.89 percent of the payroll in 1960 and increasing to 4.2 percent in 1964.[15]

These Swedish reactions seem more relevant to the U.S. experience than do the French, since the employer tax increases involved are relatively small, even though they are larger than recent U.S. increases. However, in neither country is wage restraint likely to be the only shifting vehicle. In fact, many French employers have clearly implied that they raise prices in response to tax increases; this follows from their complaints that social security burdens are undermining their international competitive position. However, it is not difficult to square such employer complaints with the argument that wages must be restrained because of hikes in the tax; indeed, it would not be surprising to find the same employer using both arguments and strategies, since each is designed to shift the burden from profits to labor's share.

In the United States explicit references to a trade-off between the employer tax and private compensation are less common than in Europe.[16] However, direct recognition of the shifting of the tax to employees can be found, for example, in the academic world. At 23 percent of the colleges and universities affiliated with the Teachers Insurance and Annuity Association, representing about 37 percent of all participants as of December 31, 1970, the institution's contribution to this private pension fund is automatically adjusted downward to offset the cost of each increase in the taxable ceiling under the social security program;[17] thus this type of tax increase is recouped

[15] U.S. Bureau of Labor Statistics, *Labor Developments Abroad* (August 1959), p. 6.

[16] There does appear to be general recognition in this country of a trade-off between the basic wage and employer contributions for private fringe benefits, since the two are negotiated in a package. The apparent narrowing of union wage differentials since World War II may be evidence of this trade-off. Younger (relatively low-paid) workers may be gaining on older workers in terms of the basic wage, as the latter are more eager to trade off wage increases against pension contributions by the employers.

[17] Letter to the author from the Teachers Insurance and Annuity Association of America–College Retirement Equities Fund (TIAA–CREF), Jan. 26, 1972.

by reduction of the total private compensation of labor. Many collective bargaining agreements concerning private pension payments have included similar offsets. In early negotiations the contract often allowed these payments to be contingent on future changes in the taxable ceiling or in social security benefits. The higher the ceiling or the future benefits, the lower the pension obligations of the employer.[18] Thus a higher employer tax caused by a higher ceiling could cut private compensation.

A rise in social security benefits could recoup taxes for the employer indirectly. Since large increases in social security benefits tend to be associated with large increases in taxes, the employer may find himself relieved from the burden of the tax increase by correspondingly lower demands from labor for contributions to the private pension program. Despite these various actual and potential trade-offs, union negotiators in the United States do not seem to consider the employer contribution a part of labor compensation. Even so, since both unions and employers may assess the company's ability to pay in terms of profits after all such costs are netted out, increases in the employer tax cut expected profits and weaken labor's case for increases in private compensation. All in all, there seem to be ample links between the tax and private compensation to assure a substantial trade-off between the two, with or without explicit recognition by the parties to collective bargaining.

### Treatment in the National Accounts

Two other opinions by practitioners who have been forced to take a position on incidence deserve mention. The social accounting convention recommended in the United Nations system of national accounts and followed by many countries other than the United States also implies that the employer tax is borne by labor. It is treated as though it were a tax deducted at the source from employees' income.[19] The General Agreement on Tariffs and Trade (GATT) treats

[18] One type of pension formula paid a fraction of past earnings up to the ceiling and a higher fraction of earnings above the ceiling. Another accomplished the private-public trade-off by agreeing to assure a given total of private and public benefits. Such formal links between the private and public schemes have been less common in recent years.

[19] Contributions on the account of employees, whether made by themselves or their employers, are classed as the social security contributions of the employees. See United Nations, Department of Economic and Social Affairs, *A System of National Accounts* (United Nations, 1968), p. 129. There are two anomalies in the treatment of these taxes

the employer tax as a direct tax, so that no border tax adjustments are made. This implies no "forward" shifting but does not indicate which factor bears the tax.

## Some Earlier Empirical Work

In an informative article Marjorie W. Hald finds that International Labour Office data show an inverse relationship between the basic wage rate and the rate of "social charges" (employer payroll tax rates) in manufacturing in thirteen European countries in the mid-1950s.[20] This suggests that increased employer contributions might tend to be substituted for increases in the basic wage. Similar conclusions were reached by G. L. Reid on the basis of data for five countries, but this sample is so small that little can be read into the numbers.[21] In any case, the Hald and Reid analyses are no more than suggestive, since other factors could have produced the observed statistical association. For example, governments in low-wage countries may be under great pressure to introduce public benefit programs. The more general model suggested in this study allows for such factors.

Other writers have looked at labor's real income and relative share

in the U.S. national income accounts. The income from which the employee tax and income tax are withheld appears in wages and salaries, but the withheld employer "contribution" appears only as a supplement. Then, the employee tax (unlike the withheld income tax) is subtracted from wages and salaries in arriving at personal income (in order to balance the outlay side, where it is not treated as a tax). It is difficult to understand why these three withheld taxes should be treated differently. Until 1966 the Council of Economic Advisers (CEA) avoided separate treatment, including all three taxes as part of wages in statistical tables. However, in 1966 the CEA apparently reversed itself by excluding the rise in the employer tax from the 3.2 percent wage guideposts on the ground that this tax was "determined by law," not bargaining. (*Economic Report of the President together with the Annual Report of the Council of Economic Advisers* [1966], pp. 92–93.) Why it should be treated differently from other taxes also "determined by law" is not explained.

[20] Marjorie W. Hald, "Social Charges in the EEC Countries: Some Economic Aspects," *Economia Internazionale*, Vol. 12 (November 1959), pp. 683–87. No statistical test was provided, but computations using the data give a Spearman rank correlation coefficient of $-0.50$, just significant at the 5 percent level on a one-tail test. Only Ireland was far out of line, with a low wage level despite a low tax rate. (International Labour Office, *Social Aspects of European Economic Co-operation* [Geneva: ILO, 1956], p. 33.)

[21] See G. L. Reid, "Supplementary Labour Costs in Europe and Britain," in G. L. Reid and D. J. Robertson (eds.), *Fringe Benefits, Labour Costs, and Social Security* (London: George Allen & Unwin, 1965), p. 111.

in the national income for clues to the incidence of the employer tax. Lorwin reports the following opinion on France in the early fifties:

Despite understandable employer complaints about the burden of social charges, the increased benefits have come, not out of profits, but essentially out of a redistribution of income within the working class, as between direct wage and social wage recipients. . . .

This phenomenon is made clearer by the fact that both (1) the total of *real* income going to wage earners (in the form of direct wages and social wage payments) and (2) wage earners' share in national income are about the same as in 1938. "Since the total mass of wage income, made up of the sum of direct wages and indirect wages (i.e., social or transfer payments) has remained stable in real value despite the considerable increase of the latter, it is evidently because the first have contracted to almost the same extent," as the *Report on the National Accounts for 1951 and 1952* points out. As for wage earners' share of national income, since 1947 that has hovered at about the same figure (50 per cent) as in 1938.[22]

The stability of labor's total compensation (including the rapidly rising employer contributions) in relation to national income is consistent with the proposition that the tax is substituted for the basic wage. However, this is a ceteris paribus interpretation, and other variables require consideration.

Using U.S. time series data, Wayne Vroman asked whether there was any evidence that the markup of price over unit labor and material costs held up in the face of rising employer taxes. Ceteris paribus, this would indicate that employers recouped the tax. He found a slight upward trend in markups, suggesting that employers did shift at least part of the tax. This widening spread between price and unit costs could be due to backward or forward shifting or to a combination of the two. In any case, Vroman cautions that other factors involved qualify the shifting interpretation.[23]

The above empirical reports are no more than suggestive, but they are very persuasive in comparison with the most recent empirical effort to appear, in which Deran[24] found that the share of property

[22] Val R. Lorwin, *The French Labor Movement* (Harvard University Press, 1955), p. 227, citing Ministry of Finance, *Rapports sur les comptes provisoires de la nation . . . de 1951 et 1952*, p. 46.

[23] Wayne G. Vroman, "The Macroeconomic Effects of Social Insurance" (Ph.D. dissertation, University of Michigan, 1967).

[24] Elizabeth Deran, "Changes in Factor Income Shares Under the Social Security Tax," *Review of Economics and Statistics*, Vol. 49 (November 1967), pp. 627–30. For a

income in the national income of Puerto Rico fell with the introduction of the social security tax. Deeming this decline statistically significant on the basis of a meaningless misapplication of the chi-square procedure, Deran then interpreted it as showing that the employee tax (as well as the employer tax) was borne by capital, even though the fall in the share of capital was six times too large to be explained by the tax alone.[25] These faulty interpretations alone are sufficient for dismissal of the conclusions of this article.

An important and elaborate empirical study was recently published by Weitenberg.[26] It uses econometric models of the Dutch Central Planning Bureau for a time series analysis of the effect of social security taxes on after-tax real wage rates. The preliminary short-run analysis shows 25 percent of the total payroll tax shifted forward by higher wages. Another short-run result shows that the initial depression of real disposable income by the tax is offset about one-third by forward shifting; this, however, has a lagged effect on prices.

On the other hand, Weitenberg states that in the long run the autonomous increase of the nominal wage rate is endogenously reduced by about 50 percent, with price increases offsetting the other half. Thus Weitenberg concludes that in the longer run a payroll tax cannot be shifted by labor in aggregate.[27] This finding offers support to the incidence hypothesis and empirical findings to be presented

---

gentle demolition of this article, see Ronald F. Hoffman, "Factor Shares and the Payroll Tax: A Comment," *Review of Economics and Statistics*, Vol. 50 (November 1968), pp. 506–08.

[25] The payroll tax in Puerto Rico increased from zero in 1950 to $6.2 million in 1952. See *Social Security Bulletin*, Vol. 17 (April 1954), Table 6, p. 28. On the basis of Deran's figures ("Changes in Factor Income Shares," Table 1, p. 628), the new tax amounted to 0.7 percent of aggregate "net income" in 1952, but the share of property income in net income fell from 37.1 percent in 1950 to 32.9 percent in 1952 (six times the rate of the new tax). Deran's figures showed a slightly smaller decline in the share of property income, since she departed from the national income accounts basis and included the employer tax as part of property income. She was assured that no "extraordinary economic events" other than the imposition of the new tax occurred at this time. Under her interpretation, therefore, the Puerto Rico labor movement must surely be the envy of the world; indeed, if it could overkill to the extent of recouping six times the tax, Puerto Rico labor should be in Washington lobbying for more and bigger payroll taxes!

[26] Johannes Weitenberg, "The Incidence of Social Security Taxes," *Public Finance*, Vol. 24 (1969), pp. 193–208.

[27] Weitenberg's statement of his conclusion could be confusing unless it is borne in mind that he is speaking of a payroll tax charged on the use of labor and that he makes no distinction with respect to the employer tax.

here. However, Weitenberg's results go even further to indicate an aggregate decline in the real before-tax wage bill of employers caused by increased unemployment resulting from the tax. (The implications of his finding of adverse employment and growth effects are considered later in this chapter.) The analysis by Weitenberg and the other discussions of European data reported earlier are useful, but further a priori and empirical considerations appear to be in order.

## Theoretical Analysis of Incidence

### Marginal Productivity Theory

The classical view that a universal employer tax is borne by labor was stated succinctly by H. G. Brown.[28] He assumes that rationality and competition lead employers to hire workers up to the point that the wage is just barely recouped by the marginal value product. If a tax is imposed on the employer in proportion to labor hired, the marginal worker will no longer be hired unless he accepts a real wage reduced by the amount of the tax. He can be expected to accept it because his labor supply function is assumed to be highly inelastic; he cannot hold out very long and has no alternative under a universal tax. Brown also sees nothing in the situation to allow the tax to be offset by higher prices, because he assumes that the tax does not increase the money supply and would have little effect on aggregate demand.[29]

Brown's underlying assumption of a fixed amount of labor supplied is subject to question. The overall effect of a tax on labor supplied cannot be forecast with any confidence, since it depends on the unknown preference functions of individual workers with respect to consumption and leisure. The substitution effect of a tax increase

[28] Harry Gunnison Brown, *The Economics of Taxation* (Lucas Brothers, 1924), pp. 160–63. One of the first considerations of a wage tax was by Ricardo. His subsistence theory of wages and assumed fixed proportions led him to conclude that profits bear such a tax. See David Ricardo, *Principles of Political Economy and Taxation*, edited, with introductory essay, notes, and appendices, by E. C. K. Gonner (London: George Bell and Sons, 1903), p. 198.

[29] Clearly, Brown assumes that the reduction of factor incomes by the tax is offset by spending of the proceeds, leaving aggregate money demand unchanged. This is the "balanced-budget" approach to incidence that is also adhered to in this study. On the alternative methodologies, see Richard A. Musgrave, *The Theory of Public Finance: A Study in Public Economy* (McGraw-Hill, 1959), pp. 211–17. Brown's assumption of a fixed money supply is not essential to analysis of incidence, as is explained in the technical note at the end of this chapter.

tends to produce a contraction of labor supplied and this in turn is counteracted by the income effect, but the relative strength of the two forces on balance is unknown.[30] Certainly, recent empirical studies in this area have produced no consensus, and this remains a qualification of Brown's case.[31]

Brown was considering a tax on labor with universal coverage—a structure approached fairly closely in this country. The incidence of a tax applied only to certain segments of the economy, such as the British selective employment tax concentrating on services, is a more complex issue. Since the empirical analysis in Chapter III relies on tax data for national social security systems with varying degrees of coverage, it is worth asking whether nonuniversality would undermine Brown's conclusion.[32]

It is possible to show with the aid of simplifying assumptions that a selective tax, despite its allocative and price effects, may also be borne entirely by labor.[33] This can be most easily demonstrated by means of a simple general equilibrium model. The simplifying assumptions are: two industries, two factors, unitary elasticity of demand for products, Cobb-Douglas production function, fixed supplies of factors, and competitive conditions.[34]

---

[30] If one finds the frequently assumed homogeneous utility function plausible, there is no problem with Brown's analysis, since the two effects are exactly offsetting. For example, for real wage rate $w$, physical consumption $C$, and leisure hours $L$, let $U = aC^m L^n$; assume only labor income, a 24-hour day, and the household budget constraint $C = w(24 - L)$. It can be shown that utility maximization subject to the budget constraint is independent of the wage rate and leads to a completely inelastic leisure demand function: $L = 24n/(m + n)$. For a more general analysis of this type of problem, see, for example, Duncan Black, *The Incidence of Income Taxes* (Macmillan, 1939), Chap. 12.

[31] For a discussion of research on the effects of taxes on labor supply, see Carl S. Shoup, "Quantitative Research in Taxation and Government Expenditure" (National Bureau of Economic Research, no date; processed), pp. 55–59.

[32] The unemployment insurance payroll tax in this country also falls substantially short of universal coverage, even in sectors covered by OASDHI.

[33] The following analysis of a selective tax on labor parallels in most respects Arnold C. Harberger's analysis of the corporate tax in "The Incidence of the Corporation Income Tax," *Journal of Political Economy*, Vol. 70 (June 1962), pp. 215–40. However, the tax is interpreted here as affecting relative labor costs of the covered and noncovered industries, rather than causing a fall in the value of the marginal product of the taxed factor.

[34] The tax specialist may note that Harberger (*ibid.*) has already shown that in a Cobb-Douglas world a tax on a factor will be borne by that factor. The following illustration is included simply to show that a selective tax on labor not only may be extracted entirely from labor's share but that this may occur despite allocative and price effects and a partial shifting of the burden to labor in the nontaxed sector.

Let $x$ represent production in the taxed sector and $y$ in the non-taxable sector. For industry $x$ let

$Q_x$ = units of output of industry $x$
$L_x$ = units of labor used in industry $x$
$K_x$ = units of capital used in industry $x$
$p_{Q_x}, p_{L_x}, p_{K_x}$ = prices
$VMP_{L_x}, VMP_{K_x}$ = values of marginal products.

Suppose the production function is:

$$Q_x = L_x^{3/4} K_x^{1/4}.$$

The symbols for industry $y$ are analogous, and the production function is the same. For industry $x$, the equilibrium conditions are:

$$VMP_{L_x} = \tfrac{3}{4}(K_x/L_x)^{1/4} p_{Q_x} = \tfrac{3}{4}p_{Q_x}Q_x/L_x = p_{L_x}$$
$$VMP_{K_x} = \tfrac{1}{4}(K_x/L_x)^{3/4} p_{Q_x} = \tfrac{1}{4}p_{Q_x}Q_x/K_x = p_{K_x}.$$

The equilibrium conditions for industry $y$ are analogous. For a particular numerical example with annual figures, assume net product (or total receipts) of each industry is fixed (due to unitary elasticity) at $400 billion, or

$$p_{Q_x}Q_x = p_{Q_y}Q_y = \$400b \text{ (billion)}.$$

Suppose the fixed factor supplies are:

$$L_x + L_y = 80m \text{ (million) man-years}$$

$$K_x + K_y = \$2,000b \text{ (billion)}.$$

Before imposition of a tax the equilibrium conditions, including equality of *VMP*s for each industry, lead to the following equilibrium solution for factor inputs and prices:

$L_x = L_y = 40m$ $\qquad$ $p_{L_x} = p_{L_y} = \$7,500$ per man-year

$K_x = K_y = \$1,000b$ $\qquad$ $p_{K_x} = p_{K_y} = 10\cent$ per dollar.

The share of labor in each industry is $300 billion, and that of capital in each industry is $100 billion.

Now assume that a tax of 10 percent of wages is imposed on the employers in industry $x$ and spent by transfer recipients, leaving industry receipts unchanged.[35] Since industry $x$ must now pay 10 per-

---

[35] It is assumed that the expenditure patterns of transfer recipients do not differ enough from those of others to cause a redistribution on the sources or uses side of real

cent more total compensation per unit of labor, a move of labor from $x$ to $y$ must occur to bring the *VMP*s into line with labor costs. The condition for the new equilibrium is:

$$VMP_{L_x} = 1.1 \ VMP_{L_y}.$$

From the original equilibrium conditions and assumptions, this leads to $L_y = 1.1L_x$. From this condition the labor allocation and prices follow:

$$L_x = 38.1m \qquad L_y = 41.9m \qquad p_L = \$7,158.$$

Owing to reallocation of labor from $x$ to $y$, the price of labor falls only about half the tax per worker. However, the new labor price and allocation yields a new total labor share less than the original by the amount of the tax:

| | |
|---|---:|
| New aggregate share of labor in $x$ | $273b$ |
| Tax on wages paid by employers in $x$ | $27b$ |
| Aggregate share of labor in $y$ | $300b$ |
| | |
| Original share of labor | $600b$ |

If incidence is interpreted in terms of the factor shares, it is clear that the entire burden of the tax is borne by labor, despite the reallocation and price adjustments to a new equilibrium. It should be carefully noted, however, that under this selective tax the burden is shared by the untaxed industry, since the price of labor in that industry falls with the rise in labor supplied to it.[36] This model has another interesting feature in light of the frequent assertion that the payroll tax is "passed on" by means of higher prices. The present formulation implies a rise in the price of $x$ and a fall in the price of $y$. However, it has been assumed that this change in relative product prices is distributionally neutral on the side of uses of income by labor and capital. Thus the burden of the tax is unambiguously on labor's share, and

---

income available for private use. It is also assumed that changes in relative product prices, if any, cause no changes in the relative positions of capital and labor on the side of uses of income. These assumptions are discussed in the technical note at the end of this chapter.

[36] Owing to the restrictive conditions of this model, there is no change in the position of capital accompanying this reallocation. More $y$ would be produced and less $x$, but total spending on each product was assumed to remain the same due to offsetting price changes. In the absence of any change in total spending the equilibrium conditions require $K_x$, $K_y$, $VMP_K$, and $p_K$ to remain unchanged.

what may appear to be "forward shifting" in the taxed sector is not inconsistent with that result. More generally, as pointed out in the technical note at the end of this chapter, a change in the absolute price of the single product $x$ is irrelevant under the incidence concept applied here.

One more point is evident from the model. It might seem likely that corporations could shift more of the payroll tax than other firms, simply because this tax is deductible for corporate income tax purposes. According to this model, the payroll tax is substituted for the basic wage with no change in total compensation, no change in income to capital, and therefore no reduction in the corporate tax liability. Only if the employers irrationally absorbed some of the tax would the deductibility feature be relevant.

### Analysis under Less Restrictive Assumptions

Theoretical analysis of the type outlined thus far has been justifiably criticized for oversimplified assumptions and dependence on the validity of the marginal productivity theory of wages.[37] It is possible to restate the argument with greater generality and with less dependence on the various assumptions of the marginal productivity theory.

The theoretical case for imputing the employer tax to labor does not depend on profit-maximizing behavior by employers. The less restrictive assumption of cost minimization is sufficient and also more generally plausible than profit maximization. A firm in a concentrated industry, for example, might hesitate to use its full market power to maximize profits by restriction of output; however, it seems valid to assume that it will seek to produce its planned output at minimum cost. This requires that the ratio of marginal value product to marginal factor cost must be the same for all factors of production. With the imposition of an employer tax in relation to labor inputs, cost minimization cannot be maintained at the given level of employment unless the tax is recouped one way or another at the expense of the basic wage. (The complication of the picture by any employment effects is considered later in this chapter.)

In practice the tax may be recouped in any of three ways or a combination of them. The employer contribution may be offset by a

---

[37] Harris, *Economics of Social Security*, pp. 291–99. See also other chapters in Part 3 of that work for detailed summaries and analysis of various incidence theories.

money wage cut. More plausibly in a dynamic context, basic wage increases could be allowed to lag behind the pace of productivity increases, while at the same time total compensation kept pace. Finally, price increases (supported, for example, by increased government spending facilitated by the tax increase) could recoup the tax without decreasing money wages. It could be argued further, however, that the shifting of the tax to labor is not even dependent on the achievement of cost minimization or on competition in the labor market. If a fixed aggregate labor supply is assumed, it is only necessary to accept the proposition that it makes no difference to employers what name is given to the sums (called "total compensation" in the national income accounts) that they must pay to hire labor.[38] Depending on product demand, labor productivity, the degree of competition, and other factors, a certain aggregate real wage bill would have been extracted from employers in the absence of the tax. If employers are blind to the composition of the employee compensation bill, no more real total compensation could be obtained for a given amount of labor with the payroll tax than without it. Both employer and employee payroll taxes must be borne by labor, since the real after-tax wage bill must be lower by the amount of the tax.

It should be added that under the above reasoning it makes no difference whether part or all of the price is called the employer's "contribution" and sent to Washington along with the employee's tax. There is no reason to expect a different employer reaction to the two components. Suppose the two taxes were suddenly combined into one package designated an employer tax but sent away by the employer just as before in the same amount. Except for short-run qualifications, such as the current labor contract, there is no reason to expect the employer to pay more real total compensation as the result of this accounting change. In terms of formal accounting, the employer would be required to pick up the employee's part, and the nominal wage—total compensation minus employer tax—that he would be willing to pay would be correspondingly reduced. Furthermore, this argument does not depend on competition; it is equally true in noncompetitive labor markets where labor may receive less than its

---

[38] It is assumed for simplicity at this stage that prices are not adjusted as a result of the tax. It will be shown later that the same outcome in real terms can be achieved if the spending of the tax proceeds permits a price increase for the given level of output (in lieu of a money wage cut).

marginal value product. Even in a labor market with monopsonistic hiring and monopolistic labor supply, where the equilibrium is indeterminate, it does not seem plausible that the employer would distinguish among the components of compensation. (This is not to imply that employees make no such distinction.)

The same point can be made another way. What would be changed if the employer tax were renamed as a tax charged to employees? The employer would presumably continue to withhold and send away the same amount of taxes from the same total compensation, leaving labor costs unchanged and the worker with the same after-tax wage as before. The required rise in the nominal wage to bring this about would seem a far likelier outcome than a fall in total compensation unjustified by any change in real economic circumstances. There would be no corporate income tax effects, since wages and taxes are both deductible. The worker would suffer a slight rise in his income tax due to the higher nominal wage, but this would only make him wish that the entire payroll tax had been renamed an employer contribution so it was subject to no income tax. About the only result of relabeling the whole payroll tax an employee's contribution would be a more general belief that it is all borne by labor, no matter what it is called.

To sum up, it seems a plausible premise that the total real compensation that can be extracted for a given amount of labor (of given quality) is fixed and independent of the labels attached to the components. If this premise is accepted, and in addition the aggregate labor supply curve is completely inelastic, both payroll taxes are clearly borne by labor, and there is no effect on the cost of labor or aggregate employment. The two taxes will be paid out of the total before-tax compensation offered to labor at the fixed level of employment. Of course, the essence of this conclusion would not be disturbed by a small degree of supply elasticity. Even if the supply of labor were substantially elastic, the same result (no employment contraction and no substitution of capital for labor) would occur at both macro and micro levels if labor regarded both of the withheld "contributions" as part of its supply price—that is, if labor thought of both taxes as part of earnings, just as they are definitely part of the employer's costs. In this case the tax would still have no employment effect, and therefore no ambiguity would develop about the outcome, even at the single-firm level.

Obviously, neither of the above requirements for complete exclusion of employment effects is likely to hold precisely in practice. However, the main point is that if labor supply were highly inelastic and/or a substantial portion of social security contributions were viewed by labor as part of its income, employment effects of the tax would be minor. Together these conditions would be reinforcing in support of the labor burden hypothesis.

## *Qualifications Due to Supply Elasticity and Employment Effects*

There is little if any evidence that payroll taxes have had substantial employment effects. For example, countries with very high taxes do not seem to have higher unemployment than countries with lower taxes. However, it will be argued next that, even if there were large employment effects, this would in no way suggest that labor is spared the burden. Before proceeding with this argument, it must be conceded that once the possibility of large employment effects is admitted the concept of the incidence of a broad-based tax becomes clouded. How are changes in both employment and the wage rate to be weighed in assessing incidence? What is the actual meaning of an aggregate labor demand function that must be invoked for the analysis?[39] Despite the intractability of these problems, a few useful points can be made. The case of an aggregate labor supply curve with some degree of positive elasticity is illustrated in Figure 2-1, which stresses a positive slope as perhaps more plausible than the rather esoteric backward-bending supply curve.

The top aggregate demand curve represents the employers' view of their offer per unit of labor—total unit labor compensation (*TULC*)—under the simplifying assumption of homogeneous units of labor, but the analysis would not be affected by the assumption of a family of demand curves pertaining to various qualities of labor. In the absence of any payroll taxes, the equilibrium wage rate and employment level are represented by point *A*. If payroll taxes are imposed, the aggregate

---

[39] It is necessary to resort with trepidation to a ceteris paribus aggregate demand concept, while conceding that general equilibrium considerations make this a crude concept. For a clarification of the meaning and problems associated with application of an aggregate labor demand function, see Don Patinkin, *Money, Interest, and Prices* (2d ed., Harper & Row, 1965), pp. 316–28. Any given demand function reflects the assumptions of firms that they can sell their output at the prevailing market price. Any disturbance invalidating this assumption produces a disequilibrium and a shift of the demand curve requiring a complex adjustment to a new equilibrium.

**FIGURE 2-1. Aggregate Labor Supply and Demand Curves before and after Payroll Tax**[a]

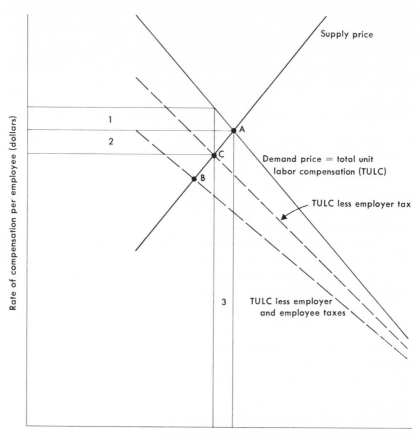

Number of employees

demand curves are lowered, as indicated in the figure. However, if labor (like employers) continues to view the demand price as measured by *TULC*, the equilibrium will remain at point *A*, and labor will bear the full amount of the taxes per worker, as indicated by the vertical distances from *A* to the curves below.

So far the cases are clear-cut, as indicated earlier. Given a meaningful labor demand function and either of two assumptions concerning labor supply and labor's evaluation of its compensation, the payroll tax has no employment effect, the burden is unambiguously on labor, and there is no aggregate substitution of capital for labor. Only if *neither* assumption holds even approximately does a substantial indeterminacy arise to prevent the real effects of the tax from being evaluated generally. Under such circumstances, the tax could reduce or increase employment substantially and complicate the net redistributive and allocative effects.

The original assumption that the employer's labor demand price is measured in terms of total compensation and is essentially independent of its accounting components seems subject to no serious objection. The belief that employer contributions are somehow "pennies from heaven" implies that the employer will greet any increase in this tax by an offer of corresponding higher total compensation for a given quantity of labor. (It is possible to reject this in its essence without adopting a rigid conception of the labor demand function, even conceding, for example, that the employer might, for rational economic reasons, pay somewhat more toward pension increases than toward increases in current wages.)

Labor's conception of the price it is actually being offered is more open to debate, however. Depending on its discounting of future income and income tax considerations, labor may prefer current cash to pension contributions, or vice versa. In the polar case, labor may view the demand price in terms of income after employer and employee taxes are withheld. This could occur if labor either discounted the expected benefits at a very high rate or viewed the taxes as adding nothing to expected benefits. If labor viewed its pay in terms of compensation after all payroll taxes, imposition of such taxes would represent a downward shift in the demand curve as viewed by labor to the lowest level in Figure 2-1. (This could have been portrayed equally well as a rise in the supply curve of labor, with the supply price measured in terms of *TULC*.) In conjunction with a nonvertical supply curve, this would affect employment; according to the particular illustration of Figure 2-1 the initial impact would be a reduction of employment to the level indicated by point *B*.[40] In such a situation no general evaluation of incidence is possible, since the redistributive and

---

[40] The adjustment portrayed in this partial analysis would not necessarily produce a new equilibrium, since the fall in employment could lead to repercussions on the aggregate demand side, unless demand were fully maintained as the result of distribution of the tax proceeds. However, such demand maintenance is assumed under the balanced budget incidence model adopted here.

allocative effects of the tax would be dependent on the various elasticities in the particular situation. The alternative possibilities are taken up later in this chapter.

On the premise that aggregate demand price is measured for employers by total unit labor compensation, the economic effects of the two payroll taxes would differ only in the special case in which labor views them differently *and* its aggregate supply curve is somewhat elastic. Although both taxes are withheld, labor might (irrationally it would seem) recognize the employee contribution as part of demand price and ignore the employer tax paid in the name of each worker. This special case is considered here because of the common presumption that only the incidence of the employer tax is in doubt.[41] In this case, from the assumed point of view of labor, the demand curve in Figure 2-1 shifts from the top position to the middle position when the employer tax is imposed. This reduces employment to the level indicated by point *C* and makes it impossible to make general statements about the economic effects of the employer tax.[42]

The total basic earnings of labor may decline by either more or less than the tax, depending on the supply and demand elasticities. The geometry of such a comparison is also illustrated in Figure 2-1.[43] In the example shown, the net share of labor has declined by more than the tax, since the decline in the basic wage bill represented by rectangles 2 and 3 is greater than the tax represented by rectangles 2 and 1. In that sense labor bears more than 100 percent of the employer tax, because the negative employment effect outweighs the increase in rate of total compensation. However, a cut in the aggregate wage bill of less than 100 percent could be illustrated by arbitrarily lowering the equilibrium intersections.

Some generalizations can now be made that hold both for the total payroll tax and for the employer tax (if it alone causes employment effects). Under the present assumption of an employment response to

[41] This could occur because labor may see the employer tax as forced saving of little value to itself. However, it is difficult to see why the employee tax would not be similarly regarded as forced saving.

[42] In a sense the tax is borne by labor in that, for the new level of employment, net unit compensation of labor is less by the amount of the tax than it otherwise would be. However, the after-tax wage rate is below the before-tax wage rate by less than the full amount of the tax rate.

[43] The same is true and the same geometrical analysis could be applied in the previously discussed case in which labor counts *neither* tax as part of its compensation.

the tax, a knowledge of the relevant elasticities is required for a more general appraisal of its impact on the basic wage bill (including private fringe benefits). In the special case of a labor demand curve of unitary elasticity, the outcome would be determinate by definition. Since the aggregate compensation of labor (including the tax) would then be invariant with respect to employment, the basic wage bill would be reduced by exactly the amount of the tax. Thus, if the aggregate wage bill is accepted as the criterion, an employment effect does not necessarily rule out the proposition that labor bears the full burden.[44] Except in this special case of unitary demand elasticity, the outcome also depends on the labor supply elasticity.

With an upward-sloping labor supply function and a demand elasticity greater (less) than one, imposition of the tax would reduce the basic wage bill by more (less) than the amount of the tax. Since employment would be reduced by the tax, a demand elasticity greater than one would result, by definition, in a reduction in aggregate compensation (including the tax) and therefore in a decline in the after-tax wage bill greater than the total employer tax. The more elastic the demand, the greater the negative employment effect relative to the positive compensation rate effect.[45] In case of a backward-sloping labor supply curve, however, these relationships are reversed, since employment would increase. With a demand elasticity greater (less) than one, imposition of the tax would reduce the basic wage bill by less (more) than the tax.

In sum, even in the polar case in which labor regards no part of the payroll tax as income, there is no particular a priori indication of a tendency for labor to bear either less or more than the full amount of the payroll tax. This depends on the relevant elasticities. However,

---

[44] Even this case is not entirely free of ambiguity concerning the impact of the tax, however. The labor supply curve (including the tax) is shifted upward. If firms are assumed to be maximizing profits before the tax, the employment adjustment will only reduce—not eliminate—the bite out of the share of capital. Thus the combined decline in the shares of labor and capital would be greater than the amount of the tax in this case of unitary demand elasticity.

[45] The crude definition, in finite difference terms, of elasticity of employment $N$ with respect to compensation rate $TULC$ approximates the ratio of the employment effect to the compensation rate effect:

$$\text{Elasticity} \cong \frac{\Delta N}{N} \bigg/ \frac{\Delta TULC}{TULC} = \frac{TULC \; \Delta N}{N \; \Delta TULC}$$

$$\cong \frac{\text{employment effect}}{\text{compensation rate effect}}.$$

two points are made in Chapter III on behalf of the far greater plausibility of the full burden hypothesis than of the zero burden hypothesis. First, it is suggested that only under extremely implausible elasticity assumptions could labor completely avoid the tax, whereas labor would bear it all under entirely believable assumptions. Second, the empirical finding in Chapter III and by Weitenberg[46] that the real wage *rate* is depressed by the amount of the tax rate is highly significant. Combined with the finding of Weitenberg and the opinion of others that the tax depresses employment, the wage rate results suggest that the after-tax real wage *bill* falls by even more than the tax. If the wage *rate* falls by the full amount of the tax rate and employment *also* falls, it would be very difficult to argue that labor does not bear at least the full amount of the tax. Thus the qualification introduced by recognition of possible elasticities of factor supply may be more academic than significant.

*Further Qualifications*

Two types of qualification of the above reasoning should be indicated. First, the stress on real factor shares abstracts from the actual mechanism of the shifting process and makes no distinction between "backward" (money wage effect) and "forward" (price effect) shifting. Neither this analysis nor the statistical case presented later takes a position in the debate between those who think labor pays the tax and those who think consumers pay it. It is argued in the technical note at the end of this chapter that such a distinction is analytically impossible. There is no way of distinguishing the effects of the tax on the general price level from the effects of associated macroeconomic policy.[47] In the context of an analysis of incidence in terms of real factor shares, this is a secondary issue. This is not to deny that price changes are important in their own right and have differing effects on various economic groups.[48] However, not only is the relative im-

---

[46] Weitenberg, "Incidence of Social Security Taxes."

[47] This distinction may have meaning in terms of what employers are trying to do. However, one reason for not stressing it is that the two outcomes are not independent. For example, if the tax is not universal, an attempt to recoup it by means of wage cuts could drive labor to the uncovered sector and could cause many adjustments, including a price increase in the taxed sector.

[48] Clearly, the differing impact of inflation on debtors and creditors, for example, could mean that forward shifting would have a differing impact on labor income and property income. However, this should not be confused with the impact of the tax on the flow of real incomes to factors.

**TABLE 2-1. Illustrative Comparison of Effect on Labor and Property Income and on Prices of the "Backward" and "Forward" Shifting of a 5 Percent Employer Tax**

*(In billions of dollars)*

| | | | After tax (year 1) | |
|---|---|---|---|---|
| | Before tax, year 0 (real dollars) | Backward shifting (real dollars) | Forward shifting | |
| | | | Current dollars | Real dollars |
| Description | | | | |
| Basic labor income, excluding tax | 600 | 570 | 600 | 571.4 |
| Government receipts from employer tax | 0 | 30 | 30 | 28.6 |
| Property income | 200 | 200 | 210 | 200.0 |
| Total income | 800 | 800 | 840 | 800.0 |
| Price index (year 0 = 100) | 100 | 100 | 105 | 105 |

Source: Calculated by the author. See text for explanation.

portance of wage and price effects in the shifting process indeterminate, but it is largely irrelevant to the adopted factor share concept of incidence.

Consider first a "selective" employment tax. It has already been shown by means of a simple marginal productivity model that a rise in product price in the taxed sector (and a fall in labor input and product output) can be compatible with the proposition that labor bears the entire tax. In that illustration total spending was assumed to be unaffected by the tax. The more general case should be considered in which the possibility of a rise in total spending sufficient to "validate" a rise in the general price level is admitted; this makes possible "passing on" or "forward shifting" of the tax. Its outcome can be illustrated most easily in the case of a universal payroll tax.[49]

Assume an economy in year 0 without taxes or government, with a labor share of $600 billion and a capital share of $200 billion, as indicated in Table 2-1; then assume that a government appears in

[49] The U.S. payroll tax for social security has neared universal coverage of employees other than those in railroads and government. With 90 percent of all wages and salaries in covered employment in 1970, it is unlikely that a rise in the tax would cause reallocation of an appreciable amount of labor to industries not covered; the 10 percent not covered represents primarily earnings of railroad and government workers for whom substantial employer contributions are already being made.

year 1, imposing on employers a tax of 5 percent of year 0 payrolls and spending the proceeds on transfer payments in year 1. If employers accomplish complete backward shifting, labor's basic income would be reduced in year 1 to $570 billion, and there would be no change in the price level. It seems most meaningful to define complete "forward shifting" as a price level increase sufficient to restore the full real share of capital, while maintaining labor income at $600 billion (in current dollars).[50] Employers recognize that they can raise their share to $210 billion by means of a general price increase of 5 percent, if the government spends its proceeds.[51] The real share of capital remains unchanged and the real share of labor is reduced by $28.6 billion, or the full amount of the tax in real terms. The real burden on labor is slightly less than it is under the backward shifting case, because the model provides no escalator clause enabling the government to reassess the tax in light of erosion caused by the inflation. However, labor still bears the full tax in year 1.

In practice the shifting mechanism is probably some combination of the backward and forward patterns. While it may be difficult for employers to cut the basic money wage, they have more leeway in a dynamic economy when productivity is rising. They can grant regular wage increases while restraining the pace of the advance to a level below that which would be justified by rising productivity in the absence of the tax. The balance of the shifting can be accomplished by cuts in real wages through product price increases.[52] Full shifting simply requires a combination of the two actions sufficient to maintain the *real* pretax share of capital. The extent to which the shifting is accomplished through inflation is, of course, not irrelevant to equity questions such as debtor versus creditor or earner versus fixed

[50] For a similar application of this concept in the case of the corporation income tax, see Joan L. Turek, "Short-Run Shifting of the Corporate Income Tax in Manufacturing, 1935–1965," *Yale Economic Essays*, Vol. 10 (Spring 1970), pp. 127–48.

[51] This conception of full forward shifting by capitalists seems more realistic than a 3.75 percent price increase sufficient only to recoup the tax in current dollars. (A price increase of only 3.75 percent would raise the money value of total output from $800 billion to $830 billion and recoup the money value of the tax, but the share of capital would be less in real terms because of the price increase.) The present full shifting interpretation also assumes that any changes in relative product prices are distributionally neutral and that the only distributional effect of the tax is on the side of sources of income.

[52] Even if labor suffered no money illusion in its bargaining, the same outcome could be achieved if labor regarded the employer contribution as part of its wage.

income recipient, but this seems a minor qualification of the analysis of incidence under the factor shares criterion.

The second main qualification of the earlier reasoning is that its aggregative focus glosses over various microeconomic effects of actual payroll tax systems. In the presence of elastic firm and industry labor supply curves and discriminatory tax structures, the tax undoubtedly has a varying impact on individual economic units. Some consideration should be given to these microeconomic effects, although they do not contradict in any way the aggregative analysis. The current payroll tax structure bears unevenly on areas, sectors, industries, and firms in at least five respects: (1) a very small sector of the economy remains in which earnings are not subject to the social security tax (or the railroad and government retirement programs), and a larger sector is excluded from the unemployment insurance tax; (2) under the unemployment insurance program tax rates vary from state to state;[53] (3) the "experience rating" criterion in the unemployment insurance program produces differential tax rates; (4) in a labor-intensive firm, area, or industry a payroll tax of a given rate yields a higher tax rate relative to total factor costs than in other situations; (5) the ceiling on taxable earnings results in a lower effective tax rate on high-paid or skilled labor than on low-paid or unskilled labor.

As firms react to these taxes with product price increases and/or wage restraint, some reallocation of labor can be expected, depending on the degree of demand elasticity and on the competition. Firms faced with relatively high tax rates tend to react more strongly than others on both price and wage fronts. Substantial price increases and/or wage restraint would lead to contraction of output and reallocation of labor to firms faced by relatively low payroll taxes; also, the differential between high-wage labor and low-wage labor may tend to widen as firms attempt to substitute the former for the latter in response to the fifth differential mentioned above. If it is assumed that there is no increase in aggregate demand, the reallocation of labor in response to the first four differentials would tend to follow the pattern illustrated earlier in this chapter by the simple marginal productivity model for the most extreme differential—that between taxable

[53] Attempting to show the difficulty of shifting this tax, Lester has stressed this factor in Richard A. Lester, *The Economics of Unemployment Compensation* (Princeton University, Department of Economics, Industrial Relations Section, 1962), pp. 60–67.

and nontaxable sectors. In that example, the adjustments to the new equilibrium left labor bearing the full burden of the tax. Of course, other models could be conceived in which the outcome would be different.

The actual degree of reallocation is likely to be rather small, as the differentials themselves are not large and the rigidities and immobility may impede the adjustments in practice. In the absence of any substantial price increases or movement of labor, backward shifting through wage restraint could accomplish a direct trade-off between the tax and the basic wage. In any case, even if allocative effects do occur, this does not point to any particular conclusion on the incidence of the tax. As shown earlier, a reallocation due to labor cost differentials and wage restraint does not necessarily clash with the proposition that the tax is borne in aggregate by labor; the marginal productivity framework can encompass both outcomes.

Finally, it might appear that the presence of a minimum wage law could prevent the shifting of an employer payroll tax to marginal workers. For example, assume a fixed, homogeneous labor supply, and suppose that prior to the introduction of the tax the equilibrium wage rate is equal to the minimum wage rate; the full labor supply is employed. Introduction of a payroll tax on employers would shift downward the after-tax demand curve. Since the minimum wage rate is stated in terms of the basic wage (not including the employer contribution), employers cannot compensate for the tax by cutting the wage rate at the given level of employment. Employment will fall, clouding the incidence of the tax. The effect on factor shares depends on the labor demand elasticity, but there is no a priori reason to expect a tendency for the wage bill to fall by either more or less than the tax.

There are other microeconomic qualifications of the broad macroeconomic argument purporting to place the incidence of the tax on labor. In particular, the effects of unionization, monopsonistic hiring, and other departures from competition in the labor market may affect the impact of the tax on individual firms and workers.[54] The resulting allocative and employment effects may be significant for the economic units involved, but a detailed analysis of these adjustments would shed little light on the overall impact of payroll taxes on factor shares and

[54] For detailed analysis of the incidence question under a myriad of assumptions, see Harris, *Economics of Social Security*, Pt. 3, Chaps. 17–20.

the allocation of capital and labor. The latter question seems of sufficient importance in its own right to justify an aggregative statistical investigation. Statistical support of the aggregative theory of payroll tax incidence would be valuable, even without a detailed knowledge of the microeconomic adjustments underlying it.

# Technical Note: Methodological Questions

In considering a priori propositions and empirical evidence concerning payroll tax incidence, several methodological questions should be discussed. This technical discussion, however, may be passed over without loss of continuity by readers more interested in the findings than the conceptual framework.

## *The Incidence Concept*

In the discussion earlier in this chapter, the terms "incidence" and "shifting" were used without explicit consideration of their intended meaning. It is now appropriate to explain the incidence concept adopted in this study.[55] The "degree of shifting" is intended to measure the extent to which the "effective incidence" on a factor share departs from the "impact incidence."[56] But what is the meaning of "incidence" itself? Here the incidence of a tax means its effect on the distribution of income available for private use.[57] More specifically, the initial emphasis is placed on the effect of the tax on relative factor shares, or real rates of return to factors. (The relation and choice between the share and rate of return criteria is discussed below.)

For the analysis of a broad-based tax in a general equilibrium context, this interpretation of incidence immediately raises methodological problems. The phrase "available for private use" indicates that the adopted incidence concept excludes the impact of the distribution

[55] For earlier and detailed consideration of the issues discussed here, see Musgrave, *Theory of Public Finance*, Chaps. 10, 15, and 16; Harberger, "The Incidence of the Corporation Income Tax"; Charles E. McLure, Jr., "Tax Incidence, Macroeconomic Policy, and Absolute Prices," *Quarterly Journal of Economics*, Vol. 84 (May 1970), pp. 254–67; and Charles E. McLure, Jr., "The Theory of Tax Incidence with Imperfect Factor Mobility," *Finanzarchiv*, Vol. 30, No. 1 (1971), pp. 27–48.

[56] See Musgrave, *Theory of Public Finance*, p. 230.

[57] This conception follows Musgrave (*ibid.*, pp. 207–08). This stress on income distribution is more general than the traditional analysis of the "burden" of the tax on individuals or factors; for Musgrave, the latter is meaningless in a general equilibrium context with elastic factor supplies. However, assuming highly inelastic factor responses, the concept of a burden on individuals or groups appears meaningful.

of benefits (and any government goods and services) financed by the tax. This emphasis is consistent with the commonsense conception of tax incidence as the distribution (among individuals or groups) of the cost of public transfers and services. Since the immediate effect of the social security payroll tax is primarily on the active population—generally widely separated both in identity and by generations from benefit recipients—it seems especially appropriate for the tax incidence problem to be considered independently of the incidence of benefits.

Although an attempt is made to isolate the effects of the tax on private incomes, abstracting from the impact of benefits, it does not follow that the complex interaction of taxing and spending policies can be ignored. In the first place a substantial tax change, with other policies held constant, would produce macroeconomic effects that would cloud the meaning of tax incidence.[58] In an attempt to avoid such ambiguities, the incidence of the payroll tax is considered in the context of an assumed balanced budget, implying spending changes corresponding to each tax change.[59]

The assumption that the proceeds of an earmarked tax, such as the social security payroll tax, are roughly offset by spending on benefits seems adequately realistic, and it largely avoids the complications that would otherwise result from macro effects. (This assumes that any macro effects due to changed consumption patterns resulting from the transfer of income from the active population to transfer recipients are negligible.) However, the methodological problems do not end there. Since the outcome of an integrated tax-expenditure process is being analyzed, some public finance specialists have argued that it is not possible in this framework to isolate the incidence of the tax per se (as distinct from other policy effects).[60] For example, Shoup

[58] Musgrave (*ibid.*, pp. 211–12) refers to this as an analysis of "specific" tax incidence that cannot separate the income distribution effects of the tax from its macroeconomic effects.

[59] For a discussion of alternative analytical frameworks, see Musgrave, pp. 211–17. The analysis of a tax-transfer scheme could also be considered under the "differential tax incidence" concept. Instead of considering substitution of the payroll tax for another tax of equal yield, a new negative tax (the benefits) would be assumed to offset the payroll tax.

[60] This methodological problem is unavoidable in the consideration of a broad-based tax that cannot be changed in vacuo. General equilibrium considerations are involved. In the case of narrowly based taxes, on the other hand, a partial ceteris paribus analysis need not face up to any major repercussions caused by tax-expenditure interactions.

argues that a change in any broad-based tax must cause a change in at least one of the following policy variables: government expenditures, other taxes, government debt, and government cash balances. He therefore views as invalid the very concept of the incidence of a broad-based tax as such.[61] That is, the effects of a large tax cannot be isolated because of its interaction with other factors, especially government spending. This limits the analyst to comparisons among broad-based taxes. Thus, for example, in the case of the payroll tax, Shoup shows that its incidence is equivalent to that of the value added tax, consumption type, but he will not generalize about the incidence of either.[62]

Despite this potential difficulty, an empirical attempt is made in Chapter III to isolate the incidence of the payroll tax per se; to do so, however, requires making a simplifying assumption. In an approximate balanced budget context with transfer payments offsetting payroll taxes, it seems realistic to assume that government expenditures are approximately distributionally neutral in their impact on money incomes available for private use, as well as on relative product prices faced by various income groups. It should be stressed that in its collection and disbursement of these taxes, the government is primarily a conduit between the active population and transfer recipients. It seems unlikely that the marginal consumption patterns of the two groups are sufficiently different to produce substantial redistribution of private incomes. Even in the case of the existing differences, there is no reason to expect that they would favor one factor over the other. Thus, it can be assumed that, in practice, the resulting changes in consumption patterns caused by transfers are not great enough or discriminatory enough to significantly change either the relative shares received by capital and labor or the relative product prices paid by capitalists and laborers.[63] The assumption of approximate distribu-

[61] Shoup, *Public Finance*, pp. 7–8, 19. The most elaborate empirical study of corporation tax incidence—Marian Krzyzaniak and Richard A. Musgrave, *The Shifting of the Corporation Income Tax: An Empirical Study of Its Short-Run Effect upon the Rate of Return* (Johns Hopkins Press, 1963)—takes note of this problem, suggesting that the tax shifting measure is "contaminated" by associated changes in government expenditures (p. 47). Nevertheless, while mentioning this qualification frequently (for example, pp. 6–7, 49, 65–66), the authors apparently conclude that they are measuring primarily the effects of tax changes; however, they do concede that their estimates probably exaggerate the effects of the tax.

[62] On the equivalence of these two taxes, see Shoup, *Public Finance*, pp. 409–11.

[63] McLure reports Shoup's view that differential incidence can represent truly general

tional neutrality of the transfer of spending power through a tax to finance transfers seems plausible—certainly more so than in the case of a tax to finance government purchases of goods and services.[64] If so, all redistribution of real income available for private use may be attributed to the tax itself.[65]

Even if the expenditure effects of the tax-transfer process can be ignored, another aspect of the incidence problem remains to be considered. Essentially, the concept of the incidence of a tax refers to its impact on the distribution of real income among economic groups. This impact has two components: the effect on the distribution of *money* income among groups and the effect on the *relative prices* paid by each group for the products it buys. Thus it is said that redistribution of real income may occur as a result of (1) changes on the side of *sources* of income such as those due to relative changes in factor incomes, and (2) changes on the side of *uses* of income due to changes in relative product prices such as those faced by factor owners.[66] For example, even if labor's share is shown to fall by the amount of the tax and there is no change in the absolute price level, this is not the whole story with respect to the burden on labor's share, since it is necessary to consider also the side of uses of income. For example, if the price of products consumed heavily by capitalists rose relative to those consumed heavily by labor, at least part of the burden would fall on capitalists.

Although no study of the incidence of a tax is truly complete if it has not examined the effects of the tax on the side of uses of income,

---

equilibrium analysis, whereas balanced budget incidence remains partial unless one is willing to accept extreme assumptions about the effects of government services on the economy or to analyze these effects explicitly (McLure, "The Theory of Tax Incidence," p. 30, note 1). It should be repeated that here the subject is basically a tax-transfer process that can itself be interpreted as differential incidence analysis, with the transfers treated as a negative tax. Insofar as goods and service spending adjustments are not associated with the tax, no extreme assumptions are necessary.

[64] For example, Harberger in "Incidence of the Corporation Income Tax" was dependent on the assumption that government expenditure patterns were roughly the same as those of individuals, or at least that any differences produce no redistributional effect between the corporate and noncorporate sectors.

[65] There may be other general equilibrium complications besides the tax-expenditure association, but in the case of the social security tax this is probably the most important because of the generally close relationship.

[66] For development and clarification of this concept, see Musgrave, *Theory of Public Finance*, pp. 217–21; and McLure, "Tax Incidence, Macroeconomic Policy, and Absolute Prices" and "The Theory of Tax Incidence."

studies of broad-based taxes, both theoretical and empirical, have in practice concentrated on incidence on the side of sources of income.[67] It has been assumed that the consumption patterns of the groups distinguished in the analysis are broadly similar. If so, any changes occurring in relative product prices will affect all groups alike in their role as consumers of products. Actually, so stringent an assumption is not required. It may simply be assumed, with respect to capitalists and laborers in the present case, that product price changes due to the tax do not affect the relative cost of the bundles of goods consumed by each group. Regardless of consumption patterns, this assumption alone rules out incidence effects on the uses side. Such an assumption seems plausible in the case of the payroll tax. There is no reason to suspect that an increase in the money cost of labor will increase the price of the "market basket" of laborers significantly more or less than it will increase that of capitalists, unless one set of goods is much more labor-intensive than the other. On this ground, incidence on the side of uses of income is assumed away in this study. Such an assumption seems realistic in the absence of evidence to the contrary.[68]

To sum up, two simplifying assumptions—both of which seem realistic to the author at least—have been made in this study. First, the alteration of consumption patterns due to the transfer process is assumed to be minor and/or virtually neutral with respect to the distribution of real income shares between labor and others. Thus all redistribution is attributed to the tax rather than to the associated expenditure. Second, changes in relative product prices due to the tax are also assumed to be minor and/or redistributionally neutral with respect to the prices paid by labor and others. Thus the only redistribution that is recognized is on the side of sources of income, or factor shares in the present case.

### *"Backward" and "Forward" Shifting*

Traditionally, discussion of the incidence of the employer payroll tax has dwelt on the relative importance of "backward shifting" through wage restraint and "forward shifting" through price mark-

[67] An exception is the case of the sales tax; analysis has concentrated on the uses side, with income source effects being assumed away.

[68] Note that the conception of incidence adopted here does not depend on changes in absolute prices per se. It is determined completely by the movements in relative factor shares and relative product prices. See McLure, "Tax Incidence, Macroeconomic Policy, and Absolute Prices," pp. 254–59.

ups. The analysis of international data in Chapter III does not permit a distinction between these two mechanisms.[69] Since it is a cross-section analysis based on the constant dollars of one period of time, the estimated relationships are entirely in real terms, and the finding is simply that, given the level of productivity (value added per worker), the higher the employer tax rate, the lower the basic wage rate by about the same amount. If the employment effects of the tax are assumed to be negligible, this is also roughly equivalent to saying that the relative share of labor in value added is lower by the relative share of the tax in value added. However, it is impossible to say, for any given country, how much of the reduction by the tax of the basic wage rate *measured in dollars* is due to (1) wage restraint as measured in local currency, and (2) price markups reducing the value of the currency as measured in dollars. The converted dollar value of the wage rate could be reduced by the tax by any combination of these two factors.

For some this inability to distinguish between what has been traditionally called forward and backward shifting may appear a great limitation. Certainly, for example, policies that reduce the basic wage rate are greatly to be preferred by fixed income groups to those that raise the general price level.[70] However, the stress here on real magnitudes and relative shares, to the exclusion of the distinction between money wage and overall price movements, has both a pragmatic and a logical defense.[71] First, nothing can be said about the effect of a tax

[69] This is also true of the less convincing time series analysis presented in Chapter III, since it is carried out in terms of real (deflated) variables.

[70] One aspect of the distinction between backward and forward shifting, which has been mentioned in the literature, is irrelevant for the present analysis. It might be thought that backward shifting puts all the burden on labor, while forward shifting shares it among factors according to the consumption patterns of their owners; if so, labor incomes would bear only part of the burden. However, incidence of the tax on labor is here interpreted as a reduction of its relative share of real income by the full amount of the tax. Thus full forward shifting requires increases in money income (by means of price increases) sufficient to restore the full real income of nonlabor factors. Although labor's share is less than 100 percent, a full recouping in this sense of an $x$ percent tax on labor would generally require an average price increase of $x$ percent. (This point was discussed earlier in this chapter; for analogous reasoning with respect to the corporation tax, see Turek, "Short-Run Shifting of the Corporate Income Tax in Manufacturing, 1935–1965.")

[71] The general position taken here draws heavily on the valuable effort by McLure in "Tax Incidence, Macroeconomic Policy, and Absolute Prices" to dispel the confusion between tax incidence and the effects of macroeconomic policies on the general price level.

per se on the absolute price level. This depends on the accompanying macroeconomic policies, including the *level* of taxation itself.

A logical alternative to a futile attempt to separate tax incidence into factor price and price level effects is to focus on *relative* factor and product prices. It was argued earlier in this technical note that, under (sometimes plausible) simplifying assumptions, it is possible to isolate these relative effects as the incidence of a tax per se. Abstraction from the nature of the shifting mechanism is also essential for consideration of the incidence of the tax as such.

It should be reiterated that the distinction between wage restraint and price markup is not unimportant. The point is that such a breakdown of the impact of a tax per se is not uniquely determined by the size and nature of the tax alone. "Redistributions of income can result from inflationary or deflationary policies, including those of taxation. But these are best considered as separate phenomena resulting from the chosen macroeconomic policy, rather than from the particular tax in question."[72]

The estimates in Chapter III suggest that the relative share of labor in value added is reduced by the relative share of the tax. Measured in this way, the incidence of the tax has direct and important implications for the size distribution of individual incomes, whatever the effects of all macroeconomic policies on prices. Taken in conjunction with estimates of the factor source breakdown of income in each bracket, the imputation of the tax to labor's share permits an estimate of the effective tax rate on each bracket. This estimated net effect of the tax itself is the basis for the analysis in Chapters IV and V of the effects of the tax on individual income distribution.

### Relative Share and Real Wage Rate Criteria

It has just been argued that the impossibility of distinguishing between money wage and price effects of the tax invites reliance on the relative share effects as the criterion of incidence. In practice, the empirical work of Chapter III focuses on the effects of the tax on the real wage rate as a criterion of incidence; the models applied there relate the wage rate to the value added and tax per worker, all measured in constant dollars. If negligible employment effects are assumed, this formulation is approximately equivalent to relating the

[72] *Ibid.*, p. 266.

relative share of the basic wage in value added to the relative share of the tax.[73] Thus, under the assumption of highly inelastic labor supply, the real wage rate and relative share criteria are closely related; they are also alike in that neither is capable of separating the money wage and price effects of the tax.

If the possibility of substantial employment effects of the tax is admitted, the entire incidence question becomes very murky, and the choice of appropriate criteria becomes much more debatable. The impact of the tax on (1) the real wage rate, (2) the relative share of labor, and (3) the real absolute share of labor all have some meaning for this question, but no one of them tells the entire story. If the (basic) real wage rate held up under the tax as the result of a collapse in employment, it would seem reasonable to say that labor had not completely avoided the burden of a nearly universal national tax. (An exception would be the extreme case in which the displaced labor could migrate and be absorbed elsewhere at the same real wage rate.) On the other hand, if the *relative* share of labor held up, in part, because capital left the country, that would not indicate complete avoidance of the tax burden either. And if labor's real absolute wage bill held up while that of capital went down by *more* than the tax, it would be incomplete to say that labor simply avoided the tax.

Conceptual ambiguities such as these would become overwhelming in the face of substantial employment effects from the tax. It was suggested earlier that a realistic and promising context within which to view this problem is under an assumed balanced budget with minimal macroeconomic effects. If this is acceptable, the redistributional impact of the tax itself on private income can be analyzed meaningfully, despite associated changes in government spending. In other words, the assumption of spending changes related to the tax minimizes employment effects without preventing isolation of the incidence of the tax per se. In this full employment framework the three criteria mentioned are roughly equivalent, and the estimates of real wage rate effects to be presented have a definite meaning, even though no distinction can be made between money wage and price effects.

Some reasons for expecting minimal employment effects of the social security tax-expenditure package were discussed earlier in this

---

[73] The models applied are somewhat more general than the latter, however, in that they do not force the estimated elasticity of substitution to equal unity.

chapter. However, the possibility cannot be ruled out that a depression of the take-home wage rate by the tax could cause a significant substitution of leisure for labor, reducing the equilibrium employment level. Even in this event, the incidence criteria discussed above retain some meaning. The demonstration in Chapter III that the equilibrium real wage rate is depressed by the full amount of the tax rate would carry an even stronger message if it could be shown that this occurs despite a contraction of employment. On the absolute real share criterion, labor would then bear even more than the full amount of the tax itself; the same would be true on the relative share criterion unless real nonwage income fell relatively more than employment. From this point of view, then, a full burden on labor under the wage rate criterion represents an even greater burden if employment contracts.[74]

### Stress on Employer Portion of Tax

An economist scanning literature on the payroll tax is likely to be struck by the frequency with which employer and employee portions are assumed to be distinctly different in their effects. Most public finance specialists would probably accept the theorem that, except for frictions and institutional peculiarities, the economic effects of a payroll tax are the same whether it is imposed on the employer or employee side of the labor market.[75] From that viewpoint, it makes no sense to analyze the employer and employee taxes separately. However, many specialists, and laymen as well, concerned with social security taxes have typically assumed that the employee tax is borne by the employee, while the employer tax is borne by the employer or "passed along" in higher prices. In this context, a strong opinion among economists that labor bears the entire payroll tax could account for the rather extensive controversy over the incidence of the employer portion.[76] Since there appears to be fairly general agree-

[74] If the income effect should outweigh the substitution effect, and equilibrium employment is increased by the tax, a full burden on labor under the wage rate criterion would generally represent less than a 100 percent burden under the other criteria.

[75] See, for example, Musgrave, *Theory of Public Finance*, pp. 350–52, and Shoup, *Public Finance*, p. 409.

[76] On the early consensus among economists, see Harris, *Economics of Social Security*, pp. 285–86. For recent thinking, see Pechman and others, *Social Security*, pp. 175–78.

ment that employees bear their portion of the tax and disagreement over the incidence of the employer portion, it is not surprising to find attention concentrated on the latter.

In this chapter and in the later empirical work, the focus is on the incidence of the employer tax. This methodological choice does not imply any assumptions with respect to the incidence of the employee portion of the tax, or of the tax imposed on the self-employed.[77] Inferences concerning the incidence of these taxes may be postponed until after consideration of the employer tax.

A concentration on the employer tax rather than separate or combined analysis of all three taxes seems appropriate for two main reasons. First, despite the plausible proposition of tax experts that an analytical distinction between taxes imposed on the two sides of the labor market is artificial, many economists and social security experts are not persuaded.[78] Rightly or wrongly, the most commonly expressed view appears to be that the employee tax is borne by the employee, but the incidence of the employer tax is in doubt. In fact, this is simply taken for granted by some public finance specialists. For example, Eckstein writes, "The employee contribution is an increasingly heavy tax on wages, particularly on low wages. . . . To the extent that the employer contribution also falls on the workers, the burden becomes even greater."[79] Since a distinction is generally made between the two taxes, the employer tax incidence being the more

[77] Only rarely has it been suggested that the burden of the tax paid by employees can be shifted forward to employers by the extraction of higher real wages and salaries. "The usual view is that direct taxes on personal income, consumption, or wealth cannot be shifted. While there are no doubt exceptional circumstances in which short-run shifting does occur, the assumption that in general the personal taxes rest on those who pay them seems reasonable." See Richard Goode, *The Individual Income Tax* (Brookings Institution, 1964), pp. 60–61. However, there are opposing opinions. For example, Shoup (*Public Finance*, p. 409) states: "Although the particular pattern of differential incidence may not be clear in any one instance, a tax on labor income cannot be said to burden only labor income."

[78] For example, see Otto Eckstein and Vito Tanzi, "Comparison of European and United States Tax Structures and Growth Implications," in *The Role of Direct and Indirect Taxes in the Federal Revenue System*, Conference Report of the National Bureau of Economic Research and the Brookings Institution (Brookings Institution, 1964), p. 222. Here the employer taxes are considered indirect taxes "because they are costs of carrying on business." However, "Employee contributions to social security are included as a direct tax."

[79] Otto Eckstein, "Financing the System of Social Insurance," in William G. Bowen and others (eds.), *The American System of Social Insurance: Its Philosophy, Impact, and Future Development* (McGraw-Hill, 1968), p. 55.

controversial, primary and direct consideration of the latter seems in order.

A second reason for concentrating on the employer tax is that such an analysis may clarify the entire picture; it can be inferred from the previously mentioned theorem that any conclusion about the employer tax must also hold for the employee tax. Even skeptics who feel that the two taxes may have different effects are unlikely to believe that labor can shift the burden of its own portion if it cannot even avoid the burden of the tax nominally paid by employers.[80] Such a finding could also be construed as evidence in support of the general neoclassical proposition that a tax on the use of a factor is borne by that factor. From this it would follow that self-employed persons also bear the entire social security tax on their income—including their imputed income from capital as well as their income from labor.[81]

[80] In the case of the old-age, survivors, disability, and health insurance (OASDHI) tax in this country, any regression finding with respect to the employer tax variable would necessarily hold also for the entire payroll tax. The latter is just double the former (except for the small excess tax, not refundable, paid by employers in the name of multiemployer earners).

[81] Earnings of the self-employed have been taxed at three-fourths the combined rate on employers and employees, as the result of a political compromise. However, the rate might be rationalized on economic grounds if it were designed to exempt one-fourth of self-employed income as nontaxable imputed return to capital. (The ratio is scheduled to decline from three-fourths because of the 7 percent ceiling on the self-employed rate.)

# CHAPTER III

# Empirical Analysis of Incidence

THE A PRIORI POSITION in Chapter II that labor bears the employer pay-roll tax—and therefore the employee tax also—is tested empirically in this chapter.[1] Widespread skepticism among those who have considered the issues and the bewildering array of potential microeconomic effects of the tax combine to call for an aggregative statistical analysis. Such an analysis was undertaken at two levels: (1) cross-section regression models fitted to country data for all manufacturing and for thirteen individual manufacturing industries, and (2) time series regression models fitted to U.S. data for twenty-seven individual industries.[2]

[1] It may be useful to repeat that the stress on the employer tax was due to the greater controversy surrounding it. This entails no assumption about the incidence of the employee tax. However, if the proposition can be sustained for the employer tax, there can be little doubt that it also holds for the employee portion.

[2] Since another empirical analysis of the incidence of a broad-based tax is attempted here, note should be taken of the heavy fire that greeted the elaborate econometric study of the corporation income tax by Marian Krzyzaniak and Richard A. Musgrave, *The Shifting of the Corporation Income Tax: An Empirical Study of Its Short-Run Effect upon the Rate of Return* (Johns Hopkins Press, 1963). For a useful summary of earlier criticism and additional points, see Carl S. Shoup, "Quantitative Research in Taxation and Government Expenditure" (National Bureau of Economic Research, no date; processed),

The objective here is to isolate quantitatively the long-run impact of employer payroll taxes on earnings and factor shares (and, by inference, the long-run impact of employee taxes as well). The primary approach builds on the relationship between the compensation and productivity of labor that has been frequently observed and is also implied under certain assumptions by the specification of a production function. The main reliance is placed on an intercountry analysis that takes statistical advantage of the wide variation in tax rates among countries. However, results of time series analysis of the U.S. experience are also reported. The analysis is carried out for the manufacturing sector in aggregate and for two-digit manufacturing industries. The overall indication is that firms react to their payroll tax as they do to any other labor cost in setting output and price and agreeing to the total compensation to be awarded a given degree of labor productivity. The long-run result appears to be that employers in the aggregate avoid the burden of their contribution by means of a trade-off between the tax and real wages and salaries.

## Hypotheses and Regression Models

### Initial Hypotheses

The degree of shifting may be defined as the fraction $s$ of the employer tax actually borne by labor. In keeping with the discussion in Chapter II, the a priori hypothesis is that the tax is borne entirely by labor; that is, $s = 1$. This follows from a competitive model of the demand for labor and an assumed zero elasticity of aggregate labor supply with respect to the real wage rate. Under pure "backward shifting" (no product price or employment effects from the tax), the fixed amount of labor would be hired only if the basic wage was lower by the amount of the tax than it would be without the tax. This is

---

pp. 55–59. So devastating was the criticism that it may seem foolhardy to undertake another empirical study, even of a different tax. However, most of the criticism of the Krzyzaniak-Musgrave study claimed that misspecification of the time series models resulted in attribution to the tax variable of influences probably due to parallel (and coincidental) cyclical developments in the economy. In the analysis here, since the primary findings are those from cross-section data, this type of misspecification, at least, is not present. Shoup adds that Krzyzaniak and Musgrave have not really separated the effects of the tax and associated spending, a limitation they themselves have repeatedly acknowledged. The relevance of the criticism to this study is discussed in the technical note at the end of Chapter II; whether it is serious depends on one's view of the two simplifying assumptions made here.

**TABLE 3-1. Dependence of Hypothesized Values of the Payroll Tax Shifting Coefficient (s) on Labor Supply and Demand Elasticities**

| Elasticity of labor supply (finite) | Elasticity of labor demand (finite, absolute values) | | | |
|---|---|---|---|---|
| | 1 | More than 1 | Less than 1 | 0 |
| Zero | s = 1 | s = 1 | s = 1 | — |
| More than zero | s = 1 | s > 1 | 0 < s < 1 | s = 0 |
| Less than zero | s = 1 | s < 1 | s > 1 | s = 0 |

Source: Author's hypothesis.

summarized in the first line of Table 3-1. If the assumption of zero supply elasticity is dropped *and* labor does not regard the employer contribution as part of its compensation, the resulting employment effect makes $s$ depend on the elasticities.[3] In the special case of a unitary demand elasticity, the outcome would be determinate by definition. Since the aggregate compensation of labor (including the tax) would be invariant with respect to employment, the basic wage bill would be reduced by exactly the amount of the tax, and $s = 1$ as indicated in the first column of Table 3-1. Thus, if the aggregate wage bill is taken as the criterion, even an employment effect does not necessarily rule out the proposition that labor bears the full burden.[4]

The alternative hypotheses of $s > 1$ and $s < 1$ can be derived from plausible assumptions, as indicated in Table 3-1. If a labor supply function with positive elasticity and a demand elasticity greater (less) than one is assumed, imposition of the tax would reduce the basic wage bill by more (less) than the amount of the tax. Since employment would be reduced by the tax, a demand elasticity greater than one would result by definition in a reduction in aggregate compensation (including the tax) and therefore a decline in the after-tax

[3] As discussed in Chapter II, once the possibility of substantial variation in labor supply and employment is admitted, the aggregative analysis becomes questionable due to general equilibrium relationships. The reasoning that follows is presented cautiously with the hope that an aggregate labor demand function has enough meaning at least to suggest directions of relationships. This is particularly true of extreme cases, such as that of zero demand elasticity.

[4] Even this case is not entirely free of ambiguity concerning the impact of the tax, however. On the assumption that firms were maximizing profits before the tax, the employment adjustment will only reduce—not eliminate—the bite out of the share of capital. Thus the combined decline in the shares of labor and capital would be greater than the amount of the tax in this case of unitary demand elasticity.

wage bill greater than the total employer tax ($s > 1$). The more elastic the demand, the greater the negative employment effect relative to the positive compensation rate effect. In the case of a backward-sloping labor supply curve, however, these relationships are reversed, since employment would increase (ignoring the unstable case in which the supply curve is less steep than the demand curve). With a demand elasticity greater (less) than one, imposition of the tax would reduce the basic wage bill by less (more) than the tax.

While values of $s$ other than unity can be derived from plausible elasticities, the hypothesis $s = 0$ (zero wage effect of the tax) seems highly implausible. This result depends on zero elasticity of demand with respect to the wage rate (in the case of an upward-sloping supply curve). As summarized in Table 3-1, under any demand elasticity greater than zero, imposition of the tax would cut employment and the after-tax wage bill ($s > 0$). Hicks has analyzed the determinants of the elasticity of derived factor demand at the industry level in a two-factor world.[5]

Under the assumptions of the competitive marginal productivity model, there is an exact relationship between the elasticity of the derived demand for labor $e_d$ and the elasticity of demand for the product $a$, the elasticity of the supply of capital $b$, the relative share of labor $c$, and the elasticity of substitution $d$:

$$e_d = \frac{d(a + b) + cb(a - d)}{a + b - c(a - d)}.$$

A zero elasticity of labor demand is implausible in itself, and this relation reinforces this a priori impression, if one accepts that it also has validity at the aggregate level. At least two of the determinants of $e_d$ (for example, product demand elasticity and elasticity of substitution) must be zero for the expression to vanish. In view of the implausibility of such extreme values, the hypothesis $s = 0$ seems untenable within the framework of the competitive model and an assumed upward-sloping supply curve. Only if the supply curve is backward sloping is zero shifting possible with a demand elasticity other than zero, and this requires a special combination of elasticities.

[5] John R. Hicks, *The Theory of Wages* (2d ed., St. Martin's Press, 1964), pp. 241–46 and 373–78. Whether or not the application of Hicks's industry demand analysis to the problem of aggregate demand is acceptable must be left to the judgment of the reader. The clues it offers are not essential to the empirical work in this study.

Even so, it seems in order to test $s = 0$ as the logical alternative to $s = 1$.

*Cross-Country Regression Models*

The first and most productive set of tests utilized cross-country regression models. The objective was to isolate the long-run impact of the employer tax on real wage rates, as distinct from the speed and process of shifting.[6] Cross-section regression analysis of aggregative data for countries can offer direct evidence on the long-run response to the tax.[7] The stress on countries rather than on states of this country was dictated by institutional realities. There are enormous inter-country differences in employer payroll tax rates but only minute differences across the states of this country.[8]

The statistical models used were variations and elaborations of the estimating equation that emerges from the constant elasticity of substitution (CES) production function.[9] The variables originally considered in statistical analysis of the CES function were:

$V$ = value added in thousands of U.S. dollars;
$L$ = labor input in man-years;
$w$ = the basic wage rate (total labor cost excluding employer contributions for social insurance, divided by $L$), in dollars per man-year.

The logarithmic transformation was generally favored, and the usual relationship estimated was:

$$(3\text{-}1) \qquad \log V/L = a_1 + b_1 \log w + u_1,$$

where $u$ (in this and succeeding equations) is a stochastic error term.

---

[6] See the technical note at the end of Chapter II for a comparison of the real wage rate with other criteria of incidence and a discussion of the analytical inseparability of forward and backward shifting.

[7] For a statement of the argument that cross-section regressions do generally yield long-run relationships, see, for example, Lawrence R. Klein, *An Introduction to Econometrics* (Prentice-Hall, 1962), pp. 52–60. On the other hand, the U.S. time series analysis presented later in this chapter must rely on the partial adaptations approach to estimate long-run reaction to the tax.

[8] The analysis of country data to be described was repeated for states, but no significant evidence was found for or against the shifting hypothesis. The estimating errors were far too large.

[9] For the original presentation of the underlying theoretical construct, see K. J. Arrow and others, "Capital-Labor Substitution and Economic Efficiency," *Review of Economics and Statistics*, Vol. 43 (August 1961), pp. 225–50.

Under assumptions of validity of the CES production function, competitive product and factor markets and equilibrium, correct measurement of variables, and an exogenous wage rate, the estimate of the slope $b_1$ is an estimate of the elasticity of substitution between labor and all capital inputs.[10] This claim has been challenged on many grounds,[11] but this interpretation of the coefficient is not essential to the present application of the model. One can acknowledge the distinguished paternity of equation (3-1) as a point of departure without being dependent in any way on the rigid assumptions needed to deduce it from the underlying theoretical construct.[12] The relationship is a commonsense one a priori, and indeed the original authors apparently tested it statistically before coming up with the CES function as a theoretical underpinning. In addition, the particular direction of association specified in equation (3-1) does not follow from the underlying model, and the reverse specification appears equally plausible. To avoid dependence on any assumption on this score, the equations have been fitted both ways.

The assumed relationship was generalized to permit explicit analysis of the impact of the employer contributions for social insurance. The new specification can be most readily rationalized for the version stating in logarithmic form that the average wage rate in a country is dependent on the productivity of its labor:

$$(3\text{-}2) \qquad \log w = a_2 + b_2 \log V/L + u_2.$$

---

[10] Since wages constitute a substantial fraction of value added, a close regression fit is to be expected on that ground alone. This fact has led researchers in the Social Security Administration to suspect that estimates of the coefficients might themselves be biased, including the tax coefficient introduced in equation (3-3). Their Monte Carlo studies showed only minor bias in the expected direction.

[11] For example, it has been argued that the CES function itself, like the Cobb-Douglas function or models with fixed input coefficients, is only a special case of a more plausible and more general model. Recognition of this would require the presence of the capital variable in the estimating equation. See, for example, George H. Hildebrand and Ta-Chung Liu, *Manufacturing Production Functions in the United States, 1957: Interindustry and Interstate Comparison of Productivity* (Cornell University, 1965).

[12] This is a pragmatic viewpoint. After the tax variable is introduced explicitly in the related equation (3-3), the estimated regression coefficient indicates that, given productivity, the higher the tax rate, the lower the basic wage rate $w$ by about the same amount. Whether or not the underlying CES rationale is accepted, this indicates a depression of the wage rate by the tax rate unless and until an overruling explanation of the statistical result, such as omitted variables, can be established. (Even an associated depression of employment would not undermine the finding, since this would indicate a fall in the real wage bill even greater than the tax.)

The question immediately arises as to whether the wage rate associated with a given level of productivity includes the employer payroll tax per unit of labor in addition to the basic wage rate.[13] This element can be incorporated as an effective tax rate $t$ applied to the basic (private) wage rate $w$. The rate of compensation of labor was assumed to be best measured by $w$ plus some unknown fraction $s$ of the employer payroll tax $tw$. This generalized model is:

$$(3\text{-}3) \qquad \log w(1 + st) = a_3 + b_3 \log V/L + u_3.$$

For estimation of $s$, this may be rewritten with the basic wage rate $w$ as the dependent variable:

$$(3\text{-}3a) \qquad \log w = a_3 + b_3 \log V/L - \log(1 + st) + u_3.$$

The coefficient $s$ in this model may be interpreted as the "shifting coefficient," or the fraction of the employer tax per worker which is actually borne by labor in the long run. For example, if $s$ should equal zero, $\log(1 + st)$ equals zero, and the estimated basic wage rate would be independent of the tax, depending solely on productivity; this would indicate no shifting. However, an $s$ value of unity would indicate that for a given level of productivity $V/L$ the presence of the tax lowers the estimated basic wage rate by just the amount of the tax.[14] This shows a direct and complete trade-off between the basic wage rate and the tax per worker, or 100 percent shifting of the tax burden at the expense of labor's basic wage.[15]

The term $\log(1 + st)$ is awkward for estimation purposes, but the parameter $s$ can be extricated by approximating $\log(1 + st)$ either by $s \log(1 + t)$ or by the first term of the Taylor expansion $s(0.434t)$;[16]

---

[13] Note that the basic wage rate $w$, as defined above, includes private fringe benefits and does not exclude payroll taxes paid by employees.

[14] If $\log w_0$ and $\log w_1$ are the regression estimates of the dependent variable before and after tax (and $w_0$ and $w_1$ are the implied basic wage rates), $\log w_1 = \log w_0 - \log(1 + t)$, and $w_1 = w_0 - tw_1$. Therefore, the new basic wage rate tends to equal the original basic wage rate less the tax per unit of labor. This interpretation may be generalized to cover values of $s$ other than zero or one. The model implies that $w_1 = w_0 - stw_1$; the new wage rate tends to fall short of the old by the fraction $s$ of the tax $tw_1$.

[15] This shifting interpretation is, of course, subject to the qualification concerning possible employment effects discussed in Chapter II. The effect of the tax on the wage *bill* could be different in relative terms from its effect on the wage *rate*. However, any such complication signals no particular direction of bias in $s$ as a measure of the degree of shifting.

[16] The first of these approximations is exactly correct when $s$ equals zero or unity, too low for $s$ values in between, and too high for $s$ greater than one. The second is correct if

results by the two methods agree closely. For estimation purposes, two approximations of the equation (3-3a) emerge:

(3-4) $\qquad \log w = a_4 + b_4 \log V/L - s_4 \log(1 + t) + u_4$

(3-5) $\qquad \log w = a_5 + b_5 \log V/L - s_5(0.434t) + u_5.$

Treatment of $\log V/L$ as the dependent variable leads by analogous reasoning to two alternative estimating equations in which $s$ continues to be interpreted as the shifting coefficient:

(3-6) $\qquad \log V/L = a_6 + b_6 \log w + b_6 s_6 \log(1 + t) + u_6$

(3-7) $\qquad \log V/L = a_7 + b_7 \log w + b_7 s_7(0.434t) + u_7.$

These four models all rely on the logarithmic transformation of the variables. From the theoretical point of view, the logarithmic form might be favored, because it was the one that emerged from the well-known CES rationale; it was also preferable for statistical reasons, since it afforded a closer approach to the property of homoscedasticity. However, the corresponding models without the transformation were also estimated in the early stages, because there was no need to approximate $\log(1 + st)$.[17] The equations are:

(3-8) $\qquad w = a_8 + b_8 V/L - s_8 tw + u_8$

(3-9) $\qquad V/L = a_9 + bw_9 + b_9 s_9 tw + u_9.$

Models (3-4) to (3-9) offer six alternative estimates of the shifting coefficient $s$. Two further elaborations of the original model were attempted, but no improvement was achieved over these six equations.[18]

---

$s = 0$ and too high for positive values of $s$. (The two approximations bracket the correct value if $s$ is between zero and one.) The absolute error in the approximations varies positively with $t$ but does not seem excessively large for extreme values of $t$, such as 0.4. In any case the results from both approximations are presented to suggest the order of magnitude of error.

[17] Equation (3-8) also offers the most direct interpretation of the coefficient $s$. For example, if the estimate of $s$ is unity, the expression says that, for a given level of productivity, the higher the tax per unit of labor $tw$, the lower the estimated basic wage rate $w$ by the same amount.

[18] Since it has been suggested that models explaining productivity, such as equations (3-6), (3-7), and (3-9), should include capital as an explanatory variable, data on energy consumed and other conceivable proxies for capital stock were sought; however, this type of information was not available for a sufficient number of countries. Although only manufacturing data were considered, another possibility was that the wage variable $w$ was understated by its exclusion of imputed wages of self-employed persons. A variable

## Cross-Country Empirical Findings

Most of the basic country data on value added, wages and salaries, and employment were taken from a manufacturing census for 1958, but any annual census in the period 1957–59 was treated as eligible for the cross-section analysis. Four alternative sets of currency conversion ratios, including estimated "purchasing power parity ratios" based on price indexes as well as official exchange rates, were used to convert other currencies to dollars. Three sets of countries were selected and studied separately. The resulting twelve sets of country data measured in dollars were used for separate estimates of each model; this was done in the belief that repeated tests based on partially independent sets of data would be more informative than one fit to a single, arbitrarily selected set. Effective payroll tax rates were estimated from statutory rates. Data sources, criteria for country selection, and processing methods are outlined in Appendix A.

### Data for All Manufacturing

Two competing hypotheses concerning the shifting coefficient—$s = 0$ and $s = 1$—were first weighed against each other on a goodness-of-fit criterion. This was done by simplifying model (3-3) in accordance with the two hypotheses and asking which of these two-variable correlations produced the higher $\bar{R}^2$. If the association between some variant of labor compensation and productivity is accepted as meaningful, this test should indicate which of the two hypotheses is more plausible. For all twelve combinations of conversion methods and sets of countries, the earnings rate measure that includes employer payroll taxes (equivalent to the hypothesis $s = 1$) is more closely associated with productivity than the basic wage rate (equivalent to the hypothesis $s = 0$), as reported in Table 3-2. Although the improvements in the relationship achieved by inclusion of the employer tax are not great, the consistency of the results offers

---

was constructed to test this. As a measure of the importance of self-employment, the ratio of the *number engaged* to the *number employed* was considered; denoting this ratio by $z$ and its coefficient as $y$, the term $(1 + yz)$ was applied to the wage rate $w$ in the same way that the tax term $(1 + st)$ was built in. The expected positive sign for $y$ predominated in the estimates, but it was significant in so few cases that the results did not merit reporting.

**TABLE 3-2.** Comparison of Two Hypotheses Concerning the Employer Tax Shifting Coefficient ($s = 0$ and $s = 1$), Using the Goodness-of-Fit Criterion ($\bar{R}^2$),[a] by Sets of Countries, 1957–59

| Currency conversion method | 64 countries | | 44 countries | | 30 countries | |
|---|---|---|---|---|---|---|
| | $s = 1$ (with tax) | $s = 0$ (without tax) | $s = 1$ (with tax) | $s = 0$ (without tax) | $s = 1$ (with tax) | $s = 0$ (without tax) |
| Purchasing power parity ratio $x_1$ | 0.931 | 0.921 | 0.933 | 0.918 | 0.944 | 0.934 |
| Official exchange rate $x_2$ | 0.926 | 0.915 | 0.921 | 0.906 | 0.926 | 0.915 |
| Official exchange rate $x_3$ | 0.921 | 0.910 | 0.909 | 0.893 | 0.922 | 0.912 |
| Purchasing power parity ratio $x_4$ | 0.938 | 0.927 | 0.933 | 0.917 | 0.937 | 0.928 |

Sources: See Appendix A for data sources, explanation of currency conversion methods, and processing information; see text for explanation of the models used to derive the results.

[a] The tabulated values of $\bar{R}^2$ measure the association of the logarithms of productivity $V/L$ and alternative measures of labor compensation $w$ and $w(1 + t)$, adjusted for degrees of freedom. See pp. 64 and 66 for definitions of $V$, $L$, $w$, and $t$.

preliminary support for the hypothesis $s = 1$ rather than $s = 0$.[19]

Table 3-3 reports explicit estimates of the shifting coefficient $s$, based on models (3-4) to (3-9) as fitted to data for aggregate manufacturing.[20] All of the models produce high multiple correlation coefficients for all sets of data, with 92 to 96 percent of the variance explained in each case. The results for the logarithmic models (3-4) to (3-7) show positive values of $s$ significantly greater than zero in every case (at the 2.5 percent level of significance or better). On the basis of this methodology, the no-shift hypothesis appears thoroughly discredited at the aggregate level. Although all twenty-four of the point estimates of $s$ (falling in the range 1.14 to 1.60) are greater than the alternative hypothetical value of unity, they are not embarrassingly

[19] It is also worth noting that the models using estimated purchasing power parity ratios $x_1$ and $x_4$ give closer fits in every case than those for the relatively arbitrary official exchange rates contained in variables $x_2$ and $x_3$.

[20] The fitting of models to aggregative data is clearly a distasteful procedure when viewed within the production function framework. However, the negative association revealed between the tax variable and the basic wage, given productivity, nevertheless seems meaningful and indicative of a trade-off between basic wages and employer taxes. Results are reported for conversion ratios $x_1$ and $x_2$ only, because they were very nearly duplicated by the results for ratios $x_4$ and $x_3$ respectively.

**TABLE 3-3.** Regression Estimates of Employer Tax Shifting Coefficient, Based on Aggregate Data for Manufacturing, Using Purchasing Power Parity Ratio $x_1$ and Official Exchange Rate $x_2$, by Sets of Countries, 1957–59

| Model | Statistic[a] | 64 countries | | 44 countries | | 30 countries | |
|---|---|---|---|---|---|---|---|
| | | $x_1$ | $x_2$ | $x_1$ | $x_2$ | $x_1$ | $x_2$ |
| (3-4) | s | 1.325[b] | 1.326[b] | 1.535[b] | 1.435[c] | 1.538[c] | 1.564[c] |
| | S(s) | (0.463) | (0.467) | (0.463) | (0.486) | (0.650) | (0.691) |
| | $\bar{R}^2$ | 0.930 | 0.924 | 0.934 | 0.921 | 0.944 | 0.926 |
| (3-5) | s | 1.149[b] | 1.140[b] | 1.317[b] | 1.224[b] | 1.392[c] | 1.413[c] |
| | S(s) | (0.408) | (0.411) | (0.405) | (0.425) | (0.580) | (0.616) |
| | $\bar{R}^2$ | 0.929 | 0.924 | 0.933 | 0.920 | 0.944 | 0.926 |
| (3-6)[d] | s | 1.517[b] | 1.533[b] | 1.597[b] | 1.471[b] | 1.527[c] | 1.561[c] |
| | S(s) | (0.473) | (0.478) | (0.478) | (0.507) | (0.673) | (0.721) |
| | $\bar{R}^2$ | 0.932 | 0.926 | 0.934 | 0.920 | 0.943 | 0.925 |
| (3-7)[d] | s | 1.313[b] | 1.313[b] | 1.370[b] | 1.252[b] | 1.380[c] | 1.407[c] |
| | S(s) | (0.416) | (0.421) | (0.418) | (0.444) | (0.600) | (0.644) |
| | $\bar{R}^2$ | 0.931 | 0.926 | 0.933 | 0.920 | 0.943 | 0.925 |
| (3-8) | s | 1.286[b] | 0.892[e] | 1.484[b] | 1.004[e] | 1.046[e] | 0.658 |
| | S(s) | (0.395) | (0.454) | (0.424) | (0.530) | (0.556) | (0.678) |
| | $\bar{R}^2$ | 0.943 | 0.932 | 0.948 | 0.927 | 0.960 | 0.934 |
| (3-9)[d] | s | 1.706[b] | 1.428[b] | 1.762[b] | 1.418[c] | 1.310[c] | 1.083 |
| | S(s) | (0.386) | (0.452) | (0.414) | (0.532 ) | (0.550) | (0.685) |
| | $\bar{R}^2$ | 0.949 | 0.938 | 0.953 | 0.933 | 0.963 | 0.937 |

Source: Same as Table 3-2.

[a] $s$ = shifting coefficient; $S(s)$ = standard error; $\bar{R}^2$ = adjusted coefficient of determination.

[b] Different from zero in the expected (positive) direction at the 0.5 percent level of significance.

[c] Different from zero in the expected (positive) direction at the 2.5 percent level of significance.

[d] The shifting coefficient $s$ in models (3-6), (3-7), and (3-9) is estimated by the ratio of the coefficients $bs$ and $b$. The standard errors $S(s)$ for these three models are derived from an abbreviated version of Taylor's expansion approximation; see Lawrence R. Klein, A Textbook of Econometrics (Row, Peterson, 1953), p. 258. The estimate used was the ratio $S(bs)/b$. This approximation ignored the variance of $b$ and the covariance of $b$ and $bs$ on the ground that they were generally small relative to the variance of $bs$.

[e] Different from zero in the expected (positive) direction at the 5 percent level of significance.

large; the estimates exceed one by a maximum of about one standard error and are therefore consistent with the hypothesis that 100 percent of the tax is borne by labor. The results for models (3-8) and (3-9) without the logarithmic transformation are somewhat more erratic, but they tell the same story. These models show estimates of $s$ significantly greater than zero in ten out of twelve cases. In only two cases were the estimates substantially greater than unity. In sum, models (3-8) and (3-9) support the shifting results of models (3-4) to (3-7) but less convincingly.

## Analysis by Industry

Wages and productivity in two-digit manufacturing industries were next analyzed for the maximum number of countries with data available. In each case, the simple correlation between the logarithms of productivity and wage rates with employer taxes ($s = 1$) and without employer taxes ($s = 0$) was first computed. The wage rate measure, which included the employer payroll tax (equivalent to the hypothesis $s = 1$), was found to give the higher correlation in all thirteen industries studied, whatever currency conversion ratio was used. This offers substantial additional evidence of the superiority of hypothesis $s = 1$ over $s = 0$.

Tax rates were next included explicitly in the regressions, and results for individual industries are presented in Table 3-4.[21] Several of the industry models fit considerably less well than the aggregate models, but on the whole the $\bar{R}^2$ estimates remain very high (falling below 0.9 for only three industries). The estimates of the shifting coefficient $s$ based on models (3-4) to (3-7) are significantly greater than zero at the 5 percent level or better in the case of seven of the thirteen industries, but in no case significantly greater than unity; thus the majority of the industries strongly support rejection of the hypothesis $s = 0$ in favor of the hypothesis $s = 1$. Only in the single case of the nonmetallic mineral products industry can the hypothesis $s = 1$ be rejected in favor of the hypothesis $s = 0$. The median estimate of $s$ is that obtained for the clothing and footwear industry, no matter which of the four models is applied; although each of these estimates of the shifting coefficient $s$ is slightly greater than one (ranging from 1.12 to 1.23), none is significantly above one. These industry results, while not unanimous, greatly favor the hypothesis $s = 1$ over the hypothesis $s = 0$, and indicate a 100 percent trade-off between payroll taxes and the basic wage rate.[22]

[21] The purchasing power parity ratio $x_1$ produced closer fits than did the exchange rate $x_2$ for all thirteen industries. However, the estimates for $s$ were so similar in the two cases that only those for $x_1$ were tabulated.

[22] The industry tabulations in Table 3-4 focus on the shifting coefficient $s$, its standard error, and the overall fit of each equation. To facilitate appraisal of the overall plausibility of the models, results for other coefficients are given in Appendix B, where the results are compared with those of previous cross-country studies of the original CES model. Although the latter did not consider the employer tax explicitly, the data and specifications are sufficiently similar to permit the judgment that the findings here are consistent in other respects with the earlier work, despite its different emphasis.

**TABLE 3-4. Estimates of Employer Tax Shifting Coefficient, by Industry, Using Currency Conversion Ratio $x_1$, in Varying Numbers of Countries, 1957–59**

| Industry | Number of countries | Statistic[a] | Model (3-4) | Model (3-5) | Model (3-6) | Model (3-7) |
|---|---|---|---|---|---|---|
| Food, beverages, and | 36 | s | 1.74[b] | 1.57[b] | 1.83[b] | 1.65[b] |
| tobacco | | S(s) | (0.86) | (0.78) | (0.90) | (0.81) |
| | | $\bar{R}^2$ | 0.907 | 0.907 | 0.907 | 0.907 |
| Textiles | 34 | s | 1.82[c] | 1.64[c] | 1.99[c] | 1.78[c] |
| | | S(s) | (0.87) | (0.77) | (0.89) | (0.79) |
| | | $\bar{R}^2$ | 0.929 | 0.929 | 0.930 | 0.930 |
| Clothing, footwear, etc. | 31 | s | 1.23[c] | 1.12[c] | 1.23[c] | 1.12[c] |
| | | S(s) | (0.52) | (0.46) | (0.53) | (0.47) |
| | | $\bar{R}^2$ | 0.971 | 0.972 | 0.971 | 0.971 |
| Wood and wood | 36 | s | 1.64[c] | 1.52[c] | 1.82[c] | 1.67[c] |
| products | | S(s) | (0.79) | (0.71) | (0.81) | (0.72) |
| | | $\bar{R}^2$ | 0.933 | 0.933 | 0.934 | 0.934 |
| Pulp and paper | 28 | s | 0.77 | 0.71 | 0.73 | 0.67 |
| products | | S(s) | (1.00) | (0.89) | (1.04) | (0.93) |
| | | $\bar{R}^2$ | 0.918 | 0.918 | 0.917 | 0.918 |
| Printing and | 34 | s | 1.37[b] | 1.20[b] | 1.43[c] | 1.25[b] |
| publications | | S(s) | (0.67) | (0.60) | (0.69) | (0.61) |
| | | $\bar{R}^2$ | 0.946 | 0.946 | 0.946 | 0.946 |
| Leather and leather | 25 | s | −0.16 | −0.08 | −0.34 | −0.23 |
| products | | S(s) | (0.79) | (0.70) | (0.82) | (0.73) |
| | | $\bar{R}^2$ | 0.929 | 0.929 | 0.929 | 0.929 |
| Rubber products | 27 | s | 1.15 | 1.07 | 1.13 | 1.05 |
| | | S(s) | (1.36) | (1.20) | (1.46) | (1.29) |
| | | $\bar{R}^2$ | 0.859 | 0.859 | 0.858 | 0.859 |
| Chemicals and chemical | 31 | s | 0.89 | 0.80 | 1.16 | 1.01 |
| products | | S(s) | (1.60) | (1.43) | (1.80) | (1.61) |
| | | $\bar{R}^2$ | 0.771 | 0.771 | 0.772 | 0.772 |
| Nonmetallic mineral | 37 | s | −0.33 | −0.24 | −0.32 | −0.23 |
| products | | S(s) | (0.71) | (0.64) | (0.73) | (0.66) |
| | | $\bar{R}^2$ | 0.942 | 0.942 | 0.942 | 0.942 |
| Basic metals | 25 | s | 2.07[b] | 1.86[b] | 2.20[b] | 1.97[b] |
| | | S(s) | (1.14) | (1.02) | (1.22) | (1.08) |
| | | $\bar{R}^2$ | 0.879 | 0.879 | 0.879 | 0.879 |
| Metal products | 35 | s | 1.56[c] | 1.40[c] | 1.67[c] | 1.49[c] |
| | | S(s) | (0.69) | (0.62) | (0.70) | (0.63) |
| | | $\bar{R}^2$ | 0.943 | 0.943 | 0.944 | 0.944 |
| Other manufacturing | 28 | s | 1.02 | 0.92 | 1.04 | 0.93 |
| | | S(s) | (1.17) | (1.04) | (1.23) | (1.09) |
| | | $\bar{R}^2$ | 0.907 | 0.908 | 0.907 | 0.907 |

Source: Same as Table 3-2.

[a] $s$ = shifting coefficient; $S(s)$ = standard error; $\bar{R}^2$ = adjusted coefficient of determination.

[b] Different from zero in the expected (positive) direction at the 5 percent level of significance.

[c] Different from zero in the expected (positive) direction at the 2.5 percent level of significance.

**TABLE 3-5. Estimates of Employer Tax Shifting Coefficient for All Manufacturing on Pooled Industry Data, Using Currency Conversion Ratios $x_1$ and $x_2$, 1957–59**[a]

| Conversion ratio | Statistic[b] | Model (3-4) plus dummies | Model (3-5) plus dummies |
|---|---|---|---|
| Purchasing power parity ratio $x_1$ | $s$ | 1.144 | 1.043 |
| | $S(s)$ | (0.263) | (0.235) |
| | $\bar{R}^2$ | 0.911 | 0.911 |
| Official exchange rate $x_2$ | $s$ | 1.176 | 1.070 |
| | $S(s)$ | (0.268) | (0.239) |
| | $\bar{R}^2$ | 0.905 | 0.905 |

Source: Same as Table 3-2.
[a] Based on 407 observations and 380 degrees of freedom, with dummy variables for industries.
[b] $s$ = shifting coefficient; $S(s)$ = standard error; $\bar{R}^2$ = adjusted coefficient of determination.

In an attempt to pin down the estimate for the aggregate shifting coefficient for manufacturing, the industry data underlying Table 3-4 were pooled for the final estimates of models (3-4) and (3-5). Dummy variables were introduced to permit the constant term and coefficient of log $V/L$ to vary by industry.[23] Results for the two models and the two exchange rates are presented in Table 3-5. Since the dummy variable technique required 27 coefficients in each model, the 407 observations yielded 380 degrees of freedom, or about six times the number available for aggregate manufacturing. The pooling device thus yielded by far the most accurate estimates of $s$ attained in this study, with standard errors reduced to about 0.25. The estimated values of the shifting coefficient in Table 3-5 are greater than zero by 4.3 to 4.5 standard errors, permitting the hypothesis that $s = 0$ to be rejected at the 0.001 percent level of significance or better. Again, although each estimate falls slightly above unity, the excess is far from significant, and the results strongly support the hypothesis that in the aggregate the entire employer tax is shifted to labor. Finally, it may be further inferred on the basis of a standard theorem as well as on a commonsense basis that labor therefore also bears the employee tax.[24]

[23] Models (3-6) and (3-7) could not be treated in this way to yield a unique estimate of $s$, because the estimate of $s$ depended on the ratio of the single estimate of $bs$ to the estimates of $b$, which were assumed to vary by industry.

[24] Reasons for assuming the incidence of the employee tax to be the same as that of the employer tax are discussed in the technical note at the end of Chapter II.

## Analysis of U.S. Time Series

Confirmation of the shifting hypothesis for the particular case of the United States was also sought on the basis of U.S. time series data. Elaborated and dynamic versions of the constant elasticity of substitution (CES) estimating equation and other models were fitted to domestic data in further tests of the shifting hypothesis.

### Two Time Series Models

The following series for two-digit industries were obtained from sources listed in Appendix A for the eighteen-year period 1947–65.

$V$ = value added;
$W$ = wages and salaries including private fringe benefits;
$T$ = employers' contributions for social security;
$P$ = price index for industry output;
$H$ = total hours paid per week;
$y$ = year;
$x = V/PH$ = real value added per labor-hour;
$w = W/PH$ = real basic wage per labor-hour (including private fringe benefits);
$t = T/W$ = effective payroll tax rate on employers;
$r = V/W$ = reciprocal of labor's share in value added.

Also specified and "explained" by the models are the annual equilibrium levels of three of the variables: $x_e$, $V_e$, $r_e$.

Four elaborations of equation (3-1)—the original CES estimating equation—were built in for the time series analysis of the incidence of the employer tax. A possible lag in the adjustment of output in a given year toward the equilibrium level $x_e$ was allowed for by the partial adaptations model:

$$(3\text{-}10) \qquad \log x - \log x_{-1} = c(\log x_e - \log x_{-1}).$$

The reaction coefficient $c$ was expected to fall between 0 and 1. The equilibrium level itself was assumed to be affected by three factors in addition to the basic wage: (1) as in the cross-section analysis, the input of labor was assumed to be best measured by $w(1 + st)$—that is, by the real basic wage rate $w$ plus some unknown fraction $s$ of employer payroll taxes $tw$; (2) trends in productivity were allowed for by the time variable $y$;[25] (3) cycles in productivity due to varying effi-

[25] A constant relative growth of $x$, given $w$, was assumed, so that $\log x$ was made to depend linearly on $y$.

ciency in the use of labor over business cycles were incorporated, using the proxy $H/H_{-1}$ to represent annual changes in total hours paid.[26] These elaborations amount to the following generalization of the earlier cross-section model (3-6) for time series purposes:

$$(3\text{-}11) \quad \log x_e = a + b_1 \log w + b_1 s \log(1 + t) + b_2 y + b_3 \log H/H_{-1}.$$

Combining (3-11) and the lag structure (3-10) and assuming a random disturbance $u$ yields:

$$(3\text{-}12) \quad \log x/x_{-1} = ca + cb_1 \log w + cb_1 s \log(1 + t)$$
$$+ cb_2 y + cb_3 \log H/H_{-1} - c \log x_{-1} + u.$$

Since there were only eighteen observations for each industry on which to base the estimates of the six coefficients in this model, erratic results were to be expected;[27] therefore, an additional shifting model was specified.

Since one criterion of tax incidence stresses its impact on relative factor shares, a factor share model seemed an appropriate vehicle and eliminated the need for price indexes and man-hour data.[28] The tax variable was introduced through an assumed equilibrium relationship between value added and labor compensation:[29]

$$(3\text{-}13) \quad V_e = r_e W(1 + st) = r_e(W + sT).$$

The coefficient $s$ retains its interpretation as the shifting measure. For example, if $s = 1$, the relation implies, for any given equilibrium situation, a straight trade-off between $W$ and $T$ (100 percent shifting of the tax); if $s = 0$, $W$ would be independent of $T$ (zero shifting).

[26] Positive values of the coefficient were expected to predominate. High values of $H/H_{-1}$ would explain high productivity (high pressure on labor); low values would explain low productivity (possible hoarding of labor). This proxy seemed to perform at least as well as others that were tried but are not reported, such as the average hourly work week, the unemployment rate, and capacity utilization rates.

[27] Model (3-12) can be viewed as a generalization of a time series model applied earlier by McKinnon. See Ronald I. McKinnon, "Wages, Capital Costs, and Employment in Manufacturing: A Model Applied to 1947–58 U.S. Data," *Econometrica*, Vol. 30 (July 1962), pp. 501–21. Model (3-12) is essentially the same as McKinnon's except for the addition of the tax and cyclical variables. McKinnon's dependent variable was log $x$ rather than the first difference. However, in subtracting log $x_{-1}$ from both sides the present version does not alter the estimates of the coefficients; it merely yields a smaller and more meaningful value of $\bar{R}^2$, since the performance of the model is unassisted by mutual trends in the variables.

[28] This particular criterion is not completely satisfactory by itself. For a comparison of alternatives, see the technical note at the end of Chapter II.

[29] The reverse formulation with labor compensation depending on value added, though more congenial, was abandoned in favor of model (3-13) because of complications in estimating.

Possible trend and cyclical components in $r_e$ were admitted by use of the same variables as in the previous model:

$$(3\text{-}14) \qquad \log r_e = a + b_2 y + b_3 \log H/H_{-1}.$$

Assuming a lag structure in $\log V$ of the same form as model (3-10), combining models (3-13) and (3-14), approximating $\log(1 + st)$ as before, and assuming a random error term $u$ yields:

$$(3\text{-}15) \qquad \log V/V_{-1} = ca + cb_2 y + cb_3 \log H/H_{-1}$$
$$+ cs \log(1 + t) + c \log W/V_{-1} + u.$$

### Time Series Results

Models (3-12) and (3-15) were fitted to 1947–65 U.S. data for twenty-seven two-digit industries. The overall fit of the models seemed good, given that the dependent variable was a first difference in each case. The median value of $\overline{R}^2$ was 0.55 for model (3-12) and 0.87 for model (3-15).[30] However, the standard errors of the estimated shifting coefficients were so high that the result for any given industry provided no evidence at all. Even so, the overall pattern of estimates for twenty-seven industries and two models yields some confirmation of the cross-country results. Collectively, they give fairly strong support for the full-shifting hypothesis over the no-shifting alternative.

In a preliminary set of tests, models (3-12) and (3-15) were simplified in accordance with the alternative hypotheses $s = 0$ and $s = 1$, representing zero shifting and complete shifting of the employer tax, respectively. Neither hypothesis produced a markedly superior fit in any given industry, but the full-shift hypothesis produced a higher $\overline{R}^2$ in a substantial majority of cases, as summarized in Table 3-6. On the goodness-of-fit criterion, the full-shift hypothesis performed better

[30] While not directly relevant to the problem at hand, the performance of the models on other counts is relevant to their evaluation. The estimated reaction coefficient $c$ fell between 0 and 1 in twenty-one of the twenty-seven cases in model (3-12) and in twenty-two cases in model (3-15). All of the eleven exceptions were greater than one, but only one was significantly greater at the 5 percent level. The trend in productivity was positive in sixteen industries according to model (3-12); the trend in labor's share was positive in nineteen of the twenty-seven industries. The cyclical variable $H/H_{-1}$ had the expected positive sign in sixteen cases under model (3-12) and twenty-three under model (3-15). While a substantial number of signs did not come out in accordance with expectations, the performance seems fairly good for the two models, utilizing only 12 and 13 degrees of freedom, respectively. If the coefficient of the total compensation variable ($s = 1$) is taken to be the estimated elasticity of substitution, model (3-12) supports most of the earlier work by producing estimates below unity for twenty-four of the twenty-seven industries (twelve significantly below unity and only one significantly above).

**TABLE 3-6. Tests of Alternative Hypotheses Concerning the Employer Tax Shifting Coefficient (s), Using the Goodness-of-Fit Criterion, 27 U.S. Industries, 1947–65**

| Model | Number of cases favoring | | Level of significance for superiority of hypothesis $s = 1$[a] (percent) |
| | Hypothesis $s = 0$ | Hypothesis $s = 1$ | |
|---|---|---|---|
| (3-12) | 9 | 18 | 6.2 |
| (3-15) | 6 | 21 | 0.4 |

Source: Same as Table 3-2.

[a] This refers to the test of the null hypothesis that the $s = 0$ and $s = 1$ hypotheses have an equal chance to produce the higher $\bar{R}^2$ in any given test; the level of significance was derived from the binomial distribution.

than the no-shift hypothesis for 67 percent of the industries under model (3-12) and 78 percent under model (3-15). The binomial test shows these majorities achieved by the $s = 1$ hypothesis to be fairly impressive evidence against the null hypothesis (that $s = 0$ and $s = 1$ have equal merit under the $\bar{R}^2$ criterion). On the basis of this sample of twenty-seven industries, the superiority of $s = 1$ is indicated at levels of significance of about 6 percent and 0.4 percent under the respective models. While this reasoning yields no estimate of the shifting coefficient for any industry, collectively the results suggest that the full-shift hypothesis is more plausible than its specified rival in a significant majority of the industries studied.

The original versions of models (3-12) and (3-15) include the shifting coefficient explicitly. However, fitting these equations yielded industry estimates of $s$ that were so erratic (standard errors ranging from about 1 to 5) that the individual magnitudes do not merit recording in this study. Collectively, they tell about the same story as results produced by the $\bar{R}^2$ criterion. The distribution of estimates of $s$ can be used to test the hypothesis that the true median value is 0.5. The production function model (3-12) showed eighteen out of twenty-seven estimates of $s$ greater than 0.5, paralleling the earlier finding of eighteen values of $\bar{R}^2$ that were higher under the assumption of $s = 1$ than under $s = 0$. The labor share model (3-15) produced twenty-one out of twenty-seven estimates of $s$ greater than 0.5, again supporting the findings on the $\bar{R}^2$ criterion reported in Table 3-6. The results support fairly strongly the conclusion that the median value of $s$ is greater than 0.5 and at the same significance levels as those given in Table 3-6 for the superiority of the hypothesis $s = 1$ over $s = 0$.[31] However, support was mixed for the specific hypothesis of a median value of $s = 1$. Model (3-12) gave it persuasive backing; estimates of $s$ were evenly balanced around unity, with fourteen industries above and thirteen below.[32] On the other hand, model (3-15) yielded a rather awkward result. It undermined the hypothesis $s = 0$ handily by showing twenty-one positive values of $s$, with only six negative, but it was guilty of overkill in showing nineteen values of $s$ also greater than one.[33]

In sum, model (3-12) shows consistent support for the full-shifting hypothesis. Model (3-15) offers an even stronger case than model (3-12) against the no-shift hypothesis but then weakens its own credibility by suggesting more than 100 percent shifting—a result for which no rationale is apparent. Still, each model clearly favors $s = 1$ over $s = 0$, and the evidence from (3-12) is entirely consistent with a median value of $s = 1$.

In order to reduce the standard errors of the estimates of $s$, data for the ten nondurable manufacturing industries and the ten durable manufacturing industries, respectively, were pooled to form one set of data for nondurable and one for durable industries. Dummy variables were used to allow all coefficients in models (3-12) and (3-15) to vary by industry, except those of the wage and tax variables.[34] Results of this exercise are reported in Table 3-7. All of the estimates of $s$ are closer to unity than to zero, although only the model (3-15) estimate for nondurables is significantly greater than zero. The estimates average considerably above unity, but in no case is the estimate significantly greater than the hypothesized value. While awkwardly high, these estimates would seem to offer one more reed of support to the full-shift hypothesis vis-à-vis the no-shift alternative.

---

[31] Although closely related, the two criteria are not identical. In the case of model (3-12) the criteria produced contradictory, but offsetting, results for two industries. Under model (3-15) the two criteria produced consistent results for all twenty-seven industries.

[32] The hypothesis that $s = 0$ is substantially discredited by nineteen positive values of $s$ and only eight negative.

[33] If the true median $s$ were actually unity, this degree of imbalance in either direction would occur by chance in only about 6 percent of samples of twenty-seven industries.

[34] In order to obtain a unique estimate of the shifting coefficient in each case, it was necessary to constrain these two coefficients to single values.

**TABLE 3-7. Estimates of Employer Tax Shifting Coefficient (s), Based on Pooled U.S. Data for Nondurable and Durable Manufacturing Industry Groups**[a]

| Industry group | Statistic[b] | Model (3-12) plus dummies | Model (3-15) plus dummies |
|---|---|---|---|
| Nondurable manufacturing | s | 2.01 | 2.54 |
| | S(s) | (1.42) | (1.20) |
| | $\bar{R}^2$ | 0.64 | 0.73 |
| Durable manufacturing | s | 1.34 | 1.56 |
| | S(s) | (1.82) | (1.17) |
| | $\bar{R}^2$ | 0.59 | 0.94 |

Source: Same as Table 3-2.

[a] There were 180 observations in all four regressions and 138 degrees of freedom with model (3-12), 148 with model (3-15). The standard errors are approximations, as described in Table 3-3, note d.

[b] s = shifting coefficient; S(s) = standard error; $\bar{R}^2$ = adjusted coefficient of determination.

On the basis of these results from U.S. time series data, neither the individual industry picture nor the outcome based on pooling offers a resounding endorsement of the full-shift hypothesis. The small variance of the tax variable over time makes such a finding unlikely, even if the hypothesis were known to be true. Viewed collectively, the U.S. time series results constitute appreciable, though modest, support for the much tighter cross-country estimates, indicating that labor bears the employer payroll tax and therefore the employee tax also.

## Implications of the Findings on Incidence

It should be reiterated at this point that neither the cross-country nor the time series analysis has shed any light on the mechanism through which the real burden of the payroll tax on employers is shifted to employees. The way in which the adopted approaches dodged this issue may be illustrated by the case of the cross-country analysis presented earlier in this chapter. Earnings and productivity variables for each country were measured in dollars by several conversion methods; the essence of the finding is that—given the level of productivity in a country—the presence of a payroll tax on employers tends to reduce the wage rate in dollars by roughly the amount of the tax. This result could be due to a lag in the basic wage (measured in local currency) in response to imposition of the tax ("backward shifting"); it could be due to price increases reducing the value of wages as measured in dollars ("forward shifting"). More likely, the outcome of both cross-section and time series analyses is achieved through a combination of the alternative employer reactions; the nature of the blend is of secondary significance.[35] In either case, the real burden of the tax falls on labor, and this has important implications no matter how it comes about.

If the conclusion that both employer and employee payroll taxes are borne by labor is accepted, several corollary propositions follow. In the first place, the economic stabilization properties of the tax are affected by its incidence. Although it is generally conceded that the typical payroll tax is a relatively weak stabilizer, it would probably be even weaker if borne by capital. For example, on the assumption that there is a higher marginal propensity to spend income from labor than income from capital, a fall in the tax on labor in response to a wage decline would be a more effective brake to limit the decline in spending than an equal decline in a tax on capital. A tax borne by labor would also presumably produce a lesser drag on growth than would a tax on capital, which would cause a greater cut in saving.

Acceptance of the labor burden hypothesis is also relevant in the collective bargaining arena. It should be recognized on both sides that the entire payroll tax is just as clearly a component of the cost of hiring labor as private fringe benefits or the nominal wage itself. Labor might then regard the employer contribution as a cost incurred in lieu of the payment of a higher basic wage.[36] Recognition of a trade-off between wages and fringes on the one hand and the payroll tax on the other would bring into more explicit focus the pros and cons of fueling social programs by this type of tax.

The appropriate treatment of labor income under the income tax also depends on payroll tax incidence. At present the employee pays tax on the income from which employee contributions are withheld but not on the income from which the employer tax is withheld. If the latter income is part of labor's share, it should be taxed just as the

---

[35] The conception of "employer reactions" implies some combination of wage restraint and/or price markup policies by individual employers. The wage rates and prices actually sustainable depend, of course, on aggregate market forces.

[36] This is not to suggest that labor would be indifferent to the mix of these components. In view of the very loose relation between individual taxes and benefits and the long wait for the latter, labor is likely to view the employer contribution as a tax on itself rather than as a part of its compensation. However, it is difficult to believe that labor would have a different conception of the employee part of the tax.

source of the employee tax is; or both parts should be exempt in favor of a tax on benefits, which are now exempt.

If labor ultimately pays the employer tax, this is also highly relevant to relative international competitive positions. Countries such as Italy and France with large "social charges" are not placed at a competitive disadvantage vis-à-vis countries where the employer tax constitutes only a small part of total compensation. This has important implications for tariff policy and for attempts to improve international economic cooperation.

The incidence of the tax is highly significant for evaluation of its effect on income distribution. The conclusion that labor bears the tax makes clear that its burden on low-income groups is greater than is generally realized. It also implies that its impact on income distribution is typically regressive. These qualities of the payroll tax offer a solid basis for proposing that this form of taxation be curtailed or eliminated. This could be done by introducing exemptions of low incomes, as under the income tax, or by substituting the income tax for all or part of the payroll tax. These issues are taken up in Chapters IV and V.

Finally, the incidence of the tax is significant for evaluation of the terms of social security programs. The finding that labor bears the tax points to a lower rate of return on contributions to participants in social security than would be the case if the employer tax could be ignored. It is difficult to understand an earlier position of the Social Security Administration which conceded that this tax is largely borne by labor in the aggregate and yet ignored it in evaluating the tax paid by individuals on the ground that no exact imputation of the tax is possible. However, if the tax is paid by employees as a group, it must also be paid by them as individuals, and it seems better to make an imperfect imputation that is roughly right than to settle for being precisely wrong.[37]

---

[37] The conclusion that the entire payroll tax falls on labor obviously shields the tax from the usual criticism that it promotes automation and aggravates the unemployment problem. Without a net cost impact on employees, there would clearly be no incentive to substitute capital for labor. However, there is a persuasive theoretical case that such a fear was largely unfounded in the first place. See Carl S. Shoup, *Public Finance* (Aldine, 1969), p. 412; Paul A. Samuelson, "A New Theorem on Nonsubstitution," in Joseph E. Stiglitz (ed.), *The Collected Scientific Papers of Paul A. Samuelson* (M.I.T. Press, 1966), Vol. 1, pp. 520–35; E. J. Mishan, "The Emperor's New Clothes: The Payroll Tax Stripped Bare," *Bankers' Magazine*, Vol. 192 (July 1961), pp. 17–22.

CHAPTER IV

# Effects on Income Inequality

THE ANALYSIS of payroll tax incidence in Chapter III stressed the effect of this tax on the per capita real income of the earning population in aggregate. This chapter is concerned with the effect of the payroll tax on the inequality of individual annual incomes. Two presumptions from which this problem is approached should be made explicit at the outset, after which some methodological questions can be taken up. First, the previous finding—that both employer and employee contributions are in reality extracted from labor's real wage rate— points to a greater regressive impact of the entire tax than is indicated by the nominal tax structure faced by employees alone.[1] This characteristic, along with other typical properties of payroll taxation such as the taxable maximum, is taken into account here.

[1] Studies of the distribution of tax burdens by income class have generally relied on arbitrary assumptions about the incidence of the payroll tax. See, for example, Richard A. Musgrave, J. J. Carroll, L. D. Cook, and L. Frane, "Distribution of Tax Payments by Income Groups: A Case Study for 1948," *National Tax Journal*, Vol. 4 (March 1951), pp. 1–53. The "standard assumption" of this study was that the employer shifted one-third of his tax to wage earners and two-thirds to consumers. The employee tax was assumed to fall on wage earners. An exception in which the entire employer tax is imputed to labor can be found in Joseph A. Pechman, Henry J. Aaron, and Michael K. Taussig, *Social Security: Perspectives for Reform* (Brookings Institution, 1968), Chart 8-2, p. 181, and Appendixes E and F, pp. 305–11. For a thorough survey of tax burden studies and some methodological criticisms, see Carl S. Shoup, "Quantitative Research in Taxation and Government Expenditure" (National Bureau of Economic Research, no date; processed), pp. 5–25.

The a priori reasoning of Chapter II, supported empirically by the analysis of Chapter III, clearly implies that the entire payroll tax paid in the name of an individual earner may appropriately be imputed to that earner.[2] Although aggregative, the analysis showed that no study of the effect of the tax on the size distribution of incomes would be meaningful without assignment of employer as well as employee portions to individual earners. While no such imputation is perfect, it is preferable to ignoring the employer tax altogether. The group burden is carried by individuals, and any errors in individual imputation due to frictions and/or short-run factors can be expected to cancel out in the grouping of many earners within a given income class, or even in the concentrations analyzed at particular income levels.

A second presumption of the approach used here is also fundamental. The effect of the tax on the distribution of current incomes among the economically active population is considered independently of the unknown benefits likely to accrue to the same taxpayers in the future.[3] This seems appropriate for two reasons. Since any benefit levels can be financed by a variety of tax structures, the latter invite comparison in their own right. Also, earners must pay their taxes now, and these are related only tenuously to benefits likely to be received many years later.[4] A young worker in the poverty range is not likely to be captivated by the thought that he is being forced to save in preparation for retirement while the payroll tax is pushing him deeper into poverty today. The more hypothetical question of lifetime income redistribution under arbitrarily projected earnings-benefit relationships is the subject of Chapter VI.

## Methodological Problems

Several methodological issues deserve early attention. (This discussion, however, may be passed over without loss of continuity by readers more interested in the findings than the conceptual framework.)

[2] For readers unable to accept the imputation of the employer tax (including the relatively small unemployment insurance tax charged to employers), the payroll tax on earners would be viewed as slightly less than one-half the levels reported.

[3] This is not to say that the redistributive effects of these transfers are unimportant. The point is that (if the reasoning of the technical note at the end of Chapter II is accepted) it is feasible and useful to separate the incidence of taxes and benefits.

[4] For earlier discussion of the frailty of the "insurance analogy," see Pechman and others, *Social Security*, especially Chap. 4.

*Imputation of the Payroll Tax Burden to Individual Incomes*

The method of application of the aggregative findings of Chapter III to the analysis of individual income distribution calls for clarification. For reasons discussed in the technical note at the end of Chapter II, it is not possible to distinguish empirically the impact of the payroll tax in the form of (1) money wage restraint and (2) product price markups. It was also suggested there that absolute price effects of the tax are irrelevant under the adopted concept of incidence that stresses the distribution of real factor incomes. This assertion may disturb readers accustomed to allocation of the tax burden according to assumptions concerning, for example, "backward" shifting to wage earners and "forward" shifting to consumers. Under this approach a portion of the tax is sometimes allocated to individuals in proportion to wages received, some in proportion to profits, and the rest according to individual consumption patterns. However, the findings of Chapter III do not lay the groundwork for such an approach, and it is suggested that this procedure is not in order in this chapter.

The key finding of Chapter III is that the entire burden of the tax rests on the per capita real factor income of labor. If accepted, this finding implies that for any given year the net effect of wage and price adjustments to the tax leaves the per capita real wage rate lower by the tax rate than it would otherwise be. What are the implications for the appropriate imputation of the tax burden to one family's income or to an annual distribution of individual incomes? In the first place, since each average product price is given for that year, the per capita money wage rate, like the real wage rate, must be lower by the amount of the tax than it would otherwise be. Thus only one assumption is required to impute the entire payroll tax rate to the labor income of individuals; it must be assumed that the effective payroll tax rate of each individual leaves his after-tax wage rate reduced proportionally, just as it does the aggregate per capita wage rate.

This allocation of the entire payroll tax paid in the name of each individual to the labor portion of his income does not imply any assumption about the shifting mechanism—either forward or backward. Nor does it imply that there were no other effects of macro policies, including the payroll tax. It is simply suggested that the only part of the impact of the payroll tax that can be attributed to the tax per se (rather than to the tax in combination with other macro policies) is its effect on individual income from the labor source. Other results, such as the depressing effect of any attendant inflation on retirement and welfare incomes, cannot be attributed to the tax alone but must be traced also to monetary policy, nonescalation of benefits, and so on. To sum up, no pattern of absolute price effects can be assigned to the tax alone. However, the real per capita wage effects that *can* be attributed to the tax itself have a major impact on the distribution of individual incomes. This aspect of the aggravation of the inequality problem is analyzed in this chapter despite the impossibility of isolating other effects of the payroll tax from those of associated macroeconomic policies.[5]

### Emphasis on Redistribution of Factor Incomes

Another significant conceptual point is that the primary emphasis in this chapter is on the redistributional impact of the tax on the *factor* income of individuals. Thus the analysis starts with the best approximation of the income distribution before the redistributional influence of the tax-spending process and asks what the tax does to that distribution.[6] This implied exclusion of transfers (adhered to in this chapter and in Chapter V) is in keeping with the previously discussed conception of incidence as the redistributional impact of the tax on "income available for private use," an ambiguous phrase that is intended to emphasize factor income and exclude transfers. This means that recipients of social security benefits and welfare transfers are excluded from the analysis, except insofar as they also receive some income from factors.

Probably the closest available approximation to a size distribution of individual factor incomes is the U.S. Internal Revenue Service distribution of "total ordinary income," that is, income that excludes

---

[5] It should be emphasized that the absence of explicit attention to price effects does not hide any depressing effect of inflation on the recipients of nonwage income. It has been suggested that, if the tax is "passed on" to consumers, labor cannot bear it all because the prices faced by others also rise. However, if the finding is accepted that the entire tax comes out of the real share of labor (and employment effects are minor), this implies that the other factors, in aggregate, have increased their money incomes sufficiently to maintain their before-tax real income. For detailed discussion of the methodological issues underlying these assertions, see the technical note at the end of Chapter II.

[6] This is admittedly a somewhat artificial question, since even incomes before the payroll tax have been affected by public policy. See Shoup, "Quantitative Research in Taxation," pp. 15–18.

most transfers and realized capital gains, but also excludes some factor income, such as undistributed corporate profits.[7] Since this income variant includes both earnings and property incomes, it offers the best basis for appraising the impact of the payroll tax on the inequality of factor incomes. The regressive impact of the tax has two components. First, it taxes high-income earners at lower rates. Second, it taxes earnings while excluding altogether property income, which is concentrated at the high end of the income scale. This chapter deals first and extensively with the payroll tax distribution among earners.[8] The effect on distributions that include property income is considered later in this chapter and in Chapter V, where reform proposals are taken up.

To sum up, the approach in this chapter concentrates on the economically active population receiving factor incomes and attempts to exclude transfer income from the analysis. As a result, the tax rates of low-income groups analyzed may appear misleadingly high to those who prefer to include transfer recipients in the same distribution. Since the latter have low average incomes and usually pay no payroll tax, the average tax rates on low money income groups (including transfer recipients) are much lower than tax rates measured with respect to factor income. All that can be said about this result is that separation of the two slightly overlapping populations is analytically useful.

The approach starts with the proposition that the payroll tax rate is negligible in its effect on transfer incomes and on individuals receiving most of their income in that form. Since the payroll tax rate is measured here with respect to factor income, the exclusion of low-income transfer recipients from coverage should not be regarded as a progressive feature of the tax. However, one point should be made very strongly in this context. The following discussion of high tax rates on the poor refers to the working poor. Millions of the poor who depend on transfers pay no payroll tax at all. Still, there are other millions who do, and it is shown later in conjunction with Table 4-1 and other evidence that the number who do and their earnings are quantitatively significant.

[7] Estimates are available from the Brookings Institution's file of approximately 90,000 individual income tax returns filed for the year 1966.

[8] Since the heavy weight of the payroll tax on low and middle ranks with little property income is its main feature, a concentration on earnings effects seems appropriate.

Three related questions are taken up in this chapter. The effects of recent payroll tax and income tax structures on income inequality are first contrasted, particularly with respect to low-income and middle-income groups, as applied to both earnings and total factor incomes of individuals.[9] The rising trend of the regressive payroll tax is then traced in its relation to the progressive income tax over the last two decades. Finally, the effect of the payroll tax itself on income inequality is weighed.

## Contrast of Payroll and Income Taxes

### *Impact on Earnings of Individuals*

In the context of a declared "war against poverty" and general acceptance of the device of progressive taxation in this country, one of the most astonishing institutional phenomena is the persistence and expansion of taxes that bear most heavily on the poor. Sales and property taxes have long been criticized on this ground,[10] but payroll taxes have generally been spared censure. This is presumably due to the common implication that taxpayers are buying an annuity comparable to that available under a private insurance program. This enables proponents to contend that the poor are "paying for their old age"— even though the link between taxes and benefits is not close.

Expressions of shock have often accompanied the recognition that many families below the officially defined poverty line have been required to pay income tax. In response to this contradiction, the Nixon administration in one of its first moves in 1969 proposed to eliminate practically all of the income tax on taxpayers in the poverty range. The illogic of collecting income tax from families in poverty was so obvious that this relatively inexpensive move gained virtually unanimous support and applause.[11] However, the payroll tax burden on the

[9] Since the tax rate is measured against the earnings base alone, the rate is virtually uniform through low-income ranges. However, it will be shown that the payroll tax is mildly progressive for incomes up to the ceiling when property income is included in the base.

[10] For example, one study found that state and local tax rates in 1965 ranged from 25 percent for incomes under $2,000 (excluding transfer payments) down to only 7 percent for incomes above $15,000. See *Economic Report of the President, January 1969*, p. 161.

[11] Even complete elimination of the income tax on the poor would no more than scratch the surface of the poverty problem. The elimination of poverty requires that families at the poverty level be assisted by a device such as the negative income tax, or by an

poor has been far greater than the income tax—even before the low-income relief under the Tax Reform Act of 1969. Surprisingly, this much deeper inequity has attracted little attention until recently, even though taxation of low incomes has grown steadily heavier during the 1950s and 1960s.[12]

With payroll taxes rising at an extraordinary rate and now second in importance (in aggregate) to the individual income tax, it seems appropriate to draw attention to the distributional effects of this levy. The promotion of income inequality by the payroll tax is most strikingly evident when it is compared with the effects of the individual income tax—often characterized as this country's "fairest tax."[13] Three main features of the current payroll tax are responsible for its tendency to counteract the progressivity of the income tax. First, while the income tax exempted in 1971 the first $650 of income per person and embraced in 1970 a liberalized minimum standard deduction that eliminated virtually all income taxes on the poor, the social security payroll tax continues to tax low incomes without exemption and at the highest effective (average) rates of all taxes.[14] Second, under the income tax, the higher the taxable income of a taxpayer, the higher his tax rate; in direct contrast, in 1973, the old-age, survivors, disability, and health insurance (OASDHI) tax rate is expected to drop to zero for income above $10,800, and unemployment insurance (UI) tax rates will fall to zero after $4,200 in most states. (The $10,800 ceiling used here and in all subsequent references to 1973 is that contained in the social security legislation enacted by Public Law 92-336 that was signed by President Nixon on July 1, 1972. Also scheduled was a $12,000 ceiling in 1974 and subsequent automatic adjustments; the ceiling will move annually in proportion to average changes in taxable earnings in the first calendar quarter.)

expanded version of the family assistance plan originally submitted to the Congress in 1969, rather than merely be exempted from the positive tax.

[12] Recent suggestions on this problem and potential reforms are found in Pechman and others, *Social Security*, Chap. 8; and Ronald F. Hoffman, "Notes on Payroll Tax Rebate Proposals," in National Tax Association, *Proceedings of the Sixty-Second Annual Conference on Taxation* (1969), pp. 356–76.

[13] Richard Goode, *The Individual Income Tax* (Brookings Institution, 1964), pp. 2, 308. See also an explicit comparison by Pechman and others, *Social Security*, Chart 8-2, p. 181.

[14] The discussion of tax rates throughout this chapter refers to average rates, or the ratio of the total tax bill to total factor income. Only in connection with some of the reform proposals of Chapter V are marginal rates considered.

Finally, the payroll tax applies only to wages, salaries, and self-employed income—exempting property income, which looms largest in the high-income brackets most heavily assessed under the income tax. Working against this is a slight tendency for the relative importance of property income to be negatively related to total income in very low-income ranges, as is shown later in this chapter.

The contrasting pattern of payroll and income taxation in 1969 is illustrated in Figure 4-1 for recipients of wages and salaries only who filed joint returns and utilized standard deductions. The income tax (including the surtax) is zero through much of the poverty range, and then the rate rises with income in all family size classes, approaching 70 percent for very high incomes paying the full statutory rate. The overall payroll tax rate is at its peak at about 11.4 percent on incomes below $3,000. The rate for a single earner declines steadily after the typical 1969 unemployment insurance ceiling is passed and more rapidly above the 1969 OASDHI ceiling of $7,800. However, the degree of regressivity is influenced somewhat by the number of earners in a family achieving a given total income. The higher payroll tax curve shows that dual earners may be taxed at a rate as much as double that on single earners. (Under the income tax dual earners filing a joint return pay a lower tax on a given family income than single earners receiving the same amount.)

The payroll and income tax curves representing the changes scheduled for 1973 are illustrated in Figure 4-2. By 1973, the social security ceiling will be $10,800, and the statutory OASDHI rate is set at 11.0 percent; in turn, the statutory income tax rates will show substantial declines and exemptions will increase. Figure 4-2 portrays this further enhanced role of the payroll tax relative to the income tax. The increasing domination of the payroll tax in low- and medium-income ranges is shown clearly. For example, in the case of a one-earner family of four, the payroll tax is greater than the income tax for incomes up to about $12,000. For a two-earner family of four, the payroll tax may exceed the income tax for incomes up to about $15,000 (this assumes both earners have equal incomes). For larger families the payroll tax dominates through even higher income ranges.

Clearly, the most important contrast shown in Figures 4-1 and 4-2 is that the payroll tax rate is highest in poverty-income ranges where the income tax rate is zero and then approaches zero for high incomes as the income tax rate approaches its maximum. The payroll tax di-

**FIGURE 4-1. Payroll and Income Tax Rates on Wages and Salaries, Various Family Sizes, 1969**

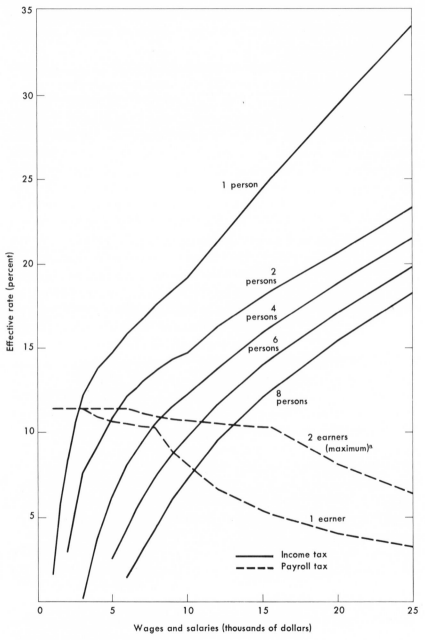

Wages and salaries (thousands of dollars)

Source: See Appendix C.
<sup>a</sup> One way to derive the maximum rate charged two earners is to assume the two had equal earnings.

**FIGURE 4-2. Payroll and Income Tax Rates on Wages and Salaries, Various Family Sizes, 1973**

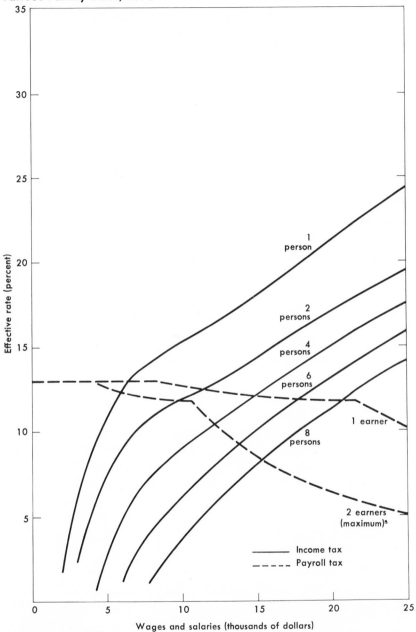

Wages and salaries (thousands of dollars)

Source: See Appendix C.
a In this figure and in all subsequent references to 1973, the OASDHI ceiling of $10,800 and the rate of 11 per cent are used, as established in Public Law 92-336, signed July 1, 1972.
b One way to derive the maximum rate charged two earners is to assume the two had equal earnings.

rectly and symmetrically counteracts the progressive income tax by
hitting the poor the hardest and by virtually sparing the rich.

The combined effect of the progressive income tax and the regressive payroll tax in 1969 and 1973 is illustrated for one-earner families
of various sizes in Figure 4-3. In 1969 the payroll tax operates alone
through almost the entire poverty range at a flat rate of about 11.4
percent—up to the $2,000 level for a family of two and $3,000 for a
family of four.[15] At these levels the income tax begins to take hold,
yielding progressive combined tax structures up to the $7,800 ceiling.
Beyond this income level (about one-sixth below the U.S. family
median of about $9,433), a striking pattern emerges. The regressive
impact of the payroll tax outweighs the progressivity of the income
tax over a substantial income range. The combined rate curve declines
from the $7,800 point until it reaches the income level of $10,200 in
the case of a two-person family ($10,000 for a four-person family).
The income tax rate then begins to dominate again, but not until the
income level of $17,200 is reached does the combined rate of the two-
person family catch up with the previous peak rate paid by the family
of two at the $7,800 income level ($12,500 in the case of a family of
four). In sum, not only did the 1969 payroll tax place more than an
11 percent burden on the wage income of families in poverty, but it
created a situation in which, for example, a two-person family earning
a lower middle level income of $7,800 faced a combined tax rate of
about 24 percent—higher than that paid by a similar family earning
more than twice that amount.[16]

By 1973 the combined payroll and income tax is scheduled to be
regressive over a considerably longer range. Figure 4-3 shows that the
combined rate curves decline after the scheduled taxable ceiling of
$10,800. Eventually the progressive income tax begins to dominate
again, but the tax rate for a family of two does not equal and surpass
the rate at $10,800 until the income level of about $23,000 is reached
($19,700 in the case of a family of four). After the temporary peak tax
rate of 24.0 percent on the $10,800 income for a family of two, the
rate falls to 22.8 percent for incomes of $15,600. Although progres-

[15] The official 1969 poverty thresholds for families of these sizes were approximately
$2,360 and $3,720, respectively.

[16] No similar dip in the maximum overall rate curve for *dual* earners is present. These
curves (not shown here) level off above the two-earner ceiling, but the downward slope
of the maximum payroll tax rate for two is not sharp enough to overcome the progressivity of the income tax rate structure.

**FIGURE 4-3. Combined Payroll and Income Tax Rates on Wages and Salaries, Various Family Sizes, One Earner, 1969 and 1973**

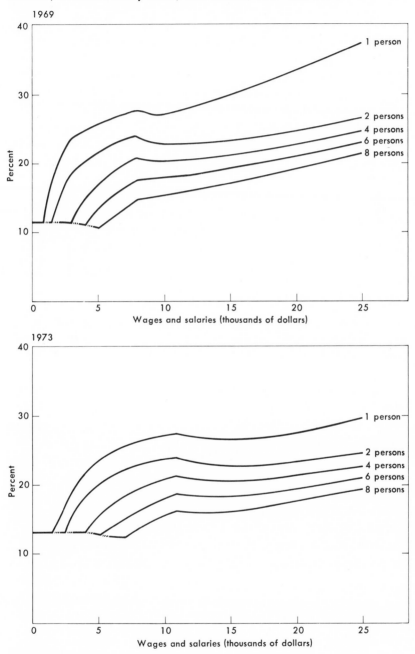

Source: See Appendix C.

sion takes over at that point, with respect to the $10,800 income the combined tax is on balance slightly regressive through a $12,000 range until a level more than double the taxable ceiling is reached.

The extent to which payroll tax regressivity swamps income tax progressivity testifies to the newly acquired importance of the former. (Trends in the importance of payroll taxation relative to income taxation are discussed later in this chapter.) A situation in which a family at the $10,800 income level will pay a higher rate than one near $23,000 calls for adjustment. While the net regressiveness is not pronounced, it violates a long-standing principle. If one adopted this combined payroll and income tax as a criterion, families in poverty and those with incomes near the middle both seem qualified for the "forgotten American" label.[17] In any case the payroll tax has led to combined tax rate patterns that are unjustifiable in these particular respects, in addition to the undesirable effect of the overall regressivity of the payroll tax itself.

*Effects on Total Factor Income*

The analysis up to this point has excluded property income. A further contrast between income tax and payroll tax structures, as applied to an income base approximating factor income, is available for the population filing income taxes in 1966.[18] The implications of tax return data for poor and nonpoor categories are considered in this chapter, and more detailed classes are discussed in connection with the reform proposals in Chapter V. Table 4-1 shows estimated average effective tax rates for filers with "ordinary income" (adjusted gross income less capital gains) below and above the officially estimated 1966 poverty lines. The rates are percentages of "ordinary income" approximating the total factor income of each person who filed a tax return. Unlike the income base in the previous discussion, this variant includes property income and is a more inclusive basis for analysis of the redistributive effect of the tax on individual factor incomes. About 18 percent of the returns were classified as receiving ordinary income

[17] It should be emphasized again that this comment is made with respect to the tax structure and without reference to the potential but unknown benefit structure in effect upon retirement.

[18] The figures reported here are taken from unpublished computations based on a sample of approximately 90,000 federal individual income tax returns made available to the Brookings Institution by the U.S. Internal Revenue Service.

**TABLE 4-1. Effective Income, Social Security, and Unemployment Insurance Tax Rates on Ordinary Income of Poor and Nonpoor Individual Federal Income Tax Filers, 1966**[a]

*(In percent)*

| | Effective rates | | |
|---|---|---|---|
| Income status of filer | Income tax | OASDHI tax | OASDHI + UI |
| Below poverty line | 0.9 | 8.2 | 10.1 |
| Above poverty line | 12.1 | 5.0 | 5.8 |

Source: The Brookings Institution's file of approximately 90,000 federal individual income tax returns filed for the year 1966. The UI tax rate was estimated on the basis of the rough assumptions that (1) each filer below the poverty line paid 2.2 percent of earnings (the average rate in 1966), and (2) each filer above the poverty line paid 2.2 percent of the typical ceiling of $3,000, or $66 on an average income of $8,000. Because of incomplete coverage, the UI rate estimates are overstated for both groups.

[a] Ordinary income is defined as adjusted gross income less realized capital gains.

less than the poverty cutoff.[19] These filers reported only about 3 percent of total reported ordinary income, but their estimated payroll tax rate of 8.2 percent (excluding unemployment insurance taxes) was considerably higher than the estimated 5 percent payroll tax paid by the better-off majority.[20] When a rough estimate of the UI tax rate is included, the 1966 payroll tax rate on incomes below the poverty line reaches about 10 percent of ordinary income, or nearly double the rate on higher incomes. In contrast, even before the low-income relief provisions of the Tax Reform Act of 1969, the 1966 income tax rate of the poor was negligible compared to the 12 percent effective rate on the nonpoor. The regressive payroll tax offsets the highly progressive income tax to the extent that the combined tax rate charged

[19] Many of these filers also received some nontaxable transfer income which, if included in tax return income, would have excluded them from the poverty category. However, given that "ordinary income" and transfers tend to be mutually exclusive, it seems unlikely that filers receive much transfer income. Subject to this qualification, the terms "poor" and "nonpoor" filers are used in Table 4-1 and elsewhere to refer to such a classification based on "ordinary income" only.

[20] The estimated payroll tax rate of 8.2 percent on ordinary income in the poverty range may be compared to the statutory rate on wages and salaries of 8.4 percent in 1966. The estimate appears to exaggerate the coverage rate somewhat. For example, the U.S. Internal Revenue Service's *Statistics of Income—1966, Individual Income Tax Returns* (1968), pp. 9–10, shows property income (dividends, interest, rent, nontaxable pensions, and royalties) totaling 15 percent of adjusted gross income in both the $1,000–$2,000 and $2,000–$3,000 classes. The 8.2 percent estimate is also biased upward, because it assumes that all earnings are taxable; however, this bias should be slight, since it is unlikely that many *earners* in this range who report income taxable under the income tax are not covered by social security.

against the poor is over one-half the rate for the rest of the filing population. In fact, if the average unemployment insurance tax rate of 2.2 percent for 1966 is included, the estimates would show that the poor paid a combined average tax rate of about 11 percent as compared to 18 percent for the nonpoor. The whole package remains mildly progressive with respect to these two groups, but it is significant that income tax filers in poverty paid a combined tax at a rate about 60 percent of that paid by the nonpoor.

The estimated 1966 tax rate of about 10 percent on the factor incomes of tax filers in the poverty range is probably a percentage point or so on the high side for the reasons given above.[21] On the other hand, statutory social security tax rates are scheduled to be about 30 percent higher by 1973, making a true effective rate on factor incomes in the poverty range of about 11 percent by that year. This is not a trivial problem, since it involved 18 percent of all income tax filers in 1966, but its importance must be qualified. It is probable that a substantial fraction of these earners, such as students, are part-time workers. A 12 percent tax on a student earning $1,000 during a summer seems more equitable than the same rate on a member of a family of four who is earning the minimum wage of $1.60 an hour, or about $3,300 a year. However, relief should be provided in both cases, and the previously demonstrated inequities involving middle-income earners should be corrected as well.

Another important estimate available from the tax data for 1966 is that about 28 million, or 40 percent of the 70 million filers, paid a higher OASDHI tax than income tax. This fraction would undoubtedly be well over 50 percent of the filers (1) if the 1970 rate and ceiling were used,[22] (2) if the tax on second earners were included, (3) if unemployment insurance taxes were included, (4) if nonfiling earners were included, (5) if the relatively well-off government and railroad workers who are not under social security were excluded from the estimates (or if their own contributions at higher rates were included), and (6) if the 1969 low-income relief under the income tax had been in effect.

An analysis of statutory tax rates for 1969 reinforces the above evidence that the payroll tax has become the dominant tax for a large

[21] See notes 19 and 20.

[22] Applying this adjustment alone to the 1966 data shows that about 50 percent of the filers had a higher OASDHI tax than income tax.

**TABLE 4-2.** Approximate Wage and Salary Levels at Which Income and Payroll Taxes Are Equal for One Earner, Amount of Tax, and Median Wage and Salary, by Family Size, 1969

*(In dollars)*

| Family size | Wage and salary level[a] | Income and payroll tax (each tax) | Estimated median wage and salary[b] |
|---|---|---|---|
| 1 | 2,770 | 316 | 2,400 |
| 2 | 4,890 | 523 | 6,000 |
| 4 | 7,707 | 794 | 8,500 |
| 6 | 9,088 | 803 | 8,700 |
| 10 | 11,754 | 803 | 8,000[c] |

[a] Assumes standard deductions claimed in computing income tax.

[b] A rough estimate obtained by multiplying the estimated overall tax return wage and salary median of $6,700 by the ratio of median money income by household size to the overall median money income. U.S. Bureau of the Census, *Current Population Reports*, Series P-60, No. 72, "Household Income in 1969 and Selected Social and Economic Characteristics of Households" (1970), p. 11.

[c] Estimated median for households of seven or more persons.

number of families. Table 4-2 shows the income levels at which the income tax and payroll tax were equal for one earner who had wage or salary income only.[23] These equal-tax earnings levels for various family sizes may be compared with $6,700, the estimated overall median wage and salary level of the tax return population in 1969,[24] and with the very rough estimates of medians by family size, also recorded in Table 4-2. The estimates suggest that one-half or more of families larger than four paid more payroll tax than income tax on their wages and salaries in 1969. Since the equal-tax point increases with family size while median wage and salary does not (in this range), the larger the family size, the larger is the size of the majority paying more payroll tax. The evidence also suggests that even among families of four or less nearly one-half may have paid more payroll tax than income tax on their wages and salaries.

While the above estimates are rather rough, it is apparent that

[23] As a representation of the entire income structure, the exclusion of property income gives these equal-tax points an upward bias (overstating payroll tax on families with this *total* income); on the other hand, ignoring the two-earner case imparts a downward bias in the case of families of four or more where the equal-tax point is above the $7,800 ceiling.

[24] This estimate is the approximate median wage and salary on income tax returns in 1966 (from *Statistics of Income—1966, Individual Income Tax Returns*, p. 9) adjusted according to the 1966–69 change in average earnings per full-time employee. See *Survey of Current Business*, Vol. 51 (July 1971), p. 36.

critics of progressivity in the federal tax system have grounds for satisfaction in recent years. Not only has the regressive payroll tax soared for those spared by the income tax, but it has surpassed the income tax as the primary burden on many others much higher in the income structure.[25]

## Trends in Taxation of the Poor and the Near-Poor

The regressive impact of payroll taxes on the distribution of individual incomes has been heightened sharply by the extremely rapid growth of these taxes since 1949. At that time their effect on the relative income shares of individuals was minor, but the expansion of these taxes since World War II has been so rapid that they now increase inequality significantly. Before weighing their effect on overall inequality, it may be useful to show the extent to which trends in payroll taxation of low-income earners have counteracted programs in behalf of other families in poverty.

Because of increases in tax rates and the taxable ceiling between 1949 and 1969, the maximum social security tax paid in the name of one wage earner rose from $60 to $749 a year; it is expected to reach $1,320 a year in 1974. Two earners in a family may be charged OASDHI taxes amounting to $2,640 in 1974. The maximum tax in 1974 is to be paid by workers with incomes at or above the taxable ceiling of $12,000. As shown above, workers with incomes near this ceiling face a combined payroll and income tax rate that discriminates against them vis-à-vis higher-income earners. However, the most disturbing aspect of payroll taxation remains its impact on lower-income groups. Trends in this taxation of the poor and near-poor deserve more detailed attention.

Definitions of the poverty range by income level have been specified and revised over the years by federal agencies. While always de-

[25] For additional analysis of recent trends in payroll taxation and income taxation, see Mary W. Smelker, "The Impact of Federal Income and Payroll Taxes on the Distribution of After-Tax Income," *National Tax Journal*, Vol. 21 (December 1968), pp. 448–56; Nancy H. Teeters, "Some Fiscal Implications of Expansion of the Social Security System," Staff Economic Studies (Board of Governors of the Federal Reserve System, no date; processed); Dorothy S. Projector, "Should the Payroll Tax Finance Higher Benefits Under OASDI? A Review of the Issues," *Journal of Human Resources*, Vol. 4 (Winter 1969), pp. 60–75.

batable, these specifications are of practical importance because, in some cases, they indicate which families are recognized as so disadvantaged as to be eligible for certain forms of government assistance. They also offer a convenient basis for emphasizing the great increase in payroll taxes withheld from families officially recognized as economically marginal or actually needing government financial support.[26] Under this contradictory process, the government helps transfer recipients with one hand but simultaneously extracts with the other hand a rapidly growing levy from wage earners in the poverty range.

Consider a hypothetical family with wages and salaries only that remains over the years at the threshold of poverty. Such a family, on the verge of eligibility for government support, may also be viewed as living at a fixed real pretax income level throughout the period.[27] Figure 4-4 pictures the upward trends in annual taxes paid by these families despite their unchanging pretax economic status. Their effective payroll tax rates in 1969 were about three times as high as the 1949 levels. The rate increased from 3.6 percent in 1949 to 11.4 percent in 1969 for small families at the poverty line and for all families with incomes below the unemployment insurance ceiling of $3,000. The peak rate for large families at the poverty line was also reached in 1969 (slightly lower than 11 percent);[28] for example, a family of eight reached a payroll tax rate of 10.5 percent in 1969—3.18 times as much as the 3.3 percent paid in 1949.

The behavior of income tax rates at the poverty line over the 1949–69 period was more complex due to discrimination against small fam-

[26] It is worth repeating at this point that much of the overall population classified as living in poverty does not have a substantial portion of its income subject to the payroll tax. Nearly a fifth of the income tax filers in 1966 had adjusted gross income below the poverty level and, as indicated in Table 4-1, the payroll tax on their wages and salaries yielded a higher effective tax rate on their adjusted gross income than that paid by other families filing a return. The fact that transfers escape the payroll tax should not obscure its burden on employed persons below the poverty line.

[27] Under the latest definitions of the poverty line, these thresholds for each family size maintain a fixed ratio to the consumer price index over time. See Bureau of the Census, *Current Population Reports*, Series P-23, No. 28, "Revision in Poverty Statistics, 1959–1968" (1969). The policy was adopted of adjusting the original 1963 figures forward and backward on the basis of the consumer price index.

[28] Poverty threshold incomes for medium-sized and large families were above $3,000, which exempted a portion of their income from the unemployment insurance tax. Families with incomes below $3,000 derived no saving from the UI or OASDHI ceiling.

**FIGURE 4-4. Payroll Tax Rates and Individual Income Tax Rates on Wage and Salary Income of Earners at the Poverty Line, Various Family Sizes, One Earner, 1949–69**

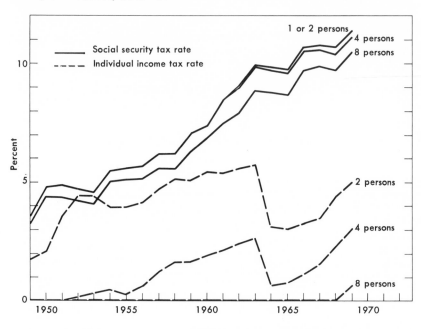

Source: See Appendix C.

ilies, especially single persons (not charted).[29] At 6.5 percent in 1949, the rates for single persons were much higher than payroll tax rates; they reached peaks of 10.1 percent in 1952 and 10.2 percent in 1963, dropped to 7.6 percent in 1968, and rose to 8.2 percent in 1969. Despite these irregularities, the contrast in trends between income and payroll tax rates is clear even for the single person at the poverty line. His income tax rate was double his payroll tax rate in 1949, remained substantially ahead until the income tax cut of 1964, and finally dropped to insignificance under the income tax relief of 1970. A substantial income tax on single persons at the poverty line has virtually

[29] The assertion of this discrimination presumes the validity of the poverty lines, or some approximation of them. If a single person and a family of eight, each at its respective poverty line, can be presumed to be about equal in economic status, the discrimination has been pronounced. For example, the single person paid a peak income tax rate of 10.2 percent in 1963, while the family of eight paid nothing. The discrimination has been due to (1) the ineligibility of the single person for income splitting, and (2) the failure of exemptions and standard deductions to exempt small families fully from income tax.

disappeared in a period during which their payroll tax rates have moved from 3.6 to 11.4 percent.

For larger families the contrast is simpler, because those at the edge of poverty have never paid much income tax. For example, rates for a family of four reached a peak of 2.7 percent in 1963 before declining, and reached a new peak of 3.0 percent in 1969; rates for a family of eight were zero until 1969. (Low-income allowances reduced rates again in 1970.) At the same time payroll tax rates were bearing down with increasing severity on the poor and the near-poor. The net result for families of four, as well as for others illustrated in Figure 4-4, is that the payroll tax is now a far greater tax on the families at the poverty threshold and below it than is the income tax.

Trends in the relative impact of payroll and income taxes on low-income groups can be contrasted more directly in another way. Consider a family with wages and salaries only whose income grew from 1949 to 1969 at such a pace that it was marginal with respect to the income tax. Figure 4-5 shows the growth and trends of payroll tax rates for families earning the maximum income completely exempt from the income tax. Since small families not subject to income tax get no benefit from payroll tax ceilings, their effective payroll tax rate is at the yearly maximum throughout, rising from 3.6 percent in 1949 to 11.4 percent in 1969. Rates for larger families are somewhat lower, especially in the early years when the ceilings reduced their effective rates substantially. However, the relative increase in their rates is greater—for example, there is a more than sevenfold increase in payroll taxes for a family of ten exempt from income tax—from 1.4 percent in 1949 to 10.2 percent in 1969.[30] In any case the main point to be stressed is that, whatever the family size, payroll tax rates have been rising rapidly for families classified by the regulations as unable to pay income tax.

The comparisons made above point out how contradictory payroll tax policy and antipoverty policy are; in addition, they show the extent to which social security taxes have become important for middle-income groups. Despite the upsurge in social security taxes, grumbling over them remains almost inaudible in comparison with the ever-present outcry over income taxes. One reason for this is that

[30] The meaning of this trend should be qualified since the low rate for 1949 is the effect of relatively liberal exemptions under the income tax as well as low payroll tax rates.

**FIGURE 4-5. Payroll Tax Rates on Wage and Salary Income of Earners Receiving Maximum Income Not Subject to Income Tax, Various Family Sizes, 1949–69**

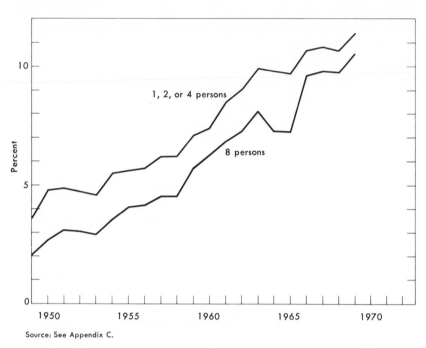

Source: See Appendix C.

payroll taxpayers do not take into account taxes nominally paid by employers; but another is that no annual payroll tax return is required of the individual. In any case, millions of taxpayers in the lower- and middle-income ranges are probably unaware that payroll taxes place a greater burden on them than the more visible income tax.

## Empirical Evidence on the Payroll Tax and Income Inequality

Some consideration should be given to the overall effect of payroll taxes on the shape of individual income distribution. It is well known that most summary indicators of the degree of inequality, such as relative shares of income ranks or the Lorenz curve, are rather insensitive to seemingly substantial changes. However, the rate of regression in recent years embodied in a tax of almost 12 percent on low incomes and practically zero on very high incomes is sufficient to produce an appreciable increase in these inequality measures.

Information on the earnings distribution in covered employment is provided by the Social Security Administration (SSA). Detailed annual estimates are available of (1) aggregate earnings, (2) aggregate earnings taxable under various hypothetical ceilings, and (3) the number of earners with earnings above each ceiling. The results for 1969 are recorded in Table 4-3, based on SSA unpublished data, April 1971.

The before-tax earnings distribution for 1969 shows a substantial degree of inequality. The 4.0 percent of earners who were in the highest class received 18.4 percent of the total earnings, while the 39.3 percent in the bottom class received only 9.0 percent of the total. The regressivity of the tax itself, with respect to earnings only, is due to the exemption above the ceiling; only 36 percent of the earnings of the top class were taxable, but the earnings of those with incomes below $7,800 were fully taxable. The regressive pattern is portrayed in the tax rate column of Table 4-3, which shows an effective rate on total earnings of 3.17 percent in the top class; the rate goes higher and higher for each lower-income class, reaching 9.41 percent for earners below the ceiling. The regressive impact of the tax may also be seen in the after-tax shares. The tax increases the relative share of the top class from 18.4 to 19.3 percent and cuts the share of the bottom group from 9.0 to 8.8 percent; that is, the top group, with 18.4 percent of pretax earnings, pays only 7.8 percent of the tax, while the bottom class, with 9.0 percent, pays about 11.3 percent of the tax. These effects of the payroll tax seem modest when viewed in terms of relative shares, but recent and scheduled rate increases enhance its regressive impact. This effect would be still more pronounced if the more regressive unemployment insurance tax were also included.

The data in Table 4-3 are pictured by means of Lorenz curves and variants of such curves in Figure 4-6. Despite the well-known stability of the Lorenz curve with respect to apparently significant changes, the tax does move the Lorenz curve appreciably farther away from the line of equality than the pretax curve. Given the regressive pattern produced by the ceiling, the degree of after-tax inequality depends on the tax rate. For illustration of this pattern, the extreme case of a 100 percent tax on taxable earnings is portrayed in the chart by the curve farthest from the line of equality. In this case, the bottom 76 percent of the earners (below $7,800 income) would have a zero share of

**TABLE 4-3. Distribution of Earners, Earnings, and Tax of Social Security Taxpayers, before and after OASDHI Tax, 1969**

| Earnings class (thousands of dollars) | Number of earners (millions) | Total earnings | Taxable earnings | Tax | Percentage cumulative frequency of earners[a] | Percentage cumulative aggregate of total earnings[b] | Percentage cumulative aggregate of earnings after tax[b] | Tax rate[c] (percent) | Percentage cumulative tax[d] |
|---|---|---|---|---|---|---|---|---|---|
| | | Billions of dollars | | | | | | | |
| 15.0 and over | 3.72 | 92.62 | 33.40 | 2.933 | 95.99 | 81.57 | 80.71 | 3.17 | 92.21 |
| 12.0–15.0 | 3.28 | 43.60 | 27.20 | 2.482 | 92.46 | 72.90 | 71.81 | 5.69 | 85.61 |
| 9.0–12.0 | 8.82 | 90.35 | 70.79 | 6.565 | 82.95 | 54.92 | 53.85 | 7.27 | 68.16 |
| 7.8–9.0 | 6.48 | 54.26 | 51.01 | 4.778 | 75.97 | 44.13 | 43.21 | 8.81 | 55.47 |
| 6.6–7.8 | 6.90 | 49.53 | 49.53 | 4.661 | 68.53 | 34.28 | 33.56 | 9.41 | 43.08 |
| 4.8–6.6 | 12.29 | 69.52 | 69.52 | 6.542 | 55.29 | 20.44 | 20.02 | 9.41 | 25.70 |
| 4.2–4.8 | 4.77 | 21.41 | 21.41 | 2.015 | 50.15 | 16.18 | 15.85 | 9.41 | 20.34 |
| 3.6–4.2 | 5.04 | 19.60 | 19.60 | 1.844 | 44.72 | 12.29 | 12.03 | 9.41 | 15.44 |
| 3.0–3.6 | 5.06 | 16.64 | 16.64 | 1.566 | 39.27 | 8.97 | 8.79 | 9.41 | 11.28 |
| Under 3.0 | 36.44 | 45.11 | 45.11 | 4.245 | 0.00 | 0.00 | 0.00 | 9.41 | 0.00 |
| Total | 92.80 | 502.64 | 404.21 | 37.631 | — | — | — | 7.49 | — |

Source: Unpublished data from the Social Security Administration, April 1971.
a Less than percentage cumulative frequency (PCF) of earners below lower limit of class.
b Less than percentage cumulative aggregate (PCA) of earnings accruing to earners below lower limit of class.
c Ratio of tax to total earnings.
d Percentage cumulative tax (PCT) charged to those below lower limit.

**FIGURE 4-6. Lorenz Curves for Earnings of Social Security Population, 1969**

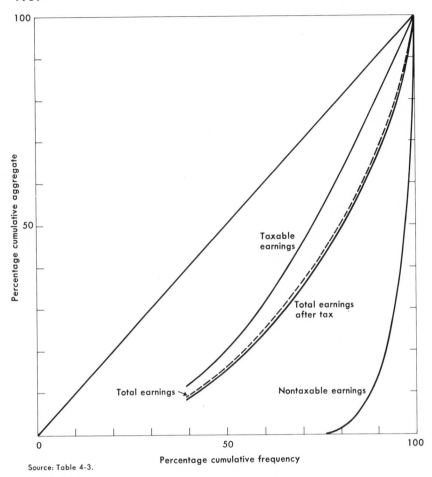

Source: Table 4-3.

after-tax earnings, while the 4 percent of the earners at the top would have a 60 percent share. A more meaningful interpretation of the bottom curve is that it represents a variant of the Lorenz curve, portraying nontaxable earnings only. This is, of course, a far less equal distribution than that of total earnings; the top 4 percent in total earnings received about 60 percent of all nontaxable earnings, and the top 17 percent cornered 97 percent of this tax-exempt income.

The other side of the picture is given by the highest curve, which is a Lorenz curve for taxable income, and therefore for the tax itself.

Taxable income (and the tax) are more equally distributed than before-tax income; low-income groups are assigned a far more generous share of the tax than of income. This highest curve shows again the reasons for the regressivity of the tax; low-income groups are permitted to bear a much greater share of the tax than of earnings, and the opposite holds for the top class.[31] Without a ceiling to accomplish this, the Lorenz curves for the tax (and the taxable income) would coincide, and the tax would be neutral with respect to relative shares and inequality.

*Trends in the Distribution of Earnings*

Postwar trends in the inequality of the earnings distribution before and after tax may also be studied by examining the annual distributions corresponding to the 1969 figures in Table 4-3. For brevity, two overall summary measures of the degree of inequality will be stressed. Table 4-4 reports annual estimates of the before-tax Gini coefficient and percentage share of the top 5 percent of the earners for 1951–69; it adds estimates of the share of the top 5 percent after social security payroll taxes.[32] On the basis of the before-tax variant of the Gini coefficient, the degree of inequality of covered earnings appears fairly stable over this nineteen-year interval. The slight upward tilt in the series does not seem significant to the naked eye, but as often happens, this stable coefficient hides important changes. The Spearman rank correlation test for trend shows that the Gini coefficient has a very convincing upward trend at a level of significance of 0.01 percent.[33] The rank correlation coefficient is 0.75, while that for the share of the top 5 percent is 0.37. The trend is less pronounced in the latter measure, although the coefficient is significant at the 5 percent level. How-

[31] The approximate break-even class in this respect was $9,000–$12,000. The 9.5 percent of all earners who had incomes in this range received about 18.0 percent of earnings and paid about 17.5 percent of the total tax. The tax was approximately neutral with respect to the relative share of this class as a whole and exactly so for some rank within it; the precise point of neutrality is at the rank at which the slopes of the two upper curves are equal.

[32] The Gini coefficient is defined as the ratio of the area between the curve and the diagonal in the Lorenz diagram to the entire area to the right of the triangle. The theoretical extremes are 0 and 1; the larger the coefficient, the higher the degree of inequality.

[33] The one-tail criterion was applied to test the a priori hypothesis that there was a significant upward trend in the degree of inequality over time. The test itself is nonparametric, testing for monotonicity without assuming normality. If there were no trend, the chance of finding a correlation as high as this would be less than one in ten thousand.

**TABLE 4-4. Earnings Inequality Measures, Social Security Population, 1951–69**[a]

| Year | Gini coefficient | Percentage share, top 5 percent | Statutory tax rate (percent) | Share of top 5 percent after payroll taxes |
|------|------|------|------|------|
| 1951 | 0.4693 | 21.15 | 2.82 | 21.46 |
| 1952 | 0.4631 | 20.52 | 2.81 | 20.82 |
| 1953 | 0.4613 | 20.03 | 2.74 | 20.32 |
| 1954 | 0.4640 | 20.54 | 3.66 | 20.94 |
| 1955 | 0.4665 | 19.51 | 3.69 | 19.87 |
| 1956 | 0.4713 | 20.74 | 3.65 | 21.14 |
| 1957 | 0.4696 | 20.36 | 4.11 | 20.80 |
| 1958 | 0.4741 | 20.63 | 4.10 | 21.07 |
| 1959 | 0.4760 | 20.70 | 4.62 | 21.20 |
| 1960 | 0.4793 | 20.80 | 5.49 | 21.41 |
| 1961 | 0.4771 | 20.50 | 5.48 | 21.10 |
| 1962 | 0.4779 | 20.51 | 5.72 | 21.12 |
| 1963 | 0.4801 | 20.58 | 6.65 | 21.30 |
| 1964 | 0.4794 | 20.21 | 6.64 | 20.90 |
| 1965 | 0.4806 | 20.32 | 6.64 | 21.01 |
| 1966 | 0.4918 | 21.52 | 7.88 | 22.41 |
| 1967 | 0.4912 | 21.73 | 8.07 | 22.69 |
| 1968 | 0.4893 | 21.34 | 8.19 | 22.27 |
| 1969 | 0.4648 | 21.07 | 8.94 | 22.08 |

Sources: Unpublished data from the Social Security Administration, April 1971. The Gini coefficient and pretax share of the top 5 percent in earnings class were estimated by the methods detailed in John A. Brittain, "Interpolation of Frequency Distributions of Aggregated Variables and Estimation of the Gini Concentration Measure," *Metron*, Vol. 22 (December 1962). The share after payroll taxes was estimated on the assumption that those in the top class each paid the maximum old-age, survivors, and disability insurance (OASDI) tax. Estimation of the tax rate for the top 5 percent of the earners relied on the tax and taxable income totals for all incomes above the lower limit of the class in which the 5 percent cutoff level was observed.

a. Data before 1966 do not include health insurance, which was introduced in that year.

ever, when this share of the top class is put on an after-payroll-tax basis, the resulting rank correlation coefficient of 0.62 is more significant—this time at the 1 percent level. The expanding payroll tax turned a barely significant trend toward greater inequality into one for which the statistical evidence is stronger. This point can be reinforced by estimating the slope of the trend line for these coefficients on a before-tax and an after-tax basis. The least squares estimates are 0.045 and 0.089, respectively. Thus the nineteen-year upward trend in inequality on an after-tax basis is nearly double that of the before-tax series.

The conclusions on the impact of the social security tax on the earnings distribution may be summed up. Inequality clearly increased in the 1951–69 period through "natural" or "market" forces.[34] However, in terms of the share of the top 5 percent of the earners, the imposition of a rising and regressive payroll tax increased the trend toward greater earnings inequality beyond that brought about by market factors.

## Payroll Tax as Related to Distribution of Total Money Income

The previous discussion has focused for the most part on the impact of the payroll tax on the distribution of wages and salaries, or on total earnings, including those of the self-employed. Evidence relating the tax to total family money income, including property income and transfers, is also available from a 1961 survey by the U.S. Bureau of Labor Statistics (BLS).[35] These data are useful, although the mixing of transfer recipients with those receiving primarily factor incomes confuses the picture. The findings in this BLS survey fall short of preferred estimates of national aggregates available in the national income accounts, as illustrated in Table 4-5. Results for the self-employed are especially low; however, the income and tax data for the quantitatively more important employee category fall less than 10 percent short of the official total. In any case, the figures appear sufficiently reliable to permit some inferences on the distributional effect of the OASDI tax.[36]

Since the payroll tax, in real terms, is paid by the active earning population, it is appropriate to study the distribution of the tax among this group.[37] A breakdown of the tabulation gives data on family heads and single consumers under the age of sixty-five—a pop-

[34] This interpretation of a rise in the inequality measures needs to be qualified. The annual distributions covered different earners and different combinations of types of earners. Part of the increase in inequality may have been due to entry into the system of high-income earners, such as physicians. The inequality measures can do no more than summarize the shape of these not altogether comparable annual distributions.

[35] Special tabulation by the U.S. Department of the Treasury of the U.S. Bureau of Labor Statistics' 1961 Consumer Expenditure Survey. A more recent survey by the U.S. Office of Economic Opportunity is now available under the title, "1967 Survey of Economic Opportunity."

[36] Since the unemployment insurance tax is nominally paid by employers, the survey offers no information on this part of the payroll tax.

[37] As discussed in the technical note at the end of Chapter II and the beginning of this chapter, price effects of the tax may also affect the real income position of others, but it is not possible to separate these effects from those of other macroeconomic policies.

**TABLE 4-5. Comparison of National Income Accounts Estimates of Earnings and Taxes with Those of the Bureau of Labor Statistics Survey, 1961**

*(In billions of dollars)*

| Type of earnings or tax | National income accounts data | Bureau of Labor Statistics survey |
|---|---|---|
| Wages and salaries | 278.08 | 260.82 |
| Self-employed income | 48.43 | 36.40 |
| Federal individual income tax | 47.57 | 38.98 |
| Old-age, survivors, and disability insurance tax on employees | 5.72 | 5.16 |
| Old-age, survivors, and disability insurance tax on self-employed persons | 0.82 | 0.58 |

Sources: U.S. Department of Commerce, Office of Business Economics, *The National Income and Product Accounts of the United States, 1929–1965: Statistical Tables* (1966), pp. 33, 53, 59; special tabulation prepared by the U.S. Department of the Treasury from the U.S. Bureau of Labor Statistics' 1961 Consumer Expenditure Survey.

ulation that should approximate the earning population considerably better than the total of all age groups. Table 4-6 therefore focuses on the under sixty-five category.[38] A further concentration on families that include both husband and wife uses most of the income information and should contribute to exclusion of most part-time and/or youthful workers whose earnings are not typical of the working population as a whole.[39] Concentration on the relatively homogeneous husband-and-wife families with husbands under sixty-five seemed appropriate.[40] The survey results reported in Table 4-6 permit a few generalizations. The payroll tax on wages and salaries per family rises with total money income until it reaches the top class, into which other income apparently put many families despite lower wages and salaries per family than in the class immediately below. The average tax of $171 for families in the $10,000–$15,000 class indicates good coverage

[38] Exclusion of the group over sixty-five eliminates about 20 percent of the families who were credited in the survey with 11.5 percent of total money income and 5.4 percent of the OASDI tax; an analysis of the progressive impact of benefits could appropriately concentrate on this group. Exclusion of income recipients over sixty-five leaves millions of other transfer recipients in the distribution.

[39] Within the class under sixty-five, the excluded single group constituting less than 19 percent of the number was credited with 12 percent of money income and paid about 11 percent of the OASDI tax.

[40] Actually, the magnitude of aggregate earnings of this group is so dominant that the findings to be presented are not much affected by inclusion of earners in the other categories, who reported only 16 percent of total OASDI taxes.

**TABLE 4-6. Taxes per Family and Tax Rates by Money Income Class, Families with Husband and Wife, Head of Family under Sixty-five, 1961**

| Money income (thousands of dollars) | Taxes per family (dollars) | | | Tax rates on income (percent) | | | Rates on earnings (percent) | |
|---|---|---|---|---|---|---|---|---|
| | OASDI on wages and salaries | Total OASDI | Federal income tax | OASDI on wages and salaries | Total OASDI | Federal income tax | OASDI on wages and salaries | Total OASDI |
| Less than 1.0 | 7.0 | 32.3 | 79.3 | —a | —a | —a | 1.18 | —a |
| 1.0–2.0 | 17.3 | 25.0 | 72.6 | 1.11 | 1.60 | 4.64 | 2.24 | 2.39 |
| 2.0–3.0 | 39.4 | 50.5 | 83.8 | 1.56 | 2.00 | 3.32 | 2.49 | 2.56 |
| 3.0–4.0 | 63.2 | 75.1 | 187.2 | 1.79 | 2.13 | 5.30 | 2.49 | 2.49 |
| 4.0–5.0 | 95.6 | 105.6 | 325.5 | 2.11 | 2.33 | 7.19 | 2.58 | 2.55 |
| 5.0–6.0 | 112.4 | 124.0 | 490.8 | 2.04 | 2.25 | 8.90 | 2.42 | 2.42 |
| 6.0–7.5 | 126.9 | 137.6 | 689.6 | 1.89 | 2.05 | 10.29 | 2.16 | 2.16 |
| 7.5–10.0 | 149.0 | 162.7 | 980.1 | 1.74 | 1.90 | 11.44 | 1.99 | 1.99 |
| 10.0–15.0 | 171.4 | 188.7 | 1,528.2 | 1.46 | 1.61 | 13.03 | 1.70 | 1.69 |
| 15.0 and over | 151.9 | 190.8 | 4,000.5 | 0.69 | 0.86 | 18.05 | 1.11 | 0.95 |
| Average per family | 119.7 | 133.6 | 874.6 | 1.59 | 1.78 | 11.65 | 1.95 | 1.91 |

Source: Special tabulation prepared by the Department of the Treasury from the Bureau of Labor Statistics' 1961 Consumer Expenditure Survey.
a Omitted because the income base was negative.

by the survey as well as a substantial number of multiple-earner families, since the maximum employee tax per person was $144 in 1961. The inclusion of self-employed earnings in the total OASDI tax showed that the top class ($15,000 and over) had the highest total OASDI tax per family—$191.[41] At that level the payroll tax is dwarfed by the average federal income tax of $4,000; this is in contrast to lower money income levels at which the OASDI tax averages as much as 60 percent of the income tax even before the employer tax is considered.

Payroll tax rates derived from the survey do not directly reflect the flat rate on earnings under the ceiling. Except for the first (negative) income class, the tax is progressive with respect to total money income up through the class containing the $4,800 ceiling, rising from 1.60 to 2.33 percent. This is due to (1) a low ratio of wages and salaries to total money income in the low brackets, and (2) a relatively low rate of coverage of wages and salaries in these brackets. As suggested at the beginning of this chapter, the very low tax rate on low total money income is due in part to the mixing of nontaxable transfers with factor income. The more appropriate criterion of progressivity of the payroll tax is its rate measured against factor income. The tax rate on total money income, excluding public benefits and pensions, is the most relevant statistic available. Aside from the first (negative) income class, the tax structure is mildly progressive on this basis also, with the rate rising from 1.6 to 2.4 percent in the ceiling class.[42] This is due to two factors. First, there is a slight progressivity in the payroll tax rate on total earnings up to the ceiling, as indicated in Table 4-6, caused by a positive association of the rate of coverage with income. Second, the importance of property income increases slightly in relation to income in the lower brackets, according to this BLS survey.

In the next chapter, Figures 5-5 to 5-7 show that the degree of progressivity below the ceiling is lower when measured against "ordinary income," even though the latter also includes some taxable pension income. The evidence for progressivity in the 1964 data is the

[41] The peculiarity that the bottom class (less than $1,000 income) reported more total OASDI tax and federal income tax per family than the $1,000–$2,000 class is apparently due to the lag in reporting self-employed earnings. Proprietors suffering a bad year in 1961 presumably paid and reported taxes for that year based on higher earnings in 1960.

[42] After this point transfers become relatively so small that the rate with respect to money income virtually equals the tax rate on estimated factor income.

rise in the fraction of ordinary income that is taxable: from a low of 83 percent to a peak of 94 percent in the ceiling class. This mild progressivity among low incomes is dwarfed by the sharp regressivity among higher incomes; for example, the fraction taxable drops to 20 percent in the $20,000–$25,000 class.

The low tax rates shown in Table 4-6 do not contradict the evidence of a high tax rate on adjusted gross income (mainly earnings) of poverty-range earners, as reported in Table 4-1. Table 4-6 may give somewhat better evidence of the importance of a tax on wages and salaries for low money incomes. The low tax rate on the bottom class applies to only a small amount of income. The effective rate on wages and salaries for incomes below $4,000, for example, is about 2.3 percent, or 4.6 percent for the combined tax when the statutory rate is 6 percent. Even more significant is the fact that *covered* wages and salaries are a major component of money income (including transfers) of these low-income groups. For example, data underlying Table 4-6 show that the mean wage income of those in the $2,000–$3,000 class was nearly $1,600. Given that statutory rates nearly doubled in the 1960s, the payroll tax burden on the working poor is clearly heavy, although slightly progressive with respect to factor income below the ceiling.

Within the range of income classes above the ceiling, the known regressivity of the OASDI tax asserts itself in all of the tax rate variants. The tax rate among money incomes over $15,000 averages about 35 to 40 percent of the rate of those in the $4,000–$5,000 class, who pay the peak rate on all variants. In sum, with respect to total money income, the OASDI tax appears progressive up to a point in the vicinity of the ceiling and regressive from that point on. In contrast the income tax rate rises smoothly and continuously from 3.3 percent on the $2,000–$3,000 class to 18 percent on the top class.

The fall in the total OASDI tax rate on money income from 2.33 percent at its peak to 0.86 percent in the top class may seem only a minor offset to the progressivity of the income tax. However, several points should be made in this context. First, imputation of the employer portion of the tax to wages and salaries doubles the tax rate on wages and salaries recorded in Table 4-6. Second, although the latest ceiling stood in 1970 at about the same point in the income distribution as in 1961, the statutory rates for OASDHI rose about 70 percent in that interval. An adjustment for these two factors, plus imputation of employer unemployment insurance tax of about 2 percent, puts the effective tax rate on money incomes in the vicinity of the ceiling at almost 10 percent. Since this rate approaches zero as the tax is applied to higher and higher money incomes, the survey data imply that the regressive and growing payroll tax is a substantial offset today to the observed and fairly stable degree of progressivity of the income tax.

One way to compare the redistributional properties of the two taxes in abstraction from their relative size is to look at their relative distribution by income rank. Consider again the distribution of total before-tax money income of the under-sixty-five group of husband-and-wife families in Table 4-6. The contrasting impact of the two taxes may be seen in the portion of each charged to various income ranks.[43] The top 5 percent in income rank received about 15 percent of total money income but paid 23 percent of the total income tax and only about 7 percent of the total payroll tax. It is clear that if the two taxes were equal in size, the top 5 percent would pay on the average just over 15 percent of the combined tax—about the same as their share in income. Therefore, the combined tax would be roughly neutral with respect to the after-tax share of the top 5 percent. Similarly, the top 20 percent in income rank received 38 percent of the total income and paid 48 percent of the total income tax and only 28 percent of the total payroll tax. At the opposite extreme, the bottom 40 percent in income rank received 21 percent of the total income, paid only 13 percent of the total income tax, but paid 27 percent of the total OASDI tax.

Lorenz curves summarizing these relationships are presented in Figure 4-7. Closest to the line of equality is the curve representing the share of total OASDI taxes accruing to each money income rank. Farthest from the line of equality is the curve representing the distribution of federal income taxes. The positions of the two curves reflect the fact that the payroll tax is distributed more equally than money incomes and results in an after-tax curve farther from the equality line than the pretax curve; the opposite is true of the income tax.[44]

---

[43] The regressivity of the payroll tax illustrated here depends heavily on the relative position of the ceiling; however, the ratio of ceiling to mean earnings at 1.288 in 1961 was rather typical of the postwar experience (see Table 7-2, below).

[44] The curve for a tax rate uniform at all levels would coincide with the Lorenz curve for incomes and be neutral with respect to the degree of inequality.

**FIGURE 4-7. Lorenz Curves for Earnings and Taxes, Families with Husband and Wife, Head under Sixty-five, 1961**

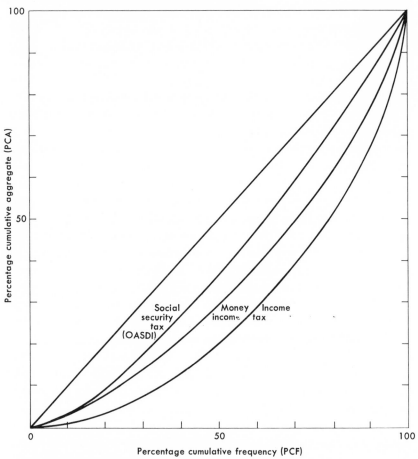

Although the actual effect on the degree of inequality depends on the size of the tax, it is worth noting that the degree of departure of the two tax curves from the income curve is about the same. Therefore, if the two taxes had the same total yield, they would have approximately offsetting effects on the degree of inequality. Thus the growth of the payroll tax relative to the income tax produces a tendency for after-tax inequality to increase over time.

CHAPTER V

# Proposals for Reform

THE HEAVY and growing weight of the social security payroll tax on the poor (detailed in Chapter IV) and the regressive nature of this tax provide a strong case for its modification or phasing out. Over the years there have been two primary lines of defense against such reforms. First, it has been inferred that the tax is inviolate on the basis of an analogy with individual purchases of private insurance contracts; the conception that the social security taxpayer "gets what he pays for" in some actuarial sense has been fostered. Second, a pragmatic corollary asserts that without benefit of this pretense authorized social security taxes would never have been sufficient to finance even the level of benefits paid to date (believed by many to have been inadequate). However, with the passage of time, the connection between individual lifetime taxes and benefits has grown steadily more tenuous. Moreover, at the aggregate level in a given year the imbalance between taxes and benefits has often been substantial; there has been a growing awareness that recent surpluses in the social security budget have exercised fortuitous (if not planned) restraint on inflation. The pretense that a close relation exists between taxes and benefits may have had a real impact on appropriations, but it is not necessary to be bound by it in evaluating the tax.[1]

[1] Alleviation of the tax burden on low incomes at a given cost is not necessarily the optimum allocation of this amount. A more general move against poverty, such as the

115

Since the tax-benefit relationship is already very loose, it seems in order to consider departures from it aimed at reducing or eliminating regressivity of the tax. Two broad classes of revision are considered: a modest internal reform of the payroll tax structure, and its complete phasing out in favor of other taxes, particularly the individual income tax.[2] It is suggested first that "floors," or exemptions and deductions virtually eliminating the burden of the payroll tax on low-income groups, may be introduced with only a modest loss of revenue, which could be recouped by rate and/or ceiling increases. The reduction by these reforms of payroll tax regressitivy is then appraised. The tax rate curve with respect to factor income (as approximated by "ordinary income") is shown to become sharply progressive below the ceiling. Finally, the effect of substitution of the individual income tax for part or all of the payroll tax is considered. This move would require substantial increases in effective income tax rates but not in the total effective rate of taxation. It would be a long step toward equity in the overall tax structure.[3]

## Definition, Costs, and Financing of Reform Proposals

### Alternative Models for Structural Reform

The modest reforms suggested here all involve "floors" or establishment of minimum taxable earnings levels analogous to the ceilings already in existence for old-age, survivors, disability, and health insurance (OASDHI) and unemployment insurance (UI). This stress on tax relief to the poor could be supplemented by ceiling increases that would also make the tax less regressive. It is shown later, however, that no ceiling increase alone would be sufficient to eliminate regressivity, owing to the decline of earnings relative to ordinary income above the $7,000–$8,000 class. Nevertheless, ceiling increases

---

negative income tax, might be a stronger weapon against inequality. However, payroll tax relief for the working poor is suggested here only as a modest reform, with no implication that more far-reaching reforms are not in order. At the same time it seems inappropriate to ignore any and all improvements that fall short of the *maximum* results per dollar. Certainly payroll tax relief is a strong candidate for a place in any broader reform package.

[2] The analysis here of proposals for general revenue financing carries no implication that only payroll taxpayers need relief. Other antipoverty actions are clearly called for.

[3] For data sources and processing underlying this chapter, see Appendix D.

are considered briefly as one device to offset the tax yield loss due to exemptions, although a ceiling increase is not considered here as a positive reform in its own right.[4] More equitable taxation of higher incomes could best be accomplished by substitution of the income tax, as discussed later in this chapter.

The exemption plans studied here are variants of the one in effect under the income tax in the 1964–69 period.[5] In practice the latter has been less liberal than would have been the conceptually more satisfactory approach that would exempt earnings below poverty lines. However, the income tax exemption structure was simpler and could be readily put into practice in payroll tax withholding. The revenue loss under nine alternative exemption plans was analyzed by computing the effect of each plan on each of approximately 100,000 individual income tax returns in a 1964 sample and extrapolating to population size.[6] The terms of the nine plans are summarized in Table 5-1. Plan 600, proposed by Walter P. Reuther in 1967,[7] allows one $600 exemption per earner, rather than including exemptions for dependents as under the income tax; it also carries no minimum standard deduction. Plan 700A yields the same total value of exemptions and standard deductions as provided for under the income tax in the period 1964–69.[8]

The formula for plan 700B computes the total as under plan 700A but allows it only to earners whose earnings are less than the com-

---

[4] Substantial ceiling increases would undoubtedly lead to a greater spreading out of the benefit scale and represent a departure from the common conception of social security as a device for "minimum" retirement support. See Joseph A. Pechman, Henry J. Aaron, and Michael K. Taussig, *Social Security: Perspectives for Reform* (Brookings Institution, 1968), Chap. 4.

[5] The methods of low-income relief discussed offer general illustrations of the costs and gains achievable under this approach. For additional analysis and alternative plans, see Ronald F. Hoffman, "Notes on Payroll Tax Rebate Proposals," in National Tax Association, *Proceedings of the Sixty-Second Annual Conference on Taxation* (1969), pp. 356–76; Pechman and others, *Social Security*, pp. 191–95 and 224–25, Donald J. Curran and John Shannon, "Positive and *Negative* Tax Credits—A New Dimension in Intergovernmental Relations," *National Tax Journal*, Vol. 19 (March 1966), pp. 18–26.

[6] For a discussion of the tax sample, see Appendix D.

[7] *President's Proposals for Revision in the Social Security System*, Hearings before the House Committee on Ways and Means, 90 Cong. 1 sess. (1967), Pt. 3, p. 1453.

[8] This statement requires qualification on two counts. First, the formula for the proposed reform assumes utilization of the minimum standard deduction by each earner and allows nothing more. Under the income tax most earners either itemize or are entitled to standard deductions above the minimum. Second, exemptions for age and blindness were excluded, since they are not regarded as essential ingredients in the exemption structure.

**TABLE 5-1. Alternative Plans for Exemptions and Deductions under the Social Security Payroll Tax**

| Exemption plan | Formula for dollar value of exemptions plus standard deductions[a] |
|---|---|
| 600 | 600 per earner[b] |
| 700A | (700 × number of exemptions) + 100 or 200[c] |
| 700B | 700A if greater than earnings; zero otherwise |
| 700A-1 | 700A − (earnings − value of 700A), or zero, whichever is greater |
| 700A-5 | 700A − 5(earnings − value of 700A), or zero, whichever is greater |
| 1050A | (1050 × number of exemptions) + 150 or 300[c] |
| 1050B | 1050A if greater than earnings; zero otherwise |
| 1050A-1 | 1050A − (earnings − value of 1050A), or zero, whichever is greater |
| 1050A-5 | 1050A − 5(earnings − value of 1050A), or zero, whichever is greater |

Source: Devised by author.
a. Exemptions exclude those for age and blindness. Earnings refer to total earnings.
b. One earner per return is assumed.
c. First figure applies for married persons filing separate returns; second figure applies in all other cases.

puted level of exemptions and deductions. While the revenue loss is greatly reduced under this plan, it produces an inequitable "notch" effect. For example, a family of four with earnings of $2,999 would pay no payroll tax, but a family of four with $3,000 income would be fully taxable and end up with substantially less income after tax than the first family. Plans 700A-1 and 700A-5 concentrate the exemptions among low-income families by phasing out the relief gradually as earnings increase. Under the formula for Plan 700A-1 the basic exemption total under plan 700A is reduced by the amount of earnings in excess of the basic exemption and disappears when the earnings level reaches twice the basic exemption. Thus, in the case of a family of four (couples that file separate returns are ignored), the effective tax rate is zero if earnings are $3,000 or less but reaches the full statutory rate for incomes of $6,000 or more (if the ceiling is $6,000 or more). For earnings between $3,000 and the ceiling, the tax rate curve is progressive, rising at a decreasing rate,[9] but it turns regressive above the ceiling, as under the present law. If the ceiling is less than twice the basic exemption level, the full statutory rate is not reached

[9] By combining the formulas for plans 700A and 700A-1, it may be shown that for levels of earnings below the ceiling the fraction taxable is given by $(2E − \$1,400N − \$400)/E$, where $N$ denotes the number of exemptions and $E$ the total earnings reported on each tax return. The second derivative of this function with respect to earnings is negative, indicating that the tax rate rises at a decreasing rate. No special brief is held for this property, which was an accidental by-product of the simple phase-out formula.

at any earnings level. For example, under the $4,800 ceiling in effect in 1964, the maximum effective tax rate that could be charged a family of four was 75 percent of the statutory rate; this maximum would have been paid by a family earning $4,800, since its basic exemption of $3,000 was reduced to $1,200, leaving taxable earnings of $3,600. Plan 700A-5 reduces the revenue loss of the basic exemption plan (700A) by phasing out the exemptions at five times the rate under plan 700A-1. Thus for a family of four the effective tax rate is zero for earnings levels through $3,000, then progressive until the statutory rate is reached at $3,600, constant at that level until the ceiling is reached, and then regressive (approaching zero as under the present law).

The formulas for plans 700A-1 and 700A-5 are two devices aimed at concentrating the benefits of exemptions among low-income families and avoiding the inequities produced by the formula for plan 700B. It is not suggested that these two plans are necessarily optimal from any point of view. However, they have the merit of simplicity, and they eliminate the main disadvantages of plans 700A and 700B.[10] Plans 700A-1 and 700A-5 illustrate a gradual and a rapid phasing out of exemptions, respectively. This type of device is computationally convenient, and unlike plan 700B, it can circumvent the situation in which an earner at a given income level may be left with less after-tax income than an earner at a lower before-tax level.[11] Finally, the four plans 1050A to 1050A-5 allow evaluation of the effect on the payroll

[10] Only in extreme cases can the marginal rate of tax under this type of phase-out scheme reach unity or above. If the phase-out multipliers 1 and 5 in the formulas for plans 700A-1 and 700A-5 are denoted generally by $m$, the payroll tax rate by $t$, total tax by $T$, and earnings by $E$, it can be shown that the marginal rate of tax in the phase-out range $dT/dE$ is given by $(1 + m)t$. This quantity must be kept below unity to avoid the notch problem. The higher the tax rate, the lower the allowable rate of phasing out. Thus, under a 10 percent tax, $m$ must be less than 9 to avoid the notch; but under a 20 percent rate, $m$ must be less than 4. In the latter case the tax is so high that the formula for plan 700A-5 in Table 5-1 would be disqualified. However, under the more realistic tax rate of 10 percent, the rapid phasing out under the formula for plan 700A-5 would escape the notch with a marginal tax rate of 60 percent over a short earnings range.

[11] This type of phasing out of exemptions also merits consideration in the case of the income tax. A scheme such as the formula for plan 700A-1 (or even a more gradual one) would yield a large increase in revenue. Alternatively it would permit substantial increases in the basic exemptions to relieve low-income families with a smaller loss in revenue than that which resulted from the increased exemptions in the 1969 legislation. Under the present structure an exemption increase is an inefficient way to aid low-income families.

tax yield of a liberalization of the 1964 exemption and deduction structure; the formulas for these plans represent a 50 percent increase in the exemption and standard deduction parameters embodied in the formulas for the four plans 700A to 700A-5, which were in effect under the income tax in 1964.

### Effects of Exemptions and Standard Deductions on Tax Yield

The objective of the exemption and deduction structures outlined in Table 5-1 is to reduce the payroll tax burden on low-income families. The cost of accomplishing this under the alternative plans depends on the tax rate, the ceiling, the number of exemptions allowed, and the extent to which higher-income groups share in the benefits. Since payroll taxes are generally assessed at a uniform statutory rate on taxable income, it is appropriate to concentrate attention on the impact of the proposed changes on the tax base rather than the tax itself. Preliminary (unadjusted) estimates of 1964 taxable earnings under various plans and ceilings were obtained from simulations with the sample of 100,000 tax returns made available by the Treasury Department; for each structure the payroll tax was estimated for each return and summed over all returns. The results are displayed in Figure 5-1; however, estimates based on the tax return sample of taxable earnings without exemptions should first be compared with Social Security Administration (SSA) estimates. The two curves nearest the top of Figure 5-1 reaffirm the need for substantial adjustment of the figures estimated from tax returns. However, it is assumed here that the estimated figures give a reliable picture of the *relative* changes in taxable earnings (and tax yield) that would have been obtained if the estimates could have been derived directly from the social security distribution (see Appendix D for the methodology used). Several generalizations are apparent from the chart. Plan 700A—the most liberal plan, allowing all earners exemptions comparable to those on individual tax returns—would have resulted in a large loss of revenue, amounting to over 50 percent loss for ceilings under about $6,000. Plan 600, allowing only one $600 exemption per return, would lose less than a third as much; however, it would relieve earners at or near the poverty line of only a small fraction of their tax burden. Plan 700A-1, which like 700A allows exemptions for dependents, is clearly more consistent with the original objective of low-income relief. Whatever the ceiling, this plan costs slightly less in lost revenue than

**FIGURE 5-1. Relationships between Social Security (OASDI) Tax Base and Ceiling on Taxable Earnings, Alternative Exemption Plans, 1964**[a]

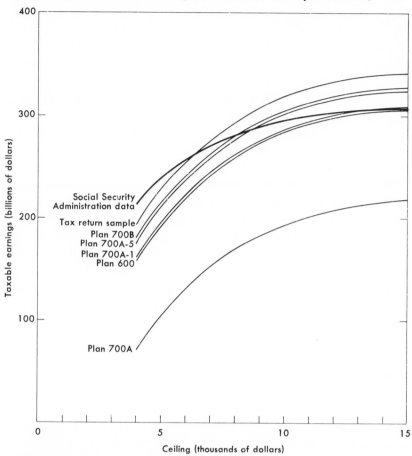

Sources: The curves based on Social Security Administration (SSA) data and the tax return sample are derived from applying actual 1964 OASDI tax rates, with no exemptions, to (1) SSA data and (2) the raw data in the Brookings Institution's file of approximately 100,000 federal individual income tax returns for 1964. The other curves are derived from applying the formulas in Table 5-1 to the tax return sample. See the text and Appendix D for descriptions of the tax return sample and the methodology used. SSA data are from Michael Resnick, "Annual Earnings and the Taxable Maximum for OASDHI," *Social Security Bulletin*, Vol. 29 (November 1966), pp. 39–40.

[a] See Table 5-1 for formulas for the exemption plans.

plan 600, even though the latter gives inadequate relief at the bottom of the income range. Under plan 700A-1 the gradual phasing out of exemptions as earnings rise saves more than enough revenue to recoup the loss due to granting exemptions for dependents to the lower-income groups.

Phasing out the exemptions at lower-income levels under plan 700A-5 results in a revenue loss only about one-half that under plan 700A-1 with its more gradual phasing out. Even the latter costs only 25–30 percent as much as the most liberal plan (700A). A comparison of the curves for plans 700B and 700A-5 also shows that the inequity due to the "notch" under the former has been banished by the phasing out of exemptions at only a small additional loss in revenue.[12]

The effects of increasing the exemptions are best illustrated numerically. Estimated ratios of tax yields under exemption plans to tax yields without exemptions are reported for various ceilings in Table 5-2. Under each plan the relative revenue loss varies substantially with the ceiling; the lower the ceiling, the lower the tax base before exemptions, and the larger the relative loss when exemptions are allowed. However, in practice over the postwar years, the ceilings of $4,800 and $6,000 in 1964 represent approximately the observed range of ceilings relative to mean earnings.[13] Thus the columns for these ceilings probably bound fairly well the likely relative revenue loss under future exemption plans bearing the same relation to mean earnings as in 1964.[14] Under the 1964 $4,800 ceiling, the liberal plan (700A) would have cut SSA revenues about 56 percent, while a 50 percent increase in the exemption and deduction parameters would have produced a net loss of about 74 percent. Under the more moderate plans, an exemption increase would be far less costly. The early-phase-out plan (700A-5) costing 8 percent seems preferable to the notch model, although the latter costs slightly less—6.2 percent. A 50 percent increase in exemptions in 1964 would have carried exemption levels well above the poverty line except for families of one or two persons. Under plan 700A-5 this would have increased the 1964 revenue loss from 8 to 20 percent. The slow-phase-out plan (700A-1) seems clearly preferable to plan 600. A 50 percent rise in exemptions would increase its revenue loss from 15 to 34 percent. These relative

[12] Avoiding the notch would also eliminate substantial disincentive effects in marginal cases.

[13] Between 1950 and 1968 the ratio ranged from a low of 1.11 in 1965 to a high of 1.52 in 1968. The $4,800 and $6,000 ceilings in 1964, in relative terms, are 1.14 and 1.43, respectively.

[14] Because average earnings have risen substantially since 1964, the relative revenue losses indicated in Table 5-2 are higher than they would be in later years if the exemption plans were unadjusted. The parameters of the exemption function must be increased at the same rate as mean earnings for application to years since 1964.

**TABLE 5-2.** Ratios of Tax Yield under Alternative Social Security Tax Exemption Plans to Tax Yield without Exemptions, Various Ceilings, 1964

*(In percent)*

| Exemption plan[a] | Taxable ceiling (dollars) | | | | | | |
|---|---|---|---|---|---|---|---|
| | 4,000 | 4,800 | 6,000 | 7,800 | 10,000 | 15,000 | No ceiling |
| 600 | 81.6 | 83.8 | 86.0 | 87.8 | 88.8 | 89.6 | 90.2 |
| 700A | 37.5 | 44.1 | 51.2 | 57.4 | 61.0 | 63.6 | 65.6 |
| 700B | 93.0 | 93.8 | 94.5 | 95.2 | 95.6 | 95.9 | 96.1 |
| 700A-1 | 83.1 | 84.9 | 86.8 | 88 5 | 89.4 | 90.2 | 90.7 |
| 700A-5 | 91.0 | 92.0 | 93.0 | 93.9 | 94.4 | 94.8 | 95.1 |
| 1050A | 20.9 | 25.8 | 32.8 | 40.3 | 45.2 | 48.9 | 51.7 |
| 1050B | 82.3 | 83.6 | 85.1 | 86.7 | 87.8 | 88.6 | 89.2 |
| 1050A-1 | 63.4 | 66.2 | 69.6 | 73.1 | 75.3 | 77.0 | 78.2 |
| 1050A-5 | 78.3 | 79.8 | 81.8 | 83.8 | 85.1 | 86.1 | 86.9 |

Source: The Brookings Institution's file of 100,000 individual income tax returns for the year 1964, processed as described in Appendix D.

[a] See Table 5-1 for formulas for exemption plans.

losses would have been up to 25 percent less under a relatively high ceiling, such as $6,000 in 1964.

### Restoration of Social Security Revenue Losses

The revenue losses under these exemption plans can be recouped within the social security tax structure itself by increases in the tax rate and/or ceiling. For 1964 the necessary increase in the tax rate alone can be derived from Table 5-2 on the assumption that the actual ceiling is fixed at $4,800. The necessary adjustment in the ceiling alone may be read from Figures 5-2 and 5-3, which display the final adjusted estimates of the percentage of covered earnings taxable under the various plans.[15] The horizontal lines represent the actual percentage taxable, and its intersections with the tax yield curves for the exemption plans identify the ceilings at which the revenue losses would be recouped. Table 5-3 summarizes the required adjustment of rate or ceiling, as well as joint adjustments allowing each to recoup one-half the loss. Compared to the actual rate of 7.25 percent on wages and salaries and the ceiling of $4,800 in effect in 1964, the new values

[15] The numerical estimates underlying these curves were derived by multiplying SSA estimates of the percentage taxable without exemptions by the revenue ratios in Table 5-2.

**FIGURE 5-2. Percentage of Earnings Taxable under Alternative Exemption Plans and Ceilings, Moderate Exemption Levels, 1964**[a]

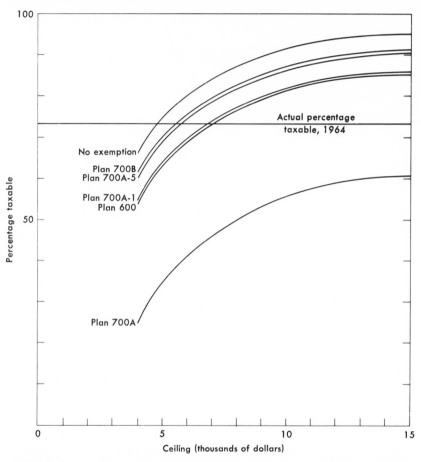

Sources: Table 5-1 and the Brookings Institution's file of approximately 100,000 individual federal income tax returns for 1964, with adjustments to conform with the relative differences between the Social Security Administration data and the tax return sample data. See the text and Appendix D for descriptions of the tax return sample and the methodology used.
    [a] See Table 5-1 for formulas for the exemption plans.

represent fairly modest increases in all except the most liberal plans (700A and 1050A), under which even a complete removal of the ceiling is not sufficient to recoup the loss. Plan 1050A-1—the next most liberal plan, involving increased exemptions and only a gradual phasing out of exemptions as earnings increase—could have been financed in 1964 with a tax rate of 9.1 percent and a ceiling of $6,940. A conservative plan like 700A-5 could have been financed by a mere

**FIGURE 5-3. Percentage of Earnings Taxable under Alternative Exemption Plans and Ceilings, High Exemption Levels, 1964**[a]

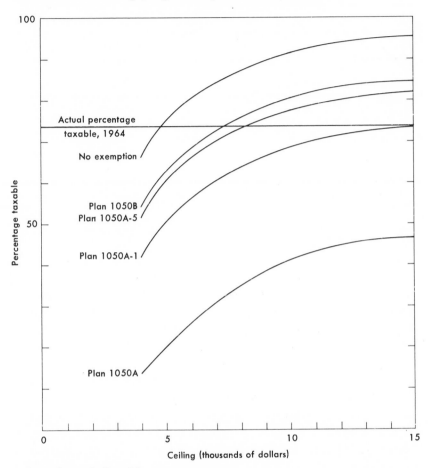

Sources: Same as for Figure 5-2.
[a] See Table 5-1 for formulas for the exemption plans.

20 percent increase in the ceiling alone. This adjustment and even those for plan 700A-1 with a more gradual phasing out seem modest enough to be feasible. They are of the same order of magnitude as other upward adjustments made in the tax structure in recent years.

### Exemption Plans for 1969

These detailed estimates for 1964 can also be used to derive approximate relationships for later years. The results for the OASDHI

**TABLE 5-3. Tax Rates and Taxable Ceilings Needed to Recoup Revenue Loss under Alternative Exemption Plans, 1964**

| Exemption plan | Rate with ceiling unchanged (percent) | Ceiling with rate unchanged (dollars) | Joint rate and ceiling changes[a] | |
|---|---|---|---|---|
| | | | Rate (percent) | Ceiling (dollars) |
| 600 | 8.6 | 7,120 | 8.0 | 5,720 |
| 700A | 16.4 | — | 10.1 | 8,760 |
| 700B | 7.7 | 5,560 | 7.5 | 5,180 |
| 700A-1 | 8.4 | 6,920 | 7.8 | 5,660 |
| 700A-5 | 7.9 | 5,760 | 7.6 | 5,260 |
| 1050A | 28.1 | — | 11.5 | 14,300 |
| 1050B | 8.7 | 7,280 | 8.0 | 5,800 |
| 1050A-1 | 11.0 | 15,000 | 9.1 | 6,940 |
| 1050A-5 | 9.1 | 8,100 | 8.2 | 6,080 |

Sources: Columns 1 and 3 are derived from Table 5-2 and actual 1964 payroll tax rate of 7.25 percent on wages and salaries, and rate of about 5.5 percent on wages and salaries of self-employed persons. Columns 2 and 4 are derived from Figures 5-2 and 5-3 and underlying data.
a. Each is adjusted to recoup one-half of the revenue loss.

tax in 1969 are presented in Figure 5-4. The parameters of the exemption plans for which estimates could be made were determined by statistical realities rather than by practical policy considerations.[16] Even so, the estimates do provide a useful updating of the analysis which clarifies the effect of low-income relief under the more current tax rate, ceiling, and income levels of 1969.

The curves in Figure 5-4 are derived from the figures underlying those for 1964 (Figure 5-2), which were based on the actual exemptions under the income tax that year. The increase in the parameters of the exemption plans is in proportion to the earnings increases between 1964 and 1969.[17] As a result, Figure 5-4 portrays the reduc-

[16] The exemption plan symbols in Figure 5-4 are to be interpreted in the same manner as those in Table 5-1, with all parameters of the plans (except the phase-out coefficients 1 and 5) increased by a fixed factor (31.4 percent) to enable the exemption levels to maintain a fixed ratio to average earnings. Since this substantially increases the money value of exemptions relative to the current Internal Revenue Service (IRS) levels, only the first five plans were considered.

[17] It was assumed that the relative distribution of earnings remained virtually unchanged in this interval. On this assumption (supported by data for earlier periods in Chapter IV), an increase in the exemption parameters and the ceilings by the same fraction as mean earnings increased would leave the relative loss of revenue under each plan unchanged. The top curve (without exemptions) was derived this way up to the vicinity of the $7,800 ceiling, where it checked almost perfectly with official estimates for 1969. Preliminary and unpublished SSA estimates, dated December 15, 1969, and available for

**FIGURE 5-4. Percentage of Earnings Taxable under Alternative Exemption Plans and Ceilings, 1969**[a]

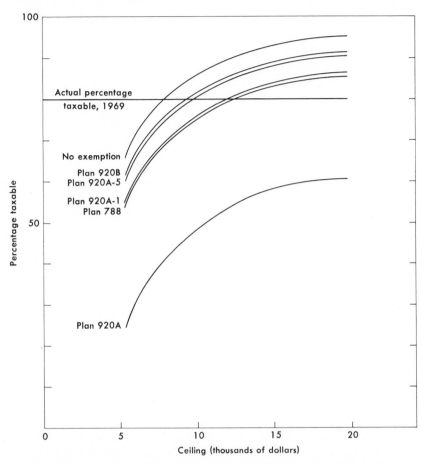

Sources: Same as for Figure 5-2, with parameters of the exemption plans increased in proportion to the earnings increases between 1964 and 1969. See text for details.
[a] The coefficients $600 and $700 from Table 5-1 have been increased by 31.4 percent. See note 16.

tion of the 1969 tax base by exemption plans that reflect increases in money terms but are at the same level relative to mean earnings as in 1964. For the actual 1969 ceiling of $7,800 the revenue effects of the exemption programs are summarized in Table 5-4. As before, the first

incomes of $7,800 and above, were used to sketch the curve for ceilings of $7,800 through $15,600. Percentage costs of exemption plans (Table 5-2) at the various 1964 ceilings (adjusted for earnings increases) were applied to the top curve to derive percentage taxable under the revised exemption plans for 1969.

**TABLE 5-4. Effects of Alternative Exemption Plans on Social Security Tax Receipts, 1969**

| Exemption plan[a] | Percentage of earnings taxable | Percentage revenue loss |
|---|---|---|
| No exemption | 79.9 | — |
| 788 | 68.7 | 14 |
| 920A | 40.8 | 49 |
| 920B | 75.4 | 6 |
| 920A-1 | 69.4 | 13 |
| 920A-5 | 74.2 | 7 |

Source: Derived from Figure 5-4.
[a] The coefficients $600 and $700 from Table 5-1 have been increased by 31.4 percent. See note 16.

plan (with one exemption per return—in this case, $788) can be rejected in favor of the slightly less costly and more effective plan, 920A-1 (similar to plan 700A-1 in Table 5-1), which provides more complete low-income relief. Plan 920B can be rejected in favor of plan 920A-5, which avoids the inequities in the former at a slight extra cost. Exemptions and standard deductions in full for all earners (plan 920A) would have virtually cut revenues in half in 1969. The contrast between the large relative loss of revenue under plan 920A and the outcome under phase-out plans 920A-1 and 920A-5 continues to be substantial, but the relative losses are lower than in 1964 due to the relatively higher ceiling in 1969. The 13 and 7 percent revenue losses under plans 920A-1 and 920A-5, respectively, seem small for low-income relief based on exemptions and deductions higher than those in effect under the income tax.

The estimates in Table 5-4 may be applied to the actual yield of $37.7 billion in 1969.[18] This shows a yield reduction of $18.5 billion under the most liberal plan compared to reductions of only $4.9 billion and $2.7 billion under the two plans that phase out exemptions for high earnings levels. Adjustments of the $7,800 ceiling in effect in 1969 needed to restore revenue forgone due to exemptions and deductions can be read from Figure 5-4. No ceiling adjustment would have been sufficient to counteract the revenue forgone under the most liberal plan, but ceiling increases to $12,400 and $9,600 would have recouped the cost of low-income relief under the slow-phase-out (920A-1) and fast-phase-out (920A-5) plans, respectively. Alterna-

[18] *Survey of Current Business*, Vol. 51 (July 1971), Table 3.8.

**TABLE 5-5.** Approximate Effects of Alternative Exemption Plans on Unemployment Insurance Tax Receipts under Ceiling of $3,000, 1969[a]

| Exemption plan | Percentage of earnings taxable | Percentage revenue loss |
|---|---|---|
| No exemption | 46 | — |
| 788 | 32 | 31 |
| 920A | 10 | 78 |
| 920B | 40 | 14 |
| 920A-1 | 33 | 29 |
| 920A-5 | 38 | 18 |

Source: Derived from rough graphical interpolation in Figure 5-4.
[a] A few states stipulated somewhat higher ceilings.

tively these two plans could have been financed by statutory rate increases of 15 and 8 percent, respectively. The size of these adjustments does not seem utopian, since the ceiling for 1973 has been adjusted to $10,800 and rate increases are also scheduled.

### Revenue Loss on Exemptions under the Unemployment Insurance Tax

Separate estimates of the effects of exemptions and deductions on unemployment insurance taxes were not constructed. However, the impact on this relatively small tax in 1969 can be adequately assessed by rough interpolation of the curves in Figure 5-4 between the zero-tax point at the origin and the points associated with the $4,800 ceiling. The estimated percentage of earnings taxable and percentage revenue loss resulting from the various plans on the assumption of a $3,000 ceiling are summarized in Table 5-5.[19] As earnings increased over the years, with most state UI tax ceilings held at $3,000, the tax has approached a fixed per capita levy, or "head tax," on most earners. The relative tax base under UI has shrunk steadily, and even before any deductions or exemptions, the fraction of total earnings covered by the tax was eroded to about 46 percent by 1969.[20] As a result of this low coverage rate and the low UI tax rate, the exemption plans

---

[19] The interpolation is crude, because no points were available in the zero to $5,260 range of hypothetical ceilings. Also the $3,000 ceiling was not the universal ceiling, and the UI earnings coverage differs even more from the income tax coverage than does the social security variant.

[20] This rough estimate based on social security data checks closely enough with the official UI estimate of 50 percent to give credence to the present exercise.

would have caused only a small revenue loss in absolute terms, whatever the relative loss.

The data suggest that granting full exemptions to every earner under UI would have further collapsed the UI tax base to a level on the order of 10 percent of covered earnings. However, phase-out plans 920A-1 and 920A-5 would have cut the fraction that was taxable more moderately—from about 46 percent to around 33 and 38 percent, respectively.[21] In the case of plans 920A-1 and 920A-5, Figure 5-4 suggests that the 46 percent coverage rate could have been restored by ceiling increases to $4,300 and $3,700, respectively. (The UI ceiling was increased to $4,200 beginning in 1972.) The ceiling is so low at present in relation to earnings that the base is comparatively elastic with respect to ceiling increases, and small adjustments can recoup the entire cost of low-income relief. Since a large majority of earners receive more than the ceiling, the burden of providing such low-income relief would be widely diffused.

The combined cost of installing exemption schemes under the OASDHI and UI taxes is moderate. Plans 920A-1 and 920A-5 would have reduced total payroll tax revenues in 1969 by $5.8 billion and $3.2 billion, respectively. Adjustments of this magnitude could be readily offset by relatively small adjustments of the payroll tax ceiling and rates and/or income tax rates.

## Effects of Taxable Floors and Ceilings on Regressivity

In the first part of this chapter, the impact of various exemption and deduction schemes in the current payroll tax structure was analyzed at the aggregate level. It was taken for granted that installation of exemption schemes would reduce the regressivity of the tax, particularly its burden on low-income groups. In this context the objectives were evaluation of the total cost of alternative reforms and of the rate and ceiling changes required to recoup revenues forgone under the specified-floor plans. It is now appropriate to examine the income distribution data and appraise the reduction of regressivity achievable by these modifications.

The concepts of progressivity and regressivity are themselves ambiguous. The payroll tax has been characterized here and elsewhere

[21] The 1969 UI tax yield of $3.2 billion would have been cut about $0.9 billion and $0.6 billion, respectively, under the two exemption plans.

as regressive in the sense that one or more overall measures of inequality (of one or more income variants) are increased by imposition of the tax. The Lorenz curves in Figure 4-6 (based on the earnings variant only) showed regressivity in this global sense. The upward slope over some ranges of the curve relating the effective tax rate to individual earnings was also interpreted as regressivity. Given the data available, the slope of the tax rate curve is the most convenient focus in the present context. However, effective tax rates are related here to "total ordinary income"[22] rather than to earnings alone, because it seems appropriate to assess the burden of a tax on a family in relation to its total factor income stream (as approximated by "ordinary income") rather than to the earnings component only.[23] Certainly total factor income is a better indicator of "ability to pay" than earnings alone.

## *Tax Rate Functions under a Given Ceiling*

The 1964 tax return sample was used to estimate the percentage of ordinary income subject to the OASDI tax in each ordinary income class. The computations were carried out for each of the 100,000 tax returns and then aggregated within income brackets. Since the statutory OASDI payroll tax rate is uniform, the relationship of the percentage taxable to ordinary income indicates the progressivity or regressivity of the tax. Estimates under the actual 1964 ceiling of $4,800 are presented in Figure 5-5.[24] In order to cover high incomes and at the same time provide detail on very low incomes, ordinary income is measured on a logarithmic scale. The overall result of each exemption

[22] The variant "total ordinary income" is defined for convenience as adjusted gross income (IRS conception) less capital gains. Omission of capital gains does not imply their irrelevance to the analysis of income distribution; because of their volatility, special treatment would be required for analysis of their role.

[23] Reasons for this focus on factor income and exclusion of transfers from the income base are given in the first section of Chapter IV.

[24] It was not possible to adjust these estimates for consistency with SSA data on taxable earnings. The present estimates relate taxable earnings to ordinary income, a variant which is not available in SSA distributions. Furthermore, the SSA provides no income distribution data based on the family as a recipient unit comparable to the "tax return family"; these factors made it impossible to adjust the IRS estimates to an SSA basis *by income class*. The best that can be done is to draw attention again to the discrepancies at the aggregate level in 1964. As indicated in Figure 5-1, taxable earnings estimated from the IRS sample fell about 7 percent short of the SSA aggregate under the $4,800 ceiling, and the distribution of the discrepancy by ordinary income bracket is unknown. (For the $7,800 ceiling considered later, the IRS estimate based on the tax file is 5 percent too high.)

**FIGURE 5-5.** Percentage of Ordinary Income Taxable for Social Security, by Income Class, Alternative Exemption Plans and Higher Exemption Plans, with Taxable Ceiling of $4,800, 1964[a]

A. ALTERNATIVE EXEMPTION PLANS

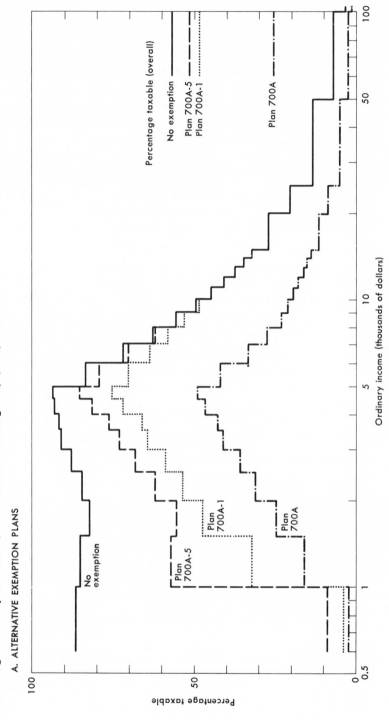

B. HIGHER EXEMPTION PLANS

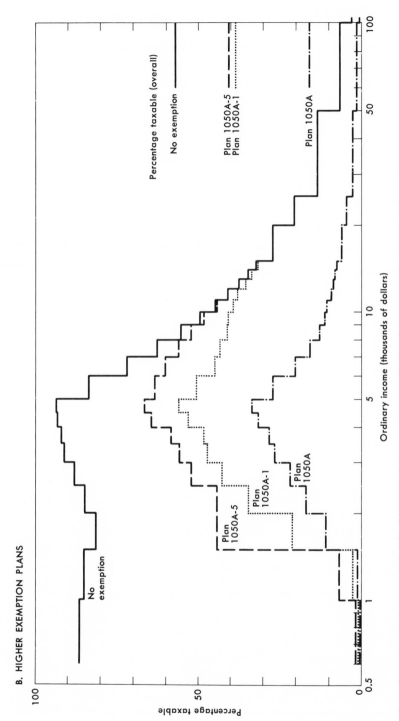

Source: Derived from the Brookings Institution's file of 100,000 individual income tax returns for 1964. See Appendix D for description of the sample.
ª See Table 5-1 for formulas for the exemption plans.

plan is shown at the right of the figure for comparison with the impact on individual income classes. Despite the deficiencies of payroll tax estimates based on tax return earnings, certain generalizations can be based with some confidence on these charts.

The top step function in each section of the figure indicates the percentage taxable in each ordinary income class in the absence of floors exempting the lower portions of taxable earnings. After an indication of slight regressivity among very low incomes, the figure confirms a range of slight progressivity of the tax among incomes up to the class containing the ceiling; this progressivity is less than indicated earlier by the U.S. Bureau of Labor Statistics (BLS) survey summarized in Table 4-6.[25] The ratio of taxable earnings to ordinary income rises from 83 to 94 percent between classes $1,500–$2,000 and $4,500–$5,000.[26] After the latter income class, where the ceiling is located, a pronounced and continuous pattern of regression is demonstrated. This is due to (1) the ceiling, which decreases the effective rate as the earnings increase, and (2) the decline of earnings relative to ordinary income above the $7,000–$8,000 class.[27]

Introduction of floors through exemptions and deductions sharply reduces the tax burden on low-income families. Over virtually the entire income range through the ceiling class, the percentage taxable, and therefore the tax rate, becomes more progressive, with the degree of change depending on the liberality of the plan. Even the least liberal plan (700A-5) shows a negligible tax rate for incomes in the $600–$1,000 class.[28] The rapid phasing out of exemptions under this plan produces a tax rate on the next income class ($1,000–$1,500) about seven times as great—only about a third less than the actual results without exemptions. It is apparent that one-exemption persons predominate in this class; under plan 700A-5 the exemption for a single person is reduced from the basic amount of $900 under plan 700A to $400 for earnings of $1,000 and eliminated completely at the earnings

[25] This progressivity is less pronounced in the IRS income variant because most transfer payments are excluded. The BLS figures show that the ratio of transfers to income excluding transfers decreases with income in low-income ranges.

[26] Since the computation assumed that all earnings below $4,800 were taxable except those of the self-employed earning under $400, this reflects primarily a decreasing relative importance of property income over that range.

[27] Data on the second relationship are presented later as evidence of the futility of any attempt to eliminate the regressivity of the payroll tax by raising the ceiling.

[28] With only about 8 percent of ordinary income taxable, the effective tax rate would have been about 0.5 percent for that group in 1964. This effective rate would have been even lower if nontaxable transfers were included in the income base.

level of $1,080. The predominance of single persons results in very little overall relief for earners in the $1,000–$1,500 class. Substitution of the slower phase-out plan (700A-1) nearly doubles the tax relief in this income class; alternatively, section B of Figure 5-5 shows that, even with fast phasing out, a 50 percent increase in the exemption parameters by means of plan 1050A-5 would have almost completely relieved this group of its payroll tax burden. However, the rapid phasing out would have struck hard at the next class ($1,500–$2,000), resulting in relief of less than one-half of its actual tax payments in 1964.

Except for the bulge in each of the step-functions depicting the rapid-phase-out plans, both parts of the figure show a smooth progressivity introduced by all floor schemes through the ceiling class of $4,500–$5,000. For higher incomes the regressive impact of the ceiling dominates the slight progressive effect of the exemption schemes at this level, resulting in a regressive tax curve from this ceiling class on up. However, plans 700A-5 and 700A-1 moderate the regressivity significantly through classes $7,000–$8,000 and $10,000–$11,000, respectively; at these levels, their curves merge with the no-exemption curve and the effect of the exemptions becomes negligible. The higher exemption schemes displayed in section B of Figure 5-5 flatten the tax rate curve considerably more and over a longer range, with plan 1050A-1 moderating the regressivity significantly up to about the $20,000 level.

Both sections of Figure 5-5 show that the plans granting exemptions at all income levels provide significant tax relief throughout the income range. However, this is accomplished only at the expense of a very much larger revenue loss than is entailed by the more modest schemes. Plan 700A-1 and its higher exemption version 1050A-1 offer a feasible compromise avoiding (1) the high cost of giving exemptions to all, and (2) the failure of the rapid-phase-out plan to adequately relieve many small families with low incomes. But the ability of the preferred exemption plans to improve the rate structure for low incomes does not extend significantly to incomes above the ceiling. The regressivity in that range calls for other remedies.

*Effects of Ceiling Increases*

The relative impotence of exemption schemes against regressivity above the ceiling invites an investigation of the effect of ceiling increases. Figure 5-6 shows the effects of the previously discussed plans

**FIGURE 5-6. Percentage of Ordinary Income Taxable for Social Security, by Income Class, Alternative Exemption Plans and Higher Exemption Plans, with Taxable Ceiling of $7,800, 1964**[a]

A. ALTERNATIVE EXEMPTION PLANS

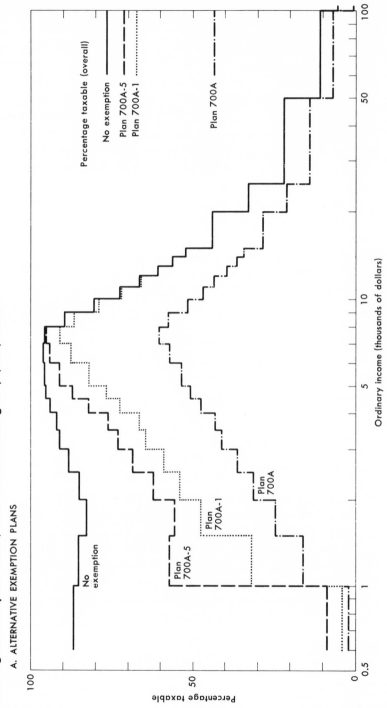

B. HIGHER EXEMPTION PLANS

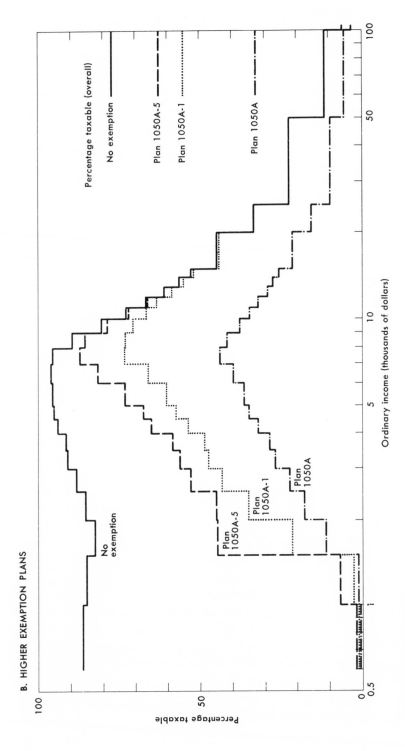

Percentage taxable (overall)

No exemption ———————

Plan 1050A-5 — — — —

Plan 1050A-1 ·················

Plan 1050A —·—·—·—

No
exemption

Plan
1050A-5

Plan
1050A-1

Plan
1050A

Percentage taxable

100

50

0
0.5        1        5        10        50        100

Ordinary income (thousands of dollars)

Source: Same as Figure 5-5.
ᵃ See Table 5-1 for formulas for the exemption plans.

for low-income relief in 1964 under a ceiling 62.5 percent higher—
$7,800 (the actual ceiling in 1968–71). The range of progressivity intro-
duced by the specified floors is extended through the $7,000–$8,000
class containing the new ceiling, and the relative revenue loss under
each floor is reduced. The slow-phase-out plans continue to yield
smooth, progressive rate curves through the ceiling class, and the
higher ceiling recoups most of the revenue that would be lost by a
50 percent increase in the exemption parameters.[29] However, the
regressivity of the payroll tax curve above the ceiling persists as
strongly as before.

The political feasibility of sharply higher ceilings is difficult to
evaluate. The $3,000 ceiling in 1938 was 3.28 times the mean earnings,
equivalent to a ceiling of about $13,700 in 1964 and $17,700 in 1969.
However, since World War II the ceiling has exceeded the mean
earnings by a maximum of 52 percent (in 1968). Even so, it seems in
order to examine the ability of a very large increase in the ceiling to
eliminate the regressive feature of the payroll tax. Figure 5-7 carries
this test to its logical extreme by showing the results of a complete
removal of the ceiling in 1964.

Without a ceiling, the progressivity introduced by the floor is extended to substantially higher earnings levels. The more liberal the
exemption scheme, the greater the range of progressivity. Under the
actual IRS exemption levels of 1964 and fast phasing out, the rate
curve rises through the $8,000–$9,000 class; under the most liberal
plan with higher exemptions and no phasing out (section B of Figure
5-7), the range of progressivity extends through the $25,000–$50,000
class. However, in all cases the rate curve eventually turns regressive.
The reason for the ultimate downturn in each rate function is apparent
in the case without exemptions (the top function in each chart). Even
without a ceiling, the function representing the fraction taxable
reaches a peak at about 97 percent in the $7,000–$8,000 ordinary income class. The percentage taxable (ratio of estimated covered wages
and salaries to ordinary income) then declines steadily with income,
reaching 82 percent in the $25,000–$30,000 class, 59 percent in the
$100,000–$150,000 class, and 6 percent in the over $1 million class.
It is clear then that, even if the ceiling were abolished, no practical
exemption scheme could eliminate the regressivity of the payroll tax.

[29] Plan 1050A-1 yields 55 percent taxable under the higher ceiling, as against 49
percent under exemption plan 700A-1 and the $4,800 ceiling.

These illustrations have shown that a modest overhaul of the payroll tax itself can alleviate the burden on the poor and achieve progressivity over a substantial range of lower and middle incomes. However, the negative relationship between the fraction taxable and income in the upper income ranges dooms to futility any attempt to eliminate regressivity as long as a uniform statutory rate is applied to earnings alone. A more substantial reform, which would entail substitution of a more equitable tax for the revenues lost through exemptions and for part or all of the remaining payroll tax revenue, will therefore be considered.[30]

## General Revenue Financing

Because undesirable properties of the payroll tax would remain after the reforms just suggested, it seems in order to turn to general revenue financing as an alternative. This would inevitably involve substantial substitution of the income tax for the payroll tax, since the former is the major source of federal revenues. Despite social security supporters' long-standing effort to liken these programs to private insurance arrangements, they have favored some degree of general revenue financing. There was an apparent consensus among the founders of social security (first called OASI) in the 1930s that the financial burden be shared by business, labor, and government. Despite this objective, the analysis in Chapters II and III suggests that, in practice, earners bore the entire burden for many years. However, general revenue financing for social security was finally accepted on a small scale in 1966 as the source of funds for Medicare,[31] and to provide special benefits for persons aged seventy-two and over. Finally, social security specialists have revealed a special tolerance for general revenue financing of "past service credits." This refers to the rationale for benefits paid to late arrivals within the system, such as the self-employed ("unearned" in terms of the "insurance principle"). Since these payments are conceded to be clearly in violation of the insurance principle, it is suggested that they might be more appropriately

---

[30] A progressive rate structure could, of course, be built into the payroll tax itself, but such an elaboration seems more cumbersome than reliance on the individual income tax.

[31] Since July 1, 1971, the Medicare program has been financed by a charge of $5.60 a month to voluntary participants, matched by an equal payment from government funds. This public financing of a portion of a social security program is unprecedented.

FIGURE 5-7. Percentage of Ordinary Income Taxable for Social Security, by Income Class, Alternative Exemption Plans and Higher Exemption Plans, with No Taxable Ceiling, 1964[a]

A. ALTERNATIVE EXEMPTION PLANS

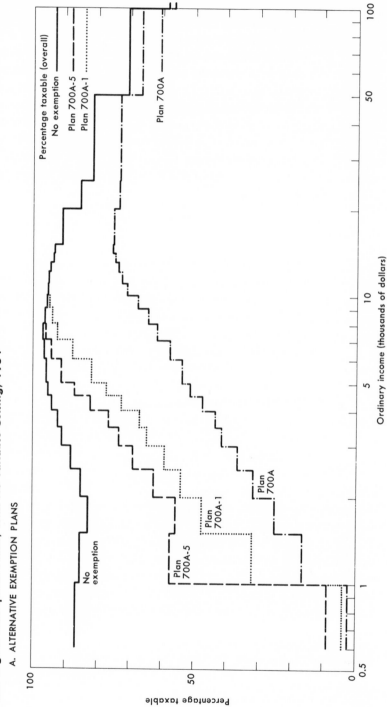

# B. HIGHER EXEMPTION PLANS

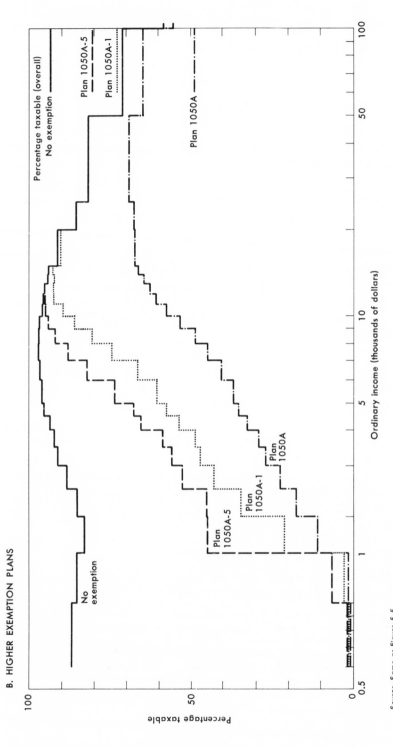

Source: Same as Figure 5-5.

a See Table 5-1 for formulas for the exemption plans.

financed from general revenues.[32] In short, there are ample precedents for considering the effects of replacing the payroll tax in whole or in part by the more equitable income tax.[33]

## Small-Scale Substitution of the Income Tax

In Figure 5-4 and Tables 5-4 and 5-5 the estimated losses of payroll tax yield under various exemption and deduction plans are presented for 1969. Internal revisions of the payroll tax through increases in the rate and/or ceiling sufficient to offset these costs were considered. However, if the income tax is assumed to be preferred on grounds of equity, it seems appropriate instead to finance payroll tax relief to low-income taxpayers by means of general revenue funds. Besides relieving the low-income groups, this approach has a more progressive effect because of the substitution of a progressive tax rather than internal revision of the payroll tax. In addition to financing a significant reform, this would constitute a logical first step toward ending reliance on the regressive OASDHI and UI taxes altogether. Table 5-6 indicates the modest adjustment of income tax rates needed to finance most of these reforms.

Although the liberal plan granting payroll tax exemptions at all income levels would require a large increase in income taxes, exemption plan 920A-1, with a gradual phasing out, would call for an increase in income tax rates of only about 6 percent. Thus a small adjustment is needed to end the worst feature of the payroll tax—its harsh treatment of low-income families—and to open up the possibility of an ultimate end to the tax. Disposing of the payroll tax altogether would require much more substantial changes, but sparing low incomes (with offsetting income tax increases) might initiate the process.

## Impact of Larger Changes on Income Distribution

Before examining the effect on inequality of ending payroll taxation, the overall impact should be summarized briefly for 1969 on the

[32] Acceptance of the element of truth in this argument does not imply agreement that other aspects of the system are akin to private pension programs. The difference between late arrivals and others, for example, is merely one of degree. As shown in Chapter VI, variations among participants in the rate of return on their contributions are great.

[33] Although only the explicit substitution of the income tax for the payroll tax is considered here, general revenue financing may take various forms, including integration of the payroll tax with the income tax. See Pechman and others, *Social Security*, pp. 188–201.

**TABLE 5-6. Income Tax Rate Increases Required to Offset Revenue Losses under Alternative Exemption Plans, with Taxable Ceiling of $7,800, 1969**

| | Percentage revenue loss | | Increase in income tax | |
|---|---|---|---|---|
| | | | Billions | |
| Exemption plan[a] | OASDHI | UI | of dollars | Percent |
| No exemption | — | — | — | — |
| 788 | 14 | 31 | 6.3 | 6.9 |
| 920A | 49 | 78 | 21.0 | 23.0 |
| 920B | 6 | 14 | 2.7 | 3.0 |
| 920A-1 | 13 | 29 | 5.8 | 6.4 |
| 920A-5 | 7 | 18 | 3.2 | 3.5 |

Sources: Revenue loss is derived from Tables 5-4 and 5-5. Tax is based on aggregated 1969 yields of $37.4 billion under OASDHI, $3.2 billion under UI, and $91 billion under the individual income tax. See *Survey of Current Business*, Vol. 51 (July 1971), Tables 3.8 and 3.1, respectively.

[a] The coefficients $600 and $700 in Table 5-1 have been increased in proportion to mean earnings (see Table 5-4).

basis of aggregate OASDHI and UI taxes adding to $41.0 billion (excluding Medicare) and the income tax yield of $91 billion. A complete substitution of income tax for payroll tax would have required a boost in income tax yield of about 45 percent. This offsetting adjustment is probably fairly typical of what would be needed in the near future, even though the income tax yield was unusually high in 1969 because of the 10 percent surcharge. The indicated income tax increase is of about the right order, because the payroll tax yield may also be viewed as unusually high. While some accumulation in the trust funds is typical, the 23 percent excess of taxes over benefits in 1969 was unusual and is not likely to be repeated.[34]

Elimination of the OASDHI and UI payroll taxes by a 45 percent across-the-board increase in income tax rates would not be feasible, since the present top statutory marginal rate of 70 percent would be changed to a rate of over 100 percent. A more feasible approach would be a 45 percent increase in yield through the *combination* of a rate increase and a broadening of the income tax base. Alternatively, the rate structure could be changed in such a way as to increase the yield

[34] Since the social security system appears to have been closer than this to a pay-as-you-go basis in recent years, such a large surplus must be regarded as abnormal. The 23 percent surplus refers to Office of Business Economics (OBE) estimates of taxes and benefits, including Medicare; the data did not permit separation of medical and hospital benefits.

by 45 percent.[35] The estimate of tax rates by ordinary income class for both types of taxes may be derived from the sample of 100,000 tax returns for 1964.[36] The objective is to use the 1964 sample to simulate the effect of changes comparable to the substitution of income taxes for payroll taxes in recent years.

Unlike previous exercises, analysis of the trade-off between the two taxes requires specification of tax *rates* in addition to the ceiling, so that the magnitude of payroll tax yield relative to income tax yield would be typical of the current experience. The combined employer-employee tax rate of 7.25 percent (5.4 percent for the self-employed) applicable in 1964 was replaced by the 1969–70 rate structure of 9.6 percent (6.9 percent for the self-employed). However, the 1964 ceiling of $4,800 was retained for the simulation on two grounds. First, its ratio to mean earnings at that time was fairly typical of the postwar experience, though slightly lower than average. Second, under these rates and ceiling the simulated social security payroll tax yield of $20.8 billion stood in about the same relation to the simulated income tax yield of $47.2 billion as it had in recent years. The ratio of the payroll tax to the income tax (44 percent) was a conservative basis for the analysis in a sense, because under that assumption payroll tax elimination would have required a slightly larger relative adjustment than in 1969, when the ratio was 41 percent.[37] Despite the inconsistencies between 1964 and 1969 data bases and rate structures, the substitution of the income tax for a payroll tax somewhat less than one-half its size in 1964 should illustrate realistically the current impact of similar trade-offs.[38]

[35] The rate curve for the small UI tax is not included here, because the relation of that tax rate to ordinary income classes could be estimated only with a lower order of accuracy than that for OASDHI. Even though the UI tax is less than 10 percent of the OASDHI tax, the exclusion of UI here should be borne in mind, since it is even more regressive in relative terms than the larger tax.

[36] Although the income tax distribution from this sample checks very well against complete *Statistics of Income* data for that year (U.S. Internal Revenue Service, *Statistics of Income—1964, Individual Income Tax Returns* [1967]), it should be reiterated that the estimated social security tax distribution is less reliable. Estimates of aggregate taxable earnings from the tax return earnings variant fall 6 percent short of SSA figures for a $4,800 ceiling (Figure 5-1), and the distribution of the error is unknown.

[37] The tax for OASDHI alone was 41 percent of federal individual income taxes in 1969 when both types of taxes were unusually high. See *Survey of Current Business*, Vol. 51 (July 1971), Tables 3.1 and 3.8.

[38] As a ratio to ordinary income, the overall effective OASDHI tax rate emerging from the simulation was about 6 percent; this is somewhat lower than the 1969 rate,

Curves relating effective tax rates to ordinary income were derived from the various simulations with 1964 returns. These curves are shown in Figure 5-8. The estimated OASDI tax rate on ordinary income is approximately proportional to the percentage-taxable function at the top of section A in Figure 5-5.[39] The rate moves in the 7.75–8.75 percent range up to about $5,000; it falls slightly at first, becomes progressive through the class containing the $4,800 ceiling, where it reaches its peak, and is then regressive throughout the higher-income range. The effective rate of income tax begins near zero in the $600–$1,000 class and rises steadily to a 35 percent average in the $50,000–$100,000 class.[40] The combined OASDHI and income tax function increases with income, reaching a preliminary peak of 17 percent in the ceiling class. The progressivity of the income tax dominates until then, but at this point regressivity due to the payroll tax ceiling turns the combined tax regressive past the $7,000–$8,000 bracket. Not until the $14,000–$15,000 class is reached does the combined tax rate exceed the previous peak attained at $4,500–$5,000. This power of the regressive payroll tax to swamp the progressive income tax over a substantial range confirms the findings in Chapter IV.[41]

The tax structure combining the rate of payroll and income taxation by income bracket is subject to criticism on two main counts of inequity.[42] First, as shown in Figure 5-8, the combined rate of taxation on incomes below the payroll tax ceiling appears unjustifiably high, especially in the case of incomes in the officially defined poverty

which produced an unusually large surplus. While of the right order for 1968–70, the 6 percent simulation figure could be left behind by future upward trends in the payroll tax rate.

[39] There is a small departure from straight proportionality caused by a slight variation in tax rates by class; this results from the different tax rates for the varying mixtures of wages and salaries and self-employed income.

[40] On the basis of the arbitrarily defined income brackets, the rate curve is progressive until it reaches a peak of 55.6 percent in the $500,000 to $1 million bracket outside the range of the chart and then falls to 45 percent in the over $1 million class. Although capital gains are excluded, those in the top income group apparently mustered sufficient deductions to turn the income tax regressive at the end.

[41] Figure 4-3 shows similar patterns, although it is based on the earnings variant only and includes UI as well as OASDHI taxes.

[42] This stress on the inequitable joint effect of payroll and income taxes does not imply that other taxes considered in conjunction with the income tax would necessarily produce a more equitable outcome. These two taxes alone are considered here because one is the subject of this study and the other is its logical substitute.

**FIGURE 5-8. Effective Payroll and Income Tax Rates and Combinations of the Two, by Income Class, Using Income Data, Ceiling, and Income Tax Structure of 1964 and Payroll Tax Rates of 1969**

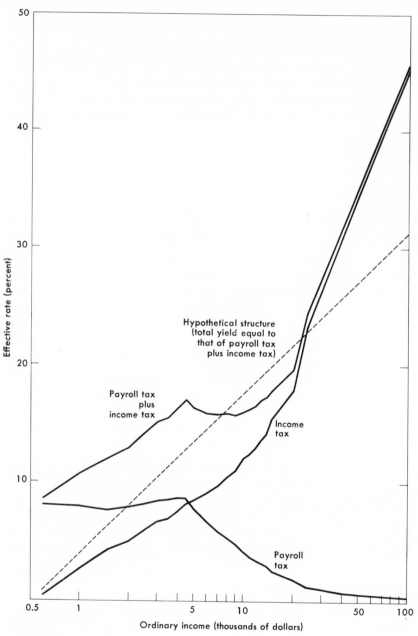

Source: Same as Figure 5-5.

range. Second, the dip in the combined rate curve for incomes above the ceiling is clearly unjustifiable; as shown in Chapter IV, regressivity in the rate curves is evident in this range above the ceiling, even for families of a given size. These inequities invite substitution of the progressive income tax for the payroll tax. It would not be feasible to do this by increasing all income tax rates by 45 percent because this would raise the top marginal rate above 100 percent. A feasible combination of rate increases and base-broadening could raise the yield by 45 percent. However, there is no need to be confined to the shape of the 1964 tax curve.

Probably a more satisfactory solution could be achieved by full substitution of an income tax in a modified form. The rate function needed for full replacement could be somewhat steeper in lower- and middle-income ranges and less steep in higher ranges. This would reduce progressivity slightly in the upper ranges, but it is obvious that a slight remodeling of the income tax curve along these lines could achieve the needed revenue with a rate curve consistently progressive and far more progressive overall than the combined rate curve in Figure 5-8.

A progressive linear rate function (with respect to the logarithm of earnings) was specified as an illustrative income tax. Such a straight-line rate function has considerable intuitive appeal in contrast with the actual combined rate curve that (1) bears heavily on low incomes, (2) displays inequity by sagging in the middle-income brackets, and (3) rises at an accelerating and nonsustainable rate in the higher brackets.

If the tax rate is denoted by $r$, earnings by $E$, and total tax by $T$:

$$r = a + b \log_{10} E \qquad (b > 0).$$

Multiplying both sides by $E$ and differentiating with respect to $E$ yields the marginal rate function:

$$dT/dE = r + b \log_{10} e = r + 0.43b.$$

Since $b$ is greater than zero, the average rate function $r$ is linear and upward sloping; the marginal rate function is also linear above the average rate and parallel to it.

The linear rate function represented by the dotted line in Figure 5-8 was derived to show that the total revenue attained from the income and payroll taxes could be raised through an alternative and more acceptable income tax structure alone. In deriving this line, the first portion of the curve representing full replacement of the payroll tax by a 45 percent income tax increase was taken as a benchmark. The rate line was determined by the point in the $1,000–$1,500 class (a tax rate of 3.9 percent) and by the slope, which produces the same total yield as the payroll and income tax together.[43] This alternative device for eliminating the payroll tax has several desirable properties. First, the combined payroll and income tax on very low incomes is largely eliminated, although families in poverty could only be completely spared by an additional device, such as the minimum standard deduction.[44] Second, the regressivity of the original combined curve (which sets in after the ceiling) is eliminated in favor of a continuously progressive tax. Third (not shown in Figure 5-8), the average effective rate in the top class (over $1 million) is about 56 percent, as against 47 percent in the class below. This eliminates the regressivity at the top under the original structure. Finally, the marginal rates derived from the substitute curve are feasible. The slope $b$ in the rate function is 15.9 percentage points, and the last equation therefore indicates that the marginal rate function is 6.8 percentage points above the average rate line. The marginal rate derived for specified incomes is:

| Ordinary income (dollars) | Marginal tax rate (percent) |
|---|---|
| 1,000 | 9 |
| 10,000 | 25 |
| 100,000 | 40 |
| 1,000,000 | 59 |
| 10,000,000 | 73 |

This illustrative income tax function replaces the regressive payroll tax with an equitable income tax structure. A comparison with the original combined tax rate curve in Figure 5-8 shows that, roughly speaking, recipients of incomes under about $7,000 would receive net tax relief. One estimate of the median family money income in 1964

[43] By coincidence the line determined by these conditions also (virtually) passes through the point representing the tax rate in the next higher class. The equation of this broken line in Figure 5-8 is $r = 2.42 + 15.9 \log E$, with $r$ measured in percentage points and $E$ measured in thousands of dollars.

[44] The average rate in the $600–$1,000 class is 0.9 percent, compared with about 8 percent under the original curve; the rate in the lowest class is effectively zero, since the rate function is slightly negative at the mean of the class.

was $6,569.[45] Thus it is clear that the new tax structure would be favored by a majority of taxpayers. Elimination of the regressivity above the ceiling leads to higher effective tax rates in roughly the $7,000–$40,000 range, with a maximum increase of about 4 percentage points in the $15,000–$20,000 class.[46] Rates on higher incomes would be reduced under this tax structure, except for the highest class, which would pay 23 percent more. The relief for high incomes below the top class seems somewhat more than is justified by the pragmatic rejection of marginal rates near 100 percent.[47] In any case the illustration shows that an income tax increase over almost all ranges can be accomplished with a reduction of total taxes for the majority and a much more equitable rate structure. It also suggests that this gain in equity must be paid for by increases in the effective rates of upper-middle-income groups by as much as 4 percentage points.

This linear rate structure (with respect to the logarithm of earnings) is only one of endless alternatives, and the statutory rate structure needed to approximate it has not been worked out. However, this illustration seems ample to show that a feasible as well as equitable income tax structure can be designed to take over completely from the payroll tax.[48]

## Conclusions on Reform and Substitution Proposals

The foregoing illustrations showed first that, for a small cost, the payroll tax on families in poverty can be ended and a progressive rate structure achieved up to the taxable ceiling. An exemption plan that gradually phases out as earnings increase could probably have largely achieved this in 1969 with a revenue loss of about $5.8 billion; this could have been recouped by a 6 percent income tax increase. However, two inequitable features would remain. The tax would continue to be regressive above the ceiling. Even if the ceiling were removed

[45] U.S. Bureau of the Census, *Current Population Reports*, Series P-60, No. 51. "Income in 1965 of Families and Persons in the United States" (1967).

[46] The total tax bill would rise a maximum of about 23 percent for some taxpayers in this class.

[47] The increased burden on middle and upper middle incomes could be reduced slightly by increasing the rather modest rates on high income.

[48] This assertion of feasibility does not imply that the taxpaying public would automatically accept this substitution with benefits held constant. Such a substantial switch to a higher income tax yield might cause the majority to favor other uses for part of the funds.

completely, the tax would still be regressive because of its exclusive application to earned income, which declines relatively as total income increases.

A second inequity would also remain—one not previously stressed. If treatment of the married couple as a taxable unit (as under the income tax) is appropriate, the separate ceilings applicable to multiple earners constitute an inequity. Two earners in a family may pay as much as twice the tax charged to a one-earner family with the same total income. Removal of the inequity could be achieved by application of a single ceiling to pooled family income.[49] Table 5-2 implies that the cost of this under the $4,800 ceiling in 1964 would have been an approximate 17 percent revenue loss.

Exemption plans, ceiling increases, and alternate treatment of multiple earner families are fairly inexpensive improvements. They may be appropriate as interim reforms. However, they do not even come close to clearing the payroll tax of its inequities. Replacement of the payroll tax by the most equitable tax available seems more appropriate. It was shown in the preceding section that a more equitable individual income tax structure of modified shape may feasibly be substituted for the present combined income and payroll tax. This constitutes an appropriate long-term objective.

---

[49] This conception of equity depends on the assumption of a family unit. From another point of view it may be regarded as inequitable for two single persons to pay as much as twice the tax a married couple with the same income pays.

# CHAPTER VI

# Lifetime Rates of Return and Income Redistribution

THIS STUDY was organized with the resolve that it would deal with the effects of the payroll tax as independently as possible of any benefits currently financed by this tax, and this policy has been followed in the discussion of current redistributive effects of the taxes on disposable income. Since social security tax and benefit structures are potentially exogenous and without essential link, this approach seems reasonable; it is meaningful to focus on the earning population that pays taxes, and disregard the retired population that receives benefits.[1] Over a lifetime, however, each person both pays and expects to receive; from this viewpoint the effects of plausible tax-benefit relationships on the distribution of lifetime incomes are worth consideration.

Note. This chapter is adapted from the author's paper, "The Real Rate of Interest on Lifetime Contributions toward Retirement under Social Security," in *Old Age Income Assurance*, Pt. 3: *Public Programs*, A Compendium of Papers on Problems and Policy Issues in the Public and Private Pension System, submitted to the Subcommittee on Fiscal Policy of the Joint Economic Committee, 90 Cong. 1 sess. (1967), pp. 109–32 (Brookings Reprint 143).

[1] This dichotomy represents a slight oversimplification, since, for example, the relatively small unemployment insurance (UI) program entails current transfers within the generally active population.

The great rise in the federal social security tax since 1949 has stirred a debate over how well workers "fare" under the system. Opinions are remarkably varied. For example, Paul Samuelson pictures a growing nation as "the greatest Ponzi game ever contrived," with its growth making possible ever-expanding social security benefits:

The beauty about social insurance is that it is *actuarially* unsound. Everyone who reaches retirement age is given benefit privileges that far exceed anything he has paid in. And exceed his payments by more than ten times as much (or five times, counting in employer payments)![2]

On the other hand, Milton Friedman speaks of a "raw deal" for young workers:

Retired persons currently enjoy a bonanza. *But* youngsters currently entering the system are getting a raw deal. . . . To finance the excess payments to the growing number of retired, taxes assessed on wages have had to be raised repeatedly. As a result, the benefits promised younger workers are much smaller than the equivalent of the taxes paid on their wages.[3]

Such disparate opinions invite a review of the arguments and a systematic evaluation of the evidence. However, the stress in this chapter is on the real rate of interest or the return on contributions under a model approximating the system, rather than on the lifetime benefit–tax ratios referred to by Samuelson and Friedman; the primary reliance here is on a growth model of tax and benefit streams. Projections by means of this abstract model suggest that even under a variety of assumptions the prospective return to most new participants under social security is far less attractive than Samuelson has indicated but better than the "raw deal" suggested by Friedman. In particular, it is argued that most participants will fare much better than investors in fixed-dollar claims have in recent decades but much less well than long-run investors in equity capital.[4]

An important qualification of these findings should be stated at this point. The analysis assumed pay-as-you-go financing of benefits, which was a good approximation of the history of the system until

[2] Paul A. Samuelson, "On Social Security," *Newsweek* (Jan. 13, 1967), p. 88.

[3] Milton Friedman, "On Social Security," *Newsweek* (April 3, 1967), p. 81.

[4] This comparison carries no implication that an option to invest in equity capital could or should be built into the present social security system. The objective here is merely to provide a yardstick against which the yield on this form of saving may be appraised, although this may well be relevant to the decision as to the appropriate ceiling on taxable earnings, maximum tax rate, and ultimate size of the system.

recent years, when surpluses have piled up. If the latter pattern should continue indefinitely, revision would be required, and the expected rates of return would be considerably lower.[5]

## Earlier Work on Lifetime Tax–Benefit Ratios

Of course, estimation of lifetime rates of return or tax–benefit ratios for individuals is a somewhat artificial exercise. Why should one ask whether a person ultimately recoups in benefits the equivalent of his taxes when the same question is rarely asked about other taxes? The essence of the retirement component of the social security system is that it is a current transfer program under which the working generation pays taxes to finance benefits to those who have retired. Since the taxes and later benefits assigned to a person are not at all closely related, as they are under private insurance, a strong case can be made for completely separate analysis and evaluation of the tax and benefit structures on their own merits. Certainly the tenuous relationship between individual taxes and benefits does not exempt the payroll tax from the criticism that it is regressive and a heavy burden on low-income groups.

Despite these methodological considerations, the attractiveness of social security to individuals has been debated on many occasions. Part of the temptation to debate this issue is due to the explicit earmarking of the tax for provision of benefits. Furthermore, participants in the system have been encouraged to believe that they are "paying for" their benefits individually, and many appear to think that they will get what they pay for, as under private insurance. On the other hand, some younger workers with a long period of taxpaying ahead of them and an even longer wait for benefits have been grumbling about rising social security taxes.[6] Others are asking congressmen whether

[5] Another qualification deserves mention. The present approach asks what yield a participant can expect on his contributions to the system; no comparison is made with his probable situation without the tax. Since members of the younger generation must pay taxes under the system, it follows that they do not need to contribute as much privately to the older generation. For a discussion of this point, see Carl S. Shoup, *Public Finance* (Aldine, 1969), pp. 164–67.

[6] " 'We aren't reaching our young people,' concedes one [AFL-CIO] politico. . . . 'For example, current . . . polls find younger union members resentful of the federation's support for increased Social Security benefits; the money is to come from taxes, and a lot of our guys don't like this money being taken from their pockets' " (John A. Grimes, "Labor's Image," *Wall Street Journal* [March 1, 1967], p. 16).

they are getting their money's worth under social security. In view of this increasing interest and concern, it seems in order to examine the issue within this framework. However, the objective of such analysis is to throw some light on the dynamic features of the overall system and its redistributive impact on lifetime incomes; it carries no implication that social security should be evaluated as a conventional insurance program.

Before turning to the proposed model and the evidence, a review of earlier thinking may be useful. The contradiction between the evaluations of Samuelson and Friedman cited above is due in part to differing assumptions. Samuelson counted on growth of real earnings of some 3 percent a year to enable the earning population to pay benefits to the retired population always much greater than the value of their accumulated taxes. However, he did not spell out the other conditions necessary to make this happen. Specifically, it is not clear whether he imputed interest to the accumulated taxes or whether he discounted the prospective benefit stream.

Friedman was referring to the type of analysis presented by Colin Campbell and others and based on current legislation.[7] Campbell took the scheduled tax and benefit structure as given and demonstrated that the value of taxes paid in the name of young workers, plus imputed interest at 4 percent, would be much greater upon retirement than the value at that time of scheduled benefits. However, his analysis did not allow for income growth and the likely corresponding increase in both taxes and benefits. This failure to allow for growth biases the estimate in favor of the "raw deal" argument, since the benefits expected by a worker grow for a longer period than the taxes he pays.

Perhaps baffled by the diversity of opinion on how individuals are faring under the system, one congressman asked social security officials how he should answer his constituents on this issue:

I would like an answer to the basic question that concerns the young person coming under the social security system as to whether this is a sound finan-

---

[7] Colin D. and Rosemary G. Campbell, "You'll Never Get Back All Those Old-Age 'Contributions,'" *Washington Post* (Nov. 7, 1965), sec. E, p. 3, and James M. Buchanan and Colin D. Campbell, "Voluntary Social Security," *Wall Street Journal*, Dec. 20, 1966. For similar calculations, see Ray M. Peterson, "The Coming Din of Inequity," *Journal of the American Medical Association*, Vol. 176 (April 8, 1961), pp. 34–40, and more recent estimates by Peterson as reported by Elizabeth Deran in "Income Redistribution under the Social Security System," *National Tax Journal*, Vol. 19 (September 1966), pp. 276–85.

cial investment or whether he is being taken—whether he could invest his money elsewhere more wisely.[8]

The Social Security Administration (SSA) responded with estimates by its chief actuary at the time, Robert J. Myers, and included a critique of the "bad-buy-for-the-young" thesis,[9] such as that set down by Campbell. It was stated that this argument is not true even if one makes the unrealistic assumption that present benefit schedules will remain unchanged.[10] Even if they were fixed, the SSA argued, social security is a good buy under present law for the young worker in terms of the tax he himself will be asked to pay; that is, ignoring the possibility that the employer tax is also paid out of potential earnings of the employee, it was argued that the value of his prospective benefits upon retirement is greater than his accumulated tax, as scheduled. On the assumption of a 3.75 percent interest rate, the employee tax was estimated to be only 80–85 percent of the value of the prospective benefits. Even earners paying the present and proposed maximum tax were said to come out about even.

Aside from the no-growth assumption, the findings of Campbell and others were indicted by the SSA on two more counts: (1) failure to take into account the value of the survivor and disability insurance protection, and (2) judging untenable the usual assumption that the employer tax belongs to, and in the absence of social security would be available to, each employee in an amount equal to his own contribution. These two points by the SSA are subject to criticism. Certainly, failure to recognize that only part of the tax is designated for retirement benefits would distort any analysis, but the writers criticized were generally aware of this problem.[11] Much more important is the second point concerning the treatment of the employer's portion

[8] Question of Congressman Al Ullman, in *President's Proposals for Revision in the Social Security System*, Hearings before the House Committee on Ways and Means, 90 Cong. 1 sess. (1967), Pt. 1, p. 329.

[9] *Ibid.*, pp. 330–41. Myers left the SSA in 1971, and the position outlined here is not necessarily that of the new chief actuary.

[10] Officials stress that earnings increases over time permit increases in benefit schedules without higher tax rates.

[11] For example, Campbell was not guilty of this error; he deducted 20 percent of the tax to remove the portion estimated to be needed to finance OASDI benefits other than those of the aged. This same 20 percent figure was mentioned by the actuary as the appropriate fraction to eliminate (*President's Proposals for Revision in the Social Security System*, Hearings, Pt. 1, p. 331).

of the tax. Estimation of the aggregate lifetime burden of social security taxes on a worker does require that a position be taken on the incidence of the employer tax.[12] The SSA has traditionally rejected the imputation of the employer tax to employees.[13] Nevertheless, on the basis of the incidence analysis and findings of Chapters II and III, the treatment in this chapter departs from this position and imputes the employer tax to employees.[14] The conclusion that the employer tax is shifted to labor calls for such an imputation and is therefore fundamental to the analysis and findings presented here.[15]

It should be emphasized that the criticism by the SSA of the imputation of the employer tax to each employee, as stated in 1967 by the chief actuary, does not imply rejection of the argument in Chapters II and III that labor as a whole bears the tax. Its criticism was on a different basis:

Even though it is true that the employer contribution in the final analysis is borne in considerable part by employees, either because they receive lower wages than they otherwise would or because as consumers they pay higher prices than they otherwise would it does not follow that the incidence of the employer tax falls on wage earners in exact proportion to the earnings on which the tax is paid. The incidence of the tax will depend in specific instances on a variety of complex factors. The employer tax, therefore, may be looked on as being for the use of the system as a whole, and not as a matching contribution that is to be credited to each particular employee on the basis of the amount he paid.[16]

[12] The incidence of the employee's tax is not at issue, since the usual view that direct taxes on individual earnings rest on those who pay them has rarely been questioned in the literature on the social security tax. However, see the technical note at the end of Chapter II.

[13] In a 1967 SSA study, one-half of the employer tax was assumed to be shifted forward to consumers, and one-half backward to employees, and the tax was imputed to "welfare classes" according to that pattern. See Benjamin Bridges, Jr., "Current Redistributional Effects of Old-Age Income Assurance Programs," in *Old-Age Income Assurance*, Pt. 2: *The Aged Population and Retirement Income Programs*, A Compendium of Papers on Problems and Policy Issues in the Public and Private Pension System submitted to the Subcommittee on Fiscal Policy of the Joint Economic Committee, 90 Cong. 1 sess. (1967), p. 110.

[14] The tax was imputed in proportion to the earnings of the individual. For a defense of this approach and a discussion of the irrelevance for this problem of the distinction between "forward" and "backward" shifting, see Chapter IV.

[15] This methodological decision is quantitatively very important. Those who support the official position will want to halve the tax–benefit ratios presented and revise upward the estimated lifetime rates of return on contributions.

[16] *President's Proposals for Revision of the Social Security System*, Hearings, Pt. 1, pp. 330–31.

On this ground the employer's tax was disregarded by the chief actuary in his 1967 memorandum suggesting that most earners are scheduled to get more than their "money's worth."[17] However, even if it is agreed that precise imputation of the burden of the employer tax to individuals is not possible, omission of this part of the tax is bound to produce seriously misleading results. Even if the proceeds are "for the use of the system as a whole," it does not follow that the tax is a burden to no one. In other words, the concern here is with the cost of the tax to the individual worker and not with the cost to the system of the ultimate benefits paid to that worker. It is difficult to understand an analysis which agrees that the employer tax "is borne in considerable part by employees" and yet ignores it in evaluating the tax paid by individuals.[18] If it is paid by employees as a group, it must also be paid by them as individuals, and it is apparent that refusal to make any kind of imputation would build a large bias into the analysis—understating the tax on employees by 50 percent, on the average.

Another implication of the exclusion of the employer tax should be noted. The Myers memorandum mentioned above discusses the tax on various earnings levels. Not imputing the employer tax to a group of earners, such as the substantial group paying the maximum employee tax, implies that lower-income earners bear more than their proportional share, if it is agreed that the tax is borne by employees as a whole. If so, the lower-income employees as a whole would pay even more than double the employee tax, and their "deal" would not be nearly as good as suggested in the memorandum. Since there is no reason to expect that this anomaly exists and since the employer tax cannot be realistically ignored, the best approach seems to be to impute to each employee an employer tax equal in amount to the employee tax—that is, the amount of the employer tax actually paid in the name of the employee. Such an imputation is in accord with the

[17] "Analysis of Whether the Young Worker Receives His Money's Worth under Social Security," in *ibid.*, pp. 331–41.

[18] This has its counterpart in the treatment by some writers of the effect of undistributed corporate profits on the size distribution of individual incomes. Although corporate returns represent the common saving of stockholders as a whole, these writers refuse to impute it to individuals. For example, Simon Kuznets in *Shares of Upper Income Groups in Income and Savings* (National Bureau of Economic Research, 1950) ultimately imputes after-tax corporate saving to individual stockholders in one income variant (not stressed by the author) but does not impute pretax corporate saving to them. This pretense that corporate saving is nobody's income understates the relative income share of high-income ranks.

incidence analysis in Chapter III, since it was asserted that even at the individual level the higher the employer tax paid in the name of the employee, the lower the compensation of other types he can expect to receive (lower by about the same amount).

The analysis in this chapter views the tax-benefit sequence under social security as a dynamic process affecting lifetime incomes. It makes some of the same assumptions as in the more aggregative approach by Henry Aaron:[19] a fixed exponential growth rate, pay-as-you-go financing, and benefits keeping pace with earnings. However, Aaron added other simplifying assumptions about population growth rate and the ratio of active to retired population. Under these assumptions his model implies a break-even tax–benefit ratio of unity if the real rate of interest equals the sum of the growth rates of per capita earnings and the population. The more detailed analysis here yields results broadly consistent with Aaron's.

## Preliminary Projections of Tax–Benefit Ratios and Rates of Return

Studies of the return to participants in the social security system have stressed lifetime tax–benefit $(T/B)$ ratios. Such projections are presented briefly here, but the main focus is on a different criterion.[20] The most arbitrary element in $T/B$ projections is the interest rate imputed to taxes and used to discount benefits. Previous studies have attempted no deflation of taxes and benefits. However, even if they had, the real interest rate is probably even more difficult to project than the real earnings growth rate, and it also varies enormously from one type of asset to another. For this reason projections of the $T/B$ ratios were not stressed. Instead, the measure sought was the real yield on contributions implied by any given tax-benefit projection.

The real rate of interest on contributions was defined as the particular rate of return that would equalize the real accumulated tax (plus imputed yield) and the present value of real benefits discounted

[19] Henry Aaron, "The Social Insurance Paradox," *Canadian Journal of Economics and Political Science*, Vol. 32 (August 1966), pp. 371–74. See also Paul A. Samuelson, "An Exact Consumption-Loan Model of Interest with or without the Social Contrivance of Money," *Journal of Political Economy*, Vol. 66 (December 1958), pp. 467–82.

[20] The assumptions and statistical models underlying the empirical analysis in this section are elaborated in the technical note at the end of this chapter.

at the same rate at the point of retirement. This yield produces a tax–benefit ratio of unity, according to previous definitions. This concept of an internal rate of return under the system is consistent with the defined yield on periodic payments toward the private purchase of a lifetime annuity.

## The Empirical Approach

The analysis assumes fixed real rates of growth of average earnings and benefits, as well as pay-as-you-go financing. The preliminary estimates are based on an average earner's paying the average tax; consequently they abstract from variations by family structure and income. Estimates of the tax–benefit ratios were based on relations (6-1) to (6-3) specified in the technical note at the end of this chapter. The computations were routine, but several aspects of the estimates are relevant to a discussion of the findings. In the first place, for simplicity the tax was assumed to be paid annually at the beginning of each calendar year, with annual benefits beginning on the sixty-fifth birthday. In effect this simplification moves both taxes and benefits half a year ahead of the pace scheduled on a monthly basis, but this does not significantly affect the ratio of the two sums. Second, since the official projections of the taxpaying population ($N_t$) and the old-age beneficiary population ($R_t$) were to be used in the computation of the annual tax per earner by equation (6-1), it was necessary to specify a starting year for the accumulation of the average tax. The year 1966 was chosen because it represented the inauguration of the latest social security tax-benefit structure available at the time.[21]

Finally, the estimates of lifetime values of taxes $T$ and benefits $B$ were obtained under two alternative official population and mortality projections for two or more specified values of each of several unmeasured variables determining $T$ and $B$. The use of various assumed values provides some indication of the manner in which variations in the factors affect the $T/B$ ratio and the yield on contributions. An attempt was made to encompass a plausible range in each of the following four variables:[22]

[21] The estimates on an average earner basis derived from relations (6-1) to (6-3) are independent of the tax-benefit structure. However, the analysis by earning levels later in this chapter depends on this structure.

[22] This numerical analysis approach was chosen because the functional form of the $T/B$ ratio appeared too complex for formal analysis. Under further simplifying assumptions (discussed later), this is not the case.

1. The projected rate of growth of average real earnings $r$ was put alternatively at 2 and at 3 percent. The past growth rates measured over relatively long periods appear generally to have fallen within this range. For example, one simple estimate shows a growth rate of 2.45 percent for 1929–65 and 2.62 percent for 1947–65.[23]

2. Two alternative sets of population and mortality projections developed by the SSA were also used. One set was prepared on "low-cost" assumptions of high birthrate and high mortality and one on "high-cost" assumptions. The projected population with taxable earnings was taken to represent $N_t$. The projected number of aged beneficiaries was used as the measure of $R_t$.[24] The low-cost and high-cost projections of $P_n$ (the probability of reaching age $n$ if one has reached sixty-five) may also be deduced from the official actuarial studies.[25]

3. Another factor in the total tax accumulation is the age when work is begun. Even if all workers paid the average annual tax, it would be necessary to distinguish between those starting early and those starting late. The taxes were accumulated from two alternative starting ages (and therefore for two different values of the length of the working career). One earner was assumed to start work on his eighteenth birthday at the beginning of 1966 and pay the average tax over his working career; the other was assumed to start at the age of twenty-two. Both were assumed to retire at sixty-five.

4. The projected real interest rate $i$ was placed alternatively at

[23] These are based on a 1929–65 time series of average annual earnings per full-time worker deflated by the consumer price index. The average earnings series was obtained from the U.S. Department of Commerce, Office of Business Economics, *The National Income and Product Accounts of the United States, 1929–1965: Statistical Tables* (1966), pp. 106–09. The consumer price index was obtained from the Department of Commerce, Office of Business Economics, *Business Statistics, 1967 Biennial Edition* (1967), p. 38. The estimated growth rates were obtained from a trend line fitted to the logarithms of the observations.

[24] These two projections are given in Robert J. Myers and Francisco Bayo, *Long-Range Cost Estimates for Old-Age, Survivors, and Disability Insurance System, 1966*, U.S. Social Security Administration, Office of the Actuary, Actuarial Study 63 (1967), Tables 3 and 8. Projections were not available annually. The average tax was assumed to grow exponentially between the years tabulated.

[25] Francisco Bayo (*United States Population Projections for OASDHI Cost Estimates*, U.S. Social Security Administration, Office of the Actuary, Actuarial Study 62 [1966], pp. 16–20) gives projected mortality rates that are assumed to have leveled off after the year 2000. These are given for age groups at five-year intervals; they are interpolated to one-year intervals according to the pattern given in U.S. Department of Health, Education, and Welfare, Public Health Service, *United States Life Tables: 1959–61* (December 1964), Vol. 1, No. 1.

1.5, 3, 5, and 8 percent to allow for the great variation among rates of return available on different types of assets in recent decades. Figure 6-1 illustrates the contrast between the real yield on fixed-value instru-

**FIGURE 6-1. Estimates of the Real Value of Alternative 1919 Investments of One Dollar, 1920–65**

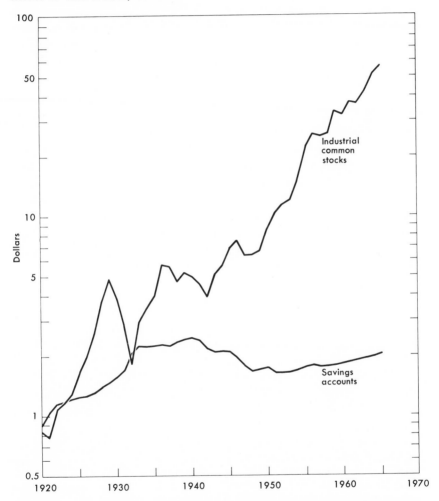

Sources: The savings account series is based on weighted averages of savings account yields from an unpublished tabulation provided by Samuel B. Chase, Jr., and deflated by the consumer price index. The 1929–65 industrial common stock series has been computed from Moody's indexes of prices and percentage dividend yields on industrial common stock. The price and dividend series were extended back to 1919 on the basis of Cowles Commission and Standard and Poor's series adjusted according to the 1929 ratio to Moody's series. The basic data are from the U.S. Bureau of the Census, *Historical Statistics of the United States, Colonial Times to 1957* (1960), pp. 656–57, and *Statistical Abstract of the United States*, various editions. The hypothetical accumulated investment has also been deflated by the consumer price index.

ments on the one hand, and equity capital on the other. The savings account and industrial common stock curves each show hypothetical annual values in real terms of a single initial investment of one dollar in 1919.[26] The annual compound yield between any two years can be derived from the slope of the line on this logarithmic chart. Some of these yields are given for selected intervals in Table 6-1. Except for a few very short intervals like 1929–32, the yield on equity greatly exceeded that on savings.[27] Even an investment in these common stocks on the eve of the 1929 crash would have greatly outperformed the savings series in the long run. Also, during the postwar rise in interest rates after 1951, savings yielded only 1.5 percent in real terms compared to 13 percent for the common stock series through 1965.

The four specified interest rates were chosen on two considerations. First, in terms of projections it was appropriate to admit the diverse options with respect to the long-run rate of return that past experience suggests are likely to be available. More important, it was essential that the assumed range be wide enough to cover the yields provided to individuals under the social security program in various circumstances. This was required for accurate interpolation of these implied rates of return on contributions. Thus these particular values of $i$ were not specified as necessarily typical or attainable; computations were carried out for each to facilitate numerical approximation of the rate of return—that which produces a tax–benefit ratio of unity and is the chief objective of the exercise.

### Results for the Recipient of Average Earnings

As indicated above, the assumptions of the model permit the lifetime average tax accumulations to be expressed as real magnitudes and as multiples of the average benefit in 1966. The nature of the

---

[26] Similar curves were also obtained for index number series for long-term government bonds, Moody's AAA corporate bonds, and all common stocks. To avoid the index number problem, the yield on mutual funds holding common stock was also considered. Government bonds generally yielded more than savings accounts, and corporate yields were still higher. However, the contrast between interest rates and the yield on equity was the most striking feature of all these comparisons, as it is in Figure 6-1. Finally, although the consumer price index has been criticized as a deflator, alternative deflators would not dispel this contrast between real interest rates and the yield on equity.

[27] If the estimates were put on an after-tax basis, the preferential treatment of capital gains would show an even greater relative performance of equity over savings.

**TABLE 6-1. Estimates of the Real Annual Rate of Return on Alternative Investments at Selected Time Intervals, 1919–65**

*(In percent)*

| | Rate of return | |
|---|---|---|
| Time interval | Savings accounts | Industrial common stocks |
| 1919–65 | 1.5 | 9.2 |
| 1929–32 | 12.0 | −38.35 |
| 1929–65 | 0.9 | 7.0 |
| 1932–37 | 1.7 | 25.1 |
| 1937–42 | −0.6 | −7.4 |
| 1942–46 | −2.6 | 17.4 |
| 1946–65 | 0.1 | 11.2 |
| 1951–65 | 1.5 | 13.0 |

Source: Same as Figure 6-1.

dependence of these on the assumptions in this study (including only the two intermediate rates of return) is indicated in Table 6-2.[28] These results show the expected relationships. The estimated lifetime tax plus imputed return is greater for high growth rates, high-cost projections, and the early starting age. The higher the assumed rate of return, the greater is the total accumulation.[29]

The present value of the benefit stream at the age of sixty-five can be conveniently and meaningfully stated as a multiple of the initial annual benefit at sixty-five. It was assumed that all earners will work long enough so that benefits will be independent of the starting age. As indicated in the technical note at the end of this chapter, the present value of this stream varies with sex and family composition because of the different mortality projections for males and females.

[28] The postulated interest rates of 1.5 and 8 percent are omitted here for brevity. However, the relationships in this range are used in later interpolated estimates of an individual's effective rate of return under the retirement program.

[29] No distinction has been made here between tax rates on the self-employed and others. Since the social security tax on the self-employed was approximately 25 percent below the combined employer-employee rate in 1966, the lifetime tax on employed workers must be somewhat higher than that shown in the table and the tax on self-employed must be 25 percent below that of the employed. The differential is scheduled to become even greater in the future—29 percent in 1973, for example. However, if the income of the self-employed were corrected for imputed profits, the tax rate on their earnings might be about the same.

**TABLE 6-2. Average Lifetime Accumulated Social Security Tax under Various Assumptions, Stated as Multiples of the Average Benefit in 1966**

| Type of cost projection[a] and starting age | 2 percent growth rate in real earnings[b] | | 3 percent growth rate in real earnings[b] | |
|---|---|---|---|---|
| | 3 percent interest rate | 5 percent interest rate | 3 percent interest rate | 5 percent interest rate |
| Low cost | | | | |
| Age 18 | 29.64 | 49.63 | 36.66 | 59.42 |
| Age 22 | 24.52 | 39.06 | 29.80 | 46.21 |
| High cost | | | | |
| Age 18 | 32.88 | 54.25 | 40.97 | 65.42 |
| Age 22 | 26.98 | 42.46 | 32.99 | 50.52 |

Source: Derived by author. See the technical note at the end of this chapter for the basic model.

[a] The low-cost projection assumes a high birthrate and high mortality; the high-cost projection a low birthrate and low mortality.

[b] Assumed average annual rate of growth of real earnings per employee.

Table 6-3 gives the present value of the benefit stream for three specified types of beneficiaries at sixty-five. These ratios are consistent with a priori expectations. The present value varies directly with the growth rate and inversely with interest rates. The high-cost (low mortality) estimates show somewhat higher values, and women have higher values than men because of their lower mortality rates. Couples eligible for the wife's benefit have almost as high values as single women with the same starting benefits, despite the reduction in benefits when one person dies. Since the values for these couples are closer to those for women than those for men, this cut in benefits appears to be more than offset by the longer period during which at least one person is expected to receive benefits.

Tables 6-2 and 6-3 form the basis for derivation of lifetime tax–benefit ratios for a recipient of average income. If it were reasonable to assume that a single benefit–earnings ratio $\bar{k}$ defined this starting benefit for the average earner it would be necessary only to restate Table 6-3 in multiples of the 1966 starting benefit[30] and take the ratio of the tax measures in Table 6-2 to the benefit measures in Table 6-3. However, a rough allowance is made here for one feature of the present social security laws—the variation of the initial benefit–earnings

[30] The adjustment factors for Table 6-3 are based on the earlier assumption of an average annual rate of growth of real benefits.

**TABLE 6-3. Present Value of Stream of Real Social Security Benefits to a Recipient at Sixty-five under Various Assumptions, Stated as a Multiple of the Initial Annual Benefit on the Sixty-fifth Birthday**

| Type of cost projection[a] and family composition | 2 percent growth rate in real earnings[b] | | 3 percent growth rate in real earnings[b] | |
|---|---|---|---|---|
| | 3 percent interest rate | 5 percent interest rate | 3 percent interest rate | 5 percent interest rate |
| **Low cost** | | | | |
| Single man or married man with wife who worked | 13.13 | 11.26 | 14.28 | 12.15 |
| Single woman or married woman with nondependent husband | 15.60 | 13.14 | 17.14 | 14.30 |
| Couple eligible for wife's benefit | 15.10 | 12.75 | 16.56 | 13.86 |
| **High cost** | | | | |
| Single man or married man with wife who worked | 13.92 | 11.86 | 15.20 | 12.84 |
| Single woman or married woman with nondependent husband | 16.39 | 13.72 | 18.08 | 14.98 |
| Couple eligible for wife's benefit | 15.89 | 13.33 | 17.50 | 14.54 |

Source: Derived by author on the basis of the specified types of projections and family composition, using the formulas in the technical note at the end of this chapter.

a The low-cost projection assumes a high birthrate and high mortality; the high-cost projection a low birthrate and low mortality.

b Assumed average annual rate of growth of real earnings per employee.

ratio according to the composition of retired-worker families. The only distinction considered was that between (1) couples in which the male retired worker is entitled to benefits for a wife, and (2) all other retired workers, whether married or not.[31] Under current law the benefit–earnings ratio is about 50 percent higher for the first group than for the second. This was taken into account in the tax–benefit ratios for average earners reported in Table 6-4 below.[32]

[31] The second category here includes the groups specified under notes *a* and *b* to Table 6-4 below. The first category is represented by the group under note *c* to the table.

[32] The 1964 *Annual Statistical Supplement* to the *Social Security Bulletin*, p. 46, indicates that about one-eighth of new retired-worker families in 1964 were headed by men entitled to benefits for aged wives or for younger wives with at least one child. Ignoring the small number who had child beneficiaries only, a rough indication of the effect of the differential can be obtained by assuming that this one-eighth of retired workers had an average starting benefit–earnings ratio 50 percent above that of all others. The original single benefit–earnings ratio $k$ is a weighted mean of the $k$s for the two subgroups, implying that these $k$s are approximately $1.41k$ and $0.94k$, respectively. These factors were used to obtain separate $T/B$ ratios for the two subgroups.

**TABLE 6-4. Estimated Average Lifetime Social Security Tax–Benefit Ratios for Recipients of Average Earnings under Various Assumptions**
*(In percent)*

| Type of cost projection, starting age, and family composition | 2 percent growth rate in real earnings | | 3 percent growth rate in real earnings | |
|---|---|---|---|---|
| | 3 percent interest rate | 5 percent interest rate | 3 percent interest rate | 5 percent interest rate |
| Low cost, age 18 | | | | |
| Man[a] | 102.6 | 200.1 | 76.6 | 146.0 |
| Woman[b] | 86.3 | 171.1 | 63.8 | 123.9 |
| Couple[c] | 59.4 | 117.8 | 44.0 | 85.3 |
| Low cost, age 22 | | | | |
| Man[a] | 84.8 | 157.6 | 62.2 | 113.5 |
| Woman[b] | 71.3 | 134.7 | 51.9 | 96.4 |
| Couple[c] | 49.1 | 92.6 | 35.7 | 66.3 |
| High cost, age 18 | | | | |
| Man[a] | 107.2 | 207.7 | 80.4 | 152.0 |
| Woman[b] | 91.1 | 179.5 | 67.7 | 130.3 |
| Couple[c] | 62.6 | 123.1 | 46.6 | 89.5 |
| High cost, age 22 | | | | |
| Man[a] | 88.0 | 162.4 | 64.8 | 117.4 |
| Woman[b] | 74.7 | 140.5 | 54.5 | 100.6 |
| Couple[c] | 51.3 | 96.4 | 37.6 | 69.1 |

Sources: Tables 6-2 and 6-3 (adjusted to multiples of 1966 starting benefit level).
[a] Single man or married man with wife who worked.
[b] Single woman or married woman with nondependent husband.
[c] Couple eligible for wife's benefit.

The estimated tax–benefit ratios show the expected relationships. High growth rates, low imputed interest rate, low-cost projections, and a late starting age make for relatively good buys.[33] The extreme cases under the particular assumptions of Table 6-4 are $T/B$ ratios of 36 and 208 percent.[34] The participant would clearly do better in many cases to obtain benefits under social security than to accumulate private savings equal to the taxes. He would do so in all cases if the growth rate were as great as the interest rate, but he would generally

[33] The phrase "relatively good buy" here refers to low tax accumulations compared to benefit expectations, with both evaluated at the specified interest rate. They might be poor buys relative to those obtainable through other available rates of return.

[34] The spread would, of course, be much wider if a wider range of rates of return, growth rates, starting ages, and cost projections had been specified.

**TABLE 6-5. Estimated Real Rates of Return on Social Security Contributions for Recipients of Average Earnings under Various Assumptions**

(In percent)

| Type of cost projection, starting age, and family composition | Growth rate in real earnings | |
|---|---|---|
| | 2 percent | 3 percent |
| Low cost, age 18 | | |
| Man[a] | 2.92 | 3.83 |
| Woman[b] | 3.43 | 4.35 |
| Couple[c] | 4.52 | 5.51 |
| Low cost, age 22 | | |
| Man[a] | 3.53 | 4.58 |
| Woman[b] | 4.06 | 5.11 |
| Couple[c] | 5.23 | 6.28 |
| High cost, age 18 | | |
| Man[a] | 2.78 | 3.68 |
| Woman[b] | 3.28 | 4.21 |
| Couple[c] | 4.38 | 5.32 |
| High cost, age 22 | | |
| Man[a] | 3.42 | 4.46 |
| Woman[b] | 3.92 | 4.98 |
| Couple[c] | 5.12 | 6.16 |

Source: Derived by author, as described in the technical note at the end of this chapter.
a Single man or married man with wife who worked.
b Single woman or married woman with nondependent husband.
c Couple eligible for wife's benefit.

fare poorly if the growth rate were substantially lower. The college graduate who starts work at twenty-two fares much better than the high school graduate who starts work at eighteen, if both earn the average wage;[35] couples with nonworking wives do relatively well. However, it is apparent that the $T/B$ ratios are so heavily dependent on the interest rate assumed that any absolute evaluation of the tax-benefit relationship provided to different groups under the system would be arbitrary. More meaningful is the implied rate of return for each group—the rate that equalizes the value of the tax and benefit streams. These rates are given in Table 6-5 and may be compared with alternative yields on investment available in the past, such as

[35] This comparison should be qualified by recognition that college graduates have a higher average wage and generally lower statutory benefit–earnings ratios. Some effects of the graduated benefit-earnings schedule are discussed later in this chapter.

those illustrated in Figure 6-1.[36] If past experience is a plausible guide, social security participants in these categories will fare much better than they would if offered the option of a private savings program. On the other hand, these relatively attractive rates of return fall considerably short of the long-run yield on equity capital in recent decades.

The yields projected for these average earners under various assumptions range from 2.78 to 6.28 percent. This spread indicates substantial income redistribution among categories of participants. However, even the least favored group (single man, starting work at eighteen, facing a high-cost system and a slow earnings growth rate) would fare much better over the long run than private savers have in the past; yet the yield of 6.28 percent to the most favored is unimpressive compared to typical yields on equity over the long run.[37] Clearly, the key assumption of the present analysis is that benefits keep pace with earnings. Insofar as the assumption holds, the social security participant has a considerable advantage over an investor in fixed dollar obligations subject to inflationary erosion, although he is likely to do less well in the long run than the investor in equities.

## Effect of Earnings Level on Rate of Return

The ceiling on taxable earnings and the relationship of benefits and past earnings have not yet been considered. In terms of transfers on a lifetime basis, another major redistributional feature of the social security system is the relatively high benefit–earnings ratios assigned to low-income groups. This feature is clearly "progressive" in the classic sense. The extent of progressivity under a given tax-benefit structure varies with the relation between the earnings ceiling and average earnings. In a departure from the emphasis on the average earner, the progressivity of the system is considered here by using the ceiling and benefit-earnings structure in effect in 1966 and 1967, as well as a hypothetical arrangement—with a higher ceiling and a more progressive tax-benefit structure.

[36] The estimated yields here and later in this chapter were obtained by semilogarithmic interpolation. Inspection showed a close linear relationship between log $T/B$ and the four specified interest rates $i$. The estimates are linear interpolation for the value of $i$ yielding log $T/B = 0$.

[37] It should be repeated that the relative performance of equity is even better on an after-tax basis, since capital gains receive preferential treatment.

Two revisions of the previous per capita analysis are required. In the first place, with a ceiling on taxable earnings it is no longer true that the recipient of average earnings pays the average tax. This mean tax is paid by a worker who earns the mean taxable income throughout his career. Second, it is now recognized that the benefit–earnings ratio $k$, though still assumed invariant over time, varies cross-sectionally with the earnings level. The revised tax–benefit ratios based on the 1966 structure were obtained in two steps. First, the average taxable amount of earnings in 1966 was fixed at \$3,700.[38] Adjustment of the $T/B$ ratios to allow for the effect of the graduated benefit-earnings schedule was then accomplished by a multiplicative correction. Each multiplier is the ratio of the statutory $k$ value for the specified earnings level to the $k$ value for the recipient of the mean taxable income of \$3,700.[39] The ratios in Table 6-4 were adjusted by these factors associated with earnings. The analysis presumes that the benefit–earnings ratios in the starting year 1966 remain fixed throughout the worker's life.

The yield under each assumption and by income level was obtained as before by interpolation. These yields are reported for selected income levels in Table 6-6. It is apparent that graduation of the benefit-earnings schedule produces a substantial graduation in the yield-earning relationship.[40] For example, the yields for those earning \$2,000 are generally 1.5 percentage points or more higher than for those earning \$6,600 or over and paying the maximum tax. However, even the most unfavorable projection for the latter continues to show

[38] This is based on the estimate for 1965 by Myers and Bayo in *Long-Range Cost Estimates*, p. 24.

[39] Estimates of these statutory $k$ values by income level were obtained by interpolation in an official table provided by the SSA (Social Security Administration, "1967 Social Security Recommendations" [Jan. 21, 1967; processed], table entitled, "Comparison of Monthly Cash Benefits Payable under Present Law and under Proposal"). The use of statutory $k$ values abstracts from details of the moving average of earnings levels on which benefits are based. However, only the slope of the benefit-earnings relationship shown in the official schedule is essential to estimation of the relationship of lifetime rate of return to the starting earnings level. This allowance for the current degree of graduation adequately serves the broad purpose of displaying this progressive feature of the system.

[40] The degree of graduation is probably somewhat exaggerated because no correction could be made for the higher mortality rates of low-income earners. This makes a given benefit stream worth less to them than is indicated by overall mortality, although they get some compensation for this in the life insurance features of social security, which are not considered here.

**TABLE 6-6. Lifetime Real Rates of Return on Social Security Contributions under Various Assumptions and Earnings Levels, 1966 Laws**

(In percent)

| Type of cost projection, starting age, growth rate of earnings, and family composition[a] | Taxable earnings levels | | | | |
|---|---|---|---|---|---|
| | $2,000 | $4,000 | $6,000 | $6,600 | Mean |
| **Low cost, age 18** | | | | | |
| (a) Growth rate of 2% | | | | | |
| Man | 3.78 | 2.82 | 2.39 | 2.30 | 2.92 |
| Woman | 4.27 | 3.34 | 2.93 | 2.85 | 3.43 |
| Couple | 5.34 | 4.43 | 4.02 | 3.94 | 4.52 |
| (b) Growth rate of 3% | | | | | |
| Man | 4.72 | 3.73 | 3.30 | 3.21 | 3.83 |
| Woman | 5.22 | 4.26 | 3.84 | 3.76 | 4.35 |
| Couple | 6.28 | 5.36 | 4.97 | 4.88 | 5.51 |
| **High cost, age 18** | | | | | |
| (a) Growth rate of 2% | | | | | |
| Man | 3.66 | 2.68 | 2.24 | 2.15 | 2.78 |
| Woman | 4.12 | 3.18 | 2.76 | 2.68 | 3.28 |
| Couple | 5.22 | 4.29 | 3.88 | 3.80 | 4.38 |
| (b) Growth rate of 3% | | | | | |
| Man | 4.59 | 3.58 | 3.15 | 3.06 | 3.68 |
| Woman | 5.06 | 4.09 | 3.67 | 3.58 | 4.21 |
| Couple | 6.16 | 5.23 | 4.82 | 4.73 | 5.32 |
| **Low cost, age 22** | | | | | |
| (a) Growth rate of 2% | | | | | |
| Man | 4.46 | 3.43 | 2.98 | 2.89 | 3.53 |
| Woman | 4.97 | 3.96 | 3.53 | 3.44 | 4.06 |
| Couple | 6.10 | 5.13 | 4.71 | 4.62 | 5.23 |
| (b) Growth rate of 3% | | | | | |
| Man | 5.51 | 4.47 | 4.02 | 3.92 | 4.58 |
| Woman | 6.00 | 5.01 | 4.57 | 4.48 | 5.11 |
| Couple | 7.17 | 6.18 | 5.75 | 5.66 | 6.28 |
| **High cost, age 22** | | | | | |
| (a) Growth rate of 2% | | | | | |
| Man | 4.36 | 3.31 | 2.86 | 2.76 | 3.42 |
| Woman | 4.83 | 3.82 | 3.39 | 3.30 | 3.92 |
| Couple | 6.06 | 5.01 | 4.58 | 4.48 | 5.12 |
| (b) Growth rate of 3% | | | | | |
| Man | 5.40 | 4.35 | 3.89 | 3.79 | 4.46 |
| Woman | 5.88 | 4.87 | 4.43 | 4.33 | 4.98 |
| Couple | 7.05 | 6.06 | 5.63 | 5.54 | 6.16 |

Source: Derived by author. See text for method.

[a] "Man" denotes a single man or a married man whose wife worked; "woman" denotes a single woman or a married woman with nondependent husband; "couple" denotes a couple eligible for the wife's benefit.

a real rate of return over 2 percent—generally better in the long run than the savings account yield shown in Figure 6-1.

Yields over 7 percent appear in Table 6-6, but these are for the unlikely case of an earner who waits to start work until he is twenty-two but nevertheless commands an income only slightly more than half the mean. However, even at the mean earnings level, yields of over 6 percent are projected for those beginning at twenty-two and eligible for wife's benefits. Despite the rather pronounced variation in these projected yields, they continue to be bounded by the poor past performance of savings accounts and the lucrative long-term results of investment in equity.

To illustrate the effect of a hypothetical and more progressive tax structure in the base year of 1966, one more set of estimates was computed under the assumption of a $10,800 ceiling and a more graduated tax-benefit schedule.[41] It was estimated that the higher ceiling would yield an average taxable income of $4,225 in 1966, as against $3,700 under the actual ceiling.[42] Allowance for this and the proposed change in the benefit-earnings schedule produce a further graduation of the yield-earnings relationship, as shown in Figure 6-2; that is, the lines are farther apart vertically.[43]

This summary portrayal in Figure 6-2 attempts to illustrate in one place the key factors affecting the yield on a participant's saving under the social security system.[44] In each individual chart the higher yield

[41] The structure used is one proposed in 1967 by the SSA ("1967 Social Security Recommendations"). Much more modest changes were actually adopted, but the effect of the hypothetical larger adjustments are illustrative. Once more there is no way of learning whether the changes are consistent with the pay-as-you-go assumption. However, the slope of the benefit-earning schedule is the key element in this exercise. The results should at least indicate the order of magnitude of changes of this type.

[42] The alternative average taxable earnings in 1966 was estimated by means of the relationship between the percentage of earnings taxable and the ratio of the ceiling to the mean available for 1964 in Michael Resnick, "Annual Earnings and the Taxable Maximum for OASDHI," *Social Security Bulletin*, Vol. 29 (November 1966), p. 39.

[43] These sketches do not indicate the relative importance of the two factors in this change. The hypothetical schedule is somewhat more graduated for income than the actual, since the minimum benefit under the hypothetical scheme represents a relatively greater increase than at other levels. However, an increase in the ceiling alone would further graduate the yields if the tax rate were adjusted to keep total tax receipts unchanged; this would increase taxes of upper income groups and lower payments of others while leaving the benefits unchanged.

[44] Despite the lines drawn on each small graph, it should be noted that each is based on only two points—one for each growth rate; the actual relation may not be linear. The relationships for only one of the two cost projections are given, because the differences between the two are so minor, as may be seen in Table 6-6.

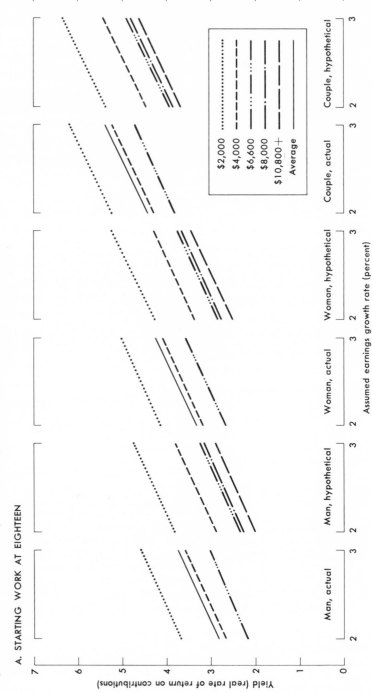

FIGURE 6-2. Lifetime Real Rates of Return on Social Security Contributions under Various Assumptions, at 1966 Earnings Levels; Actual and Proposed Ceilings and Benefit-Earnings Schedules[a]

A. STARTING WORK AT EIGHTEEN

## B. STARTING WORK AT TWENTY-TWO

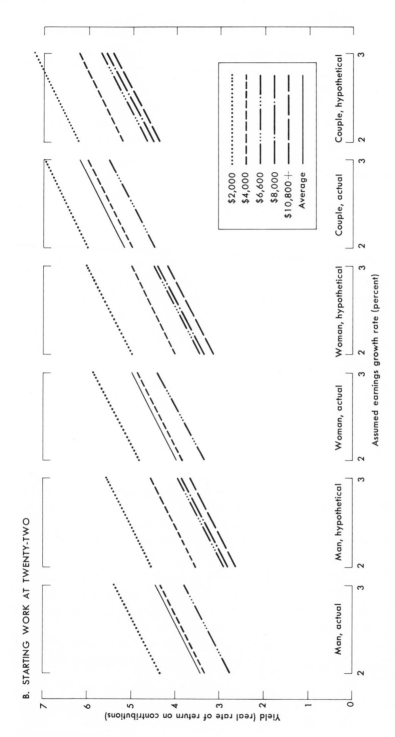

Source: Derived by author. See text for discussion.
a "Man" denotes a single man or a married man whose wife worked; "woman" denotes a single woman or a married woman with nondependent husband; "couple" denotes a couple eligible for the wife's benefit.

to low incomes is pronounced. Although not much should be made of the hypothetical projections in the figure, the greater distance between the $2,000 line and the ceiling line in the vertical direction shows the effect of a higher ceiling in the starting year and a more graduated benefit-earnings curve. The boost in the yield that accompanies a high earnings growth rate is shown in each graph for each category of worker. The relative advantage of a couple's receiving the wife's benefits[45] and of the late starter are also pointed up once again.

## Appraisal of Lifetime Rates of Return

In a citation earlier in this chapter, Congressman Ullman questioned whether social security is a sound investment for a young person or whether he is being "taken." This question has two aspects. In the first place the differentials among the yields to individuals require evaluation. Second, it must be determined whether the absolute levels of the yields are sufficient to justify this compulsory saving. The underlying model developed in the technical note at the end of this chapter and the statistical projections based on it offer no unique or unequivocal answer to these questions. However, the assumptions, reasoning, and the projected yields on savings under social security have been presented in detail so that the reader may evaluate the analysis and judge for himself the adequacy of the yield accruing to various categories of participants.

Obviously, some participants in social security are faring much better than others, but this type of differentiation also exists under the generally approved graduated income tax. The relatively high rate of return to low-income groups under social security is consistent with their being assigned a low burden under the income tax. The relatively high return to couples who did not have the benefit of a wife's income may well be consistent with the objective of redistributing income in favor of those with greater need. However, this is by no means certain, since nonworking wives may tend to be concentrated among high-income couples. It is clear, of course, that neither of these redistributional features is consistent with the insurance analogy frequently associated with the system, but that is irrelevant to their appraisal.

[45] The estimates for relatively high earnings levels must be qualified because of their failure to take into account the current practice of placing a ceiling on the wife's benefits.

Less acceptable in terms either of values or logic, if we continue to think in terms of lifetime tax-benefit relationships, are the higher yields for women[46] and late entrants into the work force. The advantage of women is minor, but the relative bargain of late starters is not trivial and would be difficult to justify within this conceptual framework. Presumably, late starters are typically college graduates, or even recipients of higher degrees, who will tend ultimately to have relatively high income but will be taxed for fewer years and thus enjoy a favorable differential, comparable to their advantage in postponement of military service.[47] This discrimination in favor of the late starter could be alleviated by increasing the tax rates and/or ceiling sufficiently to allow exemption of earners under twenty-five from the social security tax.

Another feature of the law that has not been treated explicitly in the numerical estimates is the tax differential in favor of the self-employed, who are taxed at a rate approximately 25 percent below the combined employer-employee rate. Self-employed workers have not been analyzed separately, because it seems possible that if the appropriate part of their income were imputed to them as profits their effective tax rate on *earnings* might then be on a par with that charged employees. On the other hand, a comparison of national income accounts and tax return data suggests that underreporting of self-employed income as compared with underreporting of earnings may just about offset the part of the tax self-employed workers are currently paying on profits.[48] If so, the true yield to the self-employed is considerably higher than to earners at the same reported income level. If this were established as true, it would support elimination of the present statutory tax differential that favors the self-employed.

If we depart from the lifetime tax-benefit frame of reference and consider current tax and benefit structures independently, some of

[46] As is true throughout this chapter, this point abstracts from the survivor and dependent features of the system. These are less valuable to female earners. On the other hand, women tend to receive higher yields because of less continuous coverage. The point here is simply that women fare better than men owing to the mortality factor, other things being equal.

[47] This assessment abstracts from the fact that early starters may tend to have lower incomes and greater unemployment and thereby receive favorable treatment through other features of the system. The point is that an early start, other things being equal, yields unfavorable treatment.

[48] In 1966 self-employed income reported on tax returns was 67 percent of the total given in the national income accounts.

the above appraisals no longer seem valid. For example, the progressiveness of the relationship between retirement benefits and lifetime income cannot hide the fact that the tax used to finance benefits is heavy and regressive both now and throughout the earner's working career. Even though the working poor may ultimately get out more than they put in, it does not necessarily follow that the later progressivity of the benefit structure is sufficient to compensate for the earlier hardship imposed by the payroll tax. On the other hand, the benefit advantage of women due to lower mortality may well be a progressive feature, but this depends on the assumption that women tend to have lower incomes during retirement. Finally, the extra tax paid by early starters compared to late starters with the same income may be justifiable on the grounds of ability to pay. In any case the separate appraisals of taxes and benefits generally produce different answers from those suggested by the lifetime rates of return.

Also relevant, in addition to these differentials, is the absolute level of these rates of return on contributions under the program. First, consider the aggregate or overall yield to participants as a whole. No explicit estimates have been made of this aggregate yield, but a glance at Table 6-5 suggests that it is probably on the order of 4 percent.[49] This rate of return is not inconsistent with the implications of Aaron's simple model.[50] His analysis, like the present one, assumes a fixed exponential growth rate, benefits keeping pace with earnings, and pay-as-you-go; however, he adds the further simplifying assumptions that population grows exponentially and that the active and retired population remain in fixed proportion. Under these conditions he establishes that the approximate condition for a break-even tax–benefit ratio of unity is that the real rate of interest equals the sum of the growth rates of per capita earnings and population. Putting the earnings growth rate at 2.5 percent and assuming a growth rate in the work force of 1.3 to 1.7 percent,[51] the Aaron model would also imply an overall real yield on contributions of around 4 percent. This provides rough confirmation of the more detailed analysis above which

[49] This rough approximation compromises midway between the two growth rates but weighs heavily the results for workers starting at eighteen and beneficiaries not eligible for their wives' benefits.

[50] Aaron, "Social Insurance Paradox."

[51] The growth rate for the work force is the range of growth rates in the low-cost and high-cost projections by the SSA for the intervals 1965–2000 and 1965–2025 given in Myers and Bayo, *Long-Range Cost Estimates*, p. 24.

took into account demographic projections. The empirical results for specific earner categories displayed in Figure 6-2 are also roughly consistent with Aaron's basic relationship.

It is not easy to evaluate an overall projected rate of return on social security contributions of 4 percent. It has been suggested in Figure 6-1 that this yield is very attractive in comparison with past experience with fixed dollar claims; it would probably also look good in comparison with the *real* yield on an installment purchase of a private insurance annuity. However, these are all dwarfed by past long-run yields on equity, summarized in Table 6-1.[52] It is even more difficult to evaluate the projected 2.5 percent earnings growth rate and the 1.5 percent work force growth rate, both of which are fundamental to the 4 percent projection. In any case, it should first be acknowledged that a comparison of the 4 percent projection with the yield on equity is artificial in some respects. A public retirement scheme comparable to a private plan such as that developed by the Teachers Insurance and Annuity Association (TIAA), which provides for equity investment,[53] is not feasible under a pay-as-you-go system; the present active population would not only have to finance pensions for the currently retired but also would contribute to a mammoth equity trust fund. Furthermore, there is no reason to believe that the high real yields earned on equity in the past would be impervious to the large new demand for securities that would be generated. The bidding up of price–earnings ratios (while cutting dividend rates) would probably yield real capital gains at the outset, but a highly unstable situation would be in prospect as selling of equities by the retired population began to offset buying on behalf of earners.

As a substantial improvement over the past yields on fixed claims, a 4 percent real return under a pay-as-you-go social security program seems tolerable for provision of the basic retirement floor. This avoids the uncertainties connected with a funded equity program and permits retention of some generally acceptable redistributive features not likely to survive the more precise individual earmarking to be expected under funding. On the other hand, the larger this compulsory saving under social security, the less earners will have to invest pri-

[52] This contrast would be somewhat less pronounced for estimates ending with the 1969–70 bear market. However, the recovery had erased most of the loss by 1971.

[53] As of July 1, 1971, participants in TIAA were permitted to allocate up to 100 percent of contributions in their name to the College Retirement Equity Fund.

vately in mutual funds or similar devices for periodic investment in higher-yielding equity capital. This consideration is at least relevant to determination of the optimum size of the social security program.

It is essential to stress also that the 4 percent yield itself is hardly a riskless proposition. Aside from the fallible growth rate projections, there is no guarantee that benefits will keep pace with earnings as postulated in the present model. The social insurance package would look more attractive if the taxpaying population were guaranteed that future earners would pay enough to allow their retirement income to keep pace indefinitely with their earnings. In the absence of such assurances, younger workers are likely to be more impressed by Colin Campbell's analysis of existing and proposed tax and benefit schedules than by the hypothetical projections of the model discussed here. The raw deals Campbell portrays cannot be ruled out without a public commitment to tie current benefits to current earnings indefinitely. Without such guarantees, continued grumbling by younger workers can be expected.

The lack of intergenerational contractual obligations is not the only ground for discontent on the part of social security taxpayers. Although there is a modest degree of progression in the yield-earnings relationship, the yields at the low end of the income scale are highly unattractive to the poor. Low-income families frequently must borrow at very high interest rates. It is therefore difficult to justify forcing them to save, even at a real interest rate of 7 percent under social security; they may at the same time (and in part as a consequence) be borrowing at 36 percent or more. In the context of a war against poverty it is an anomaly that a 10 percent combined employer-employee payroll tax was collected on a $5,000 income of a family of six in 1970, even though this family was recognized as incapable of paying any income tax. The payroll tax is regressive because of the earnings ceiling and other factors; it is especially burdensome to the working poor, who get little offsetting help from welfare. Whatever the ultimate payoff at age sixty-five, the magnitude of this compulsory saving can hardly be regarded as trivial by workers living in the officially defined poverty range.

It seems appropriate to accept as a working hypothesis that the young poor family discounts its projected retirement income at a very high rate. A 6 or 7 percent ultimate real yield on the 10 percent contribution paid by the young $5,000 earner may sound attractive to some policy makers, but who would presume to call such a worker a profligate glutton if he would rather have the 10 percent *now*?

There is no intent to imply that participation in the social security program should be made voluntary; this would have the virtually certain result that many people would reach retirement age with few resources and poor prospects. Rather, it is shown that the heavy and regressive burden of the present payroll tax structure on the working poor deserves recognition and should be either alleviated or eliminated through the various devices analyzed in Chapter V. In any case the main point is that families found to be in poverty should not be forced to contribute substantially, even though their projected return under social security may appear attractive to others more fortunately situated in the income distribution.[54]

In conclusion, it should be reiterated that the projected yields reported above are based on an abstract model of earnings and benefit growth that is no more than a rough approximation of past reality. If the model and the official demographic projections are fairly realistic, new contributors will in the aggregate get neither a very good "buy" nor a very bad one, but they will fare moderately well. The evaluation of the redistributive features of the system is more subjective and depends on whether one thinks in terms of lifetime rates of return or of separate tax and benefit structures. From either viewpoint, however, guaranteeing that benefits will keep pace with earnings and alleviating the burden of the payroll tax on the poor would contribute to making social security a substantially more attractive institution.

## Technical Note: The Basic Model

If the reasoning presented in the first section of this chapter is correct, the method underlying the tax–benefit ratios found in the Myers statement[55] is biased in two opposite directions. Failure to allow for the longer growth of benefits than of taxes during a worker's lifetime undervalues the "deal" expected for a participant in the system, whereas excluding the employer tax presumably borne by the

---

[54] Elimination of the payroll tax on the working poor is, of course, only one of many needed moves against poverty. A "negative tax" may also be called for to supplement earnings, just as such aid is clearly required by the nonworking poor, who are free of the payroll tax burden.

[55] See note 9.

worker overvalues it. An attempt is made in this technical note to circumvent these opposing biases.[56]

The stress here is on *average* taxes and benefits per worker under assumed growth patterns, and it is assumed that the average earner pays the average tax. This per capita approach focuses on overall earner-beneficiary transfers, abstracting temporarily from the ceiling on taxable earnings and variations in the relative position of different types of earners. Assumptions concerning growth of the system also introduce an element of arbitrariness into the analysis. However, it seems likely that almost any plausible growth assumptions provide a more realistic analytical basis than the static assumptions concerning taxes and benefits accepted reluctantly in previous studies. Similarly, it is believed that imputation to the employee of the employer tax paid in his name is preferable to ignoring its burden altogether. At this stage, however, the only imputation is at the aggregate level, since only average taxes and benefits per worker are being considered. If it is assumed that workers as a whole bear the entire tax, it follows that the *average* tax per worker must include the tax nominally assigned to employers, regardless of how it is distributed among workers.

The suggested model approximates certain features of the current and developing social security system and incorporates official data, such as SSA projections of population by age group and mortality rates by sex, resulting in a mixture of theoretical and empirical elements. It abstracts from many of the details of the present tax-benefit structure in an effort to focus on the key effects of the growth process. In addition to assuming growth patterns, the present analysis also departs from earlier work in stressing the criterion of the estimated yield to a particular type of participant on his "investment" in social security, instead of assuming specific rates of return.

The basic assumptions of this simple growth model are: (1) real earnings per employee grow at a fixed rate $r$; (2) real retirement benefits per beneficiary grow at the same rate $r$, and therefore are related to average earnings by a fixed factor $k$;[57] and (3) the system is financed

[56] This section reports the methodology developed to estimate the lifetime rates of return, and may be omitted by readers more interested in the findings than in their technical basis.

[57] Despite some irregularities, this is roughly the experience of the system in the 1940–64 interval. For example, when benefits began to be paid in 1940, the mean payment for a beneficiary and wife was about 43 percent of mean earnings of covered workers. In 1964 the ratio was 38 percent. The ratio lagged between 1940 and 1949 as coverage wid-

on a pay-as-you-go basis.[58] The particular trade-off between the tax rate and the taxable earnings ceiling to be used in raising the required tax is left unspecified at this stage. Nonretirement benefits and the taxes needed to raise them are both excluded from this model to avoid the bias produced by weighing old-age benefits alone against taxes raised for more general purposes.

The pay-as-you-go financing and the fixed benefit–earning ratio postulated for the model are intended to provide an approximate skeleton of the dynamic features of the actual detailed social security structure. They should permit a more meaningful analysis of the projected system than that possible with earnings, tax rates, and benefit rates held constant.

This preliminary framework abstracts completely from the detailed differentials in tax and benefit rates by income levels and family type and is concerned only with per capita taxes and per capita benefits. Let

$\bar{E}_t$ = average (mean) real earnings in year $t$

---

ened, then jumped to the 1964 level and remained relatively stable (Social Security Administration, *Social Security Bulletin, Annual Statistical Supplement, 1964*, pp. 27 and 29). The 1972 legislation enacted by Public Law 92-366 provided for no real increase in average benefits; the average is to be tied to the consumer price index. However, the automatic ceiling adjustment process also included can be expected to generate a surplus; thus legislated increases in real benefits seem likely. It should also be noted that the assumption concerning the growth rate of *average* benefits abstracts from the pattern at the individual level under the present system. Average benefits promised to each earner grow with the rise in his taxable earnings and with statutory increases; only the latter raise benefits after retirement. Thus the benefits of a newly retired worker tend to start out above the average level but lag behind the average in later years. Allowance for this time path would yield a somewhat higher estimate of the present value of the benefit stream upon retirement. However, this might well be offset by the higher tax estimate that would result from allowing for below-average earnings in early years and above-average earnings in later years.

[58] Some growth in the actual trust fund is foreseen by the SSA over and above the interest accumulated, but it is generally agreed that the system is far closer to a pay-as-you-go basis than a fully funded basis. In fact, the former chief actuary, Robert J. Myers, has interpreted the financing basis as unchanged from the beginning "insofar as general principles are concerned—namely, that full actuarial reserves are not developed; rather, over a long-range future period, the income is estimated to meet the outgo" (letter to David Lawrence reproduced in *The 1967 Economic Report of the President*, Hearings before the Joint Economic Committee, 90 Cong. 1 sess. [1967], Pt. 2, p. 354). As mentioned in note 57, the automatic adjustment features embodied in the 1972 legislation appear likely to generate a surplus; however, past experience suggests that such accumulations tend to lead to higher benefits so that pay-as-you-go may still be the approximate result.

$\bar{b}_t = k\bar{E}_t$ = average real benefit in year $t$ (where $k$ is fixed ratio of current $\bar{E}_t$ to $\bar{b}_t$)

$N_t$ = total earning (taxpaying) population

$R_t$ = total old-age beneficiary (largely retired) population

$\bar{T}_t$ = average real tax in year $t$ (including both employer and employee contributions).

Under assumptions of pay-as-you-go financing[59] and an exponential growth rate $r$ for $\bar{E}_t$,

$$(6\text{-}1) \qquad \bar{T}_t = \frac{k\bar{E}_t R_t}{N_t} = \frac{k\bar{E}_0(1+r)t_{R_t}}{N_t}.$$

Given $k$ and projections of $\bar{E}$, $R$, and $N$, the projected average tax can be obtained and accumulated along with imputed interest.

The present value of the average benefit stream beginning at sixty-five[60] may then be compared to the accumulated tax. Let

$\bar{b}_n$ = average benefit during the year at age $n$

$B$ = present value of the average benefit stream at age sixty-five

$P_n$ = probability of reaching age $n$ if one has reached sixty-five

$L$ = length of working career

$i$ = interest rate.

The discounted present value of the still-growing benefit stream is given by:

$$(6\text{-}2) \qquad B = \sum_{n=65}^{\infty} \frac{\bar{b}_{65}(1+r)^{n-65}}{(1+i)^{n-65}} \cdot P_n.$$

However, the first annual benefit at sixty-five is:

$$\bar{b}_{65} = k\bar{E}_0 (1+r)^L.$$

Therefore equation (6-2) may be rewritten as:

$$(6\text{-}3) \qquad B = k\bar{E}_0 \sum_{n=65}^{\infty} \frac{(1+r)^{L+n-65}}{(1+i)^{n-65}} \cdot P_n.$$

---

[59] As pointed out earlier, this approximated well the history of the system until recent years, when surpluses have piled up. A continuation of the latter approach would require revision of the model.

[60] Estimates are given for this typical retirement age only, although the SSA puts the average retirement age at sixty-seven. This avoids the complexities of the "earnings test" but qualifies the results, since later retirement leads to more taxes and less benefits. On the other hand, it seems likely that the standard retirement age will eventually be lowered, so that sixty-five may be a plausible compromise.

It is apparent from equation (6-1) that the accumulated tax must be directly proportional to (a multiple of) $k\bar{E}_0$ which is the average benefit in the initial year. Since equation (6-3) shows this to be true also of the present value of benefits at retirement, the initial benefit factor cancels out in computation of the tax–benefit ratio; since the latter is therefore independent of the initial benefit, the accumulated tax can be stated generally as a multiple of the starting benefit level, and no estimate is needed of the latter. Under the assumptions of the model, the ratio of the accumulated average tax to the present value of average benefits at age sixty-five depends only on the assumed values of the growth rate, the interest rate, the type of demographic projections (including $P_n$), and the length of the working career $L$.

The values of $P_n$ to be used in equation (6-3) for single men and single women are derived directly from the official projected mortality rates for males and females. However, the probabilities to be used in evaluating the benefit stream of a couple (eligible for wife's benefits) are compound probabilities involving the mortality rates of both sexes.[61] This evaluation necessitated special treatment requiring for the first time certain assumptions about the internal benefit structure.

First, consider such a couple with a given starting benefit. (Allowance is ultimately made for the fact that on the average couples have higher starting benefits than single earners.) Assume that upon the death of a wife a widower's benefits become two-thirds of the level originally received by the couple and that a widow's benefits are 82.5 percent of two-thirds, or 55 percent, as under the present law. Then the present value becomes the sum of three components—benefits as a couple and potential benefits as widower and as widow. With the probability of living from sixty-five to age $n$ denoted as $P_{nm}$ and $P_{nf}$ for men and women, respectively, the present value of the stream received as a couple is obtained by replacing $P_n$ in equation (6-3) by $P_{nm}P_{nf}$. The potential stream in the widower status is evaluated by replacing $P_n$ by $P_{nm}(1 - P_{nf})$ and multiplying by two-thirds. For the widow status, the probability term is $(1 - P_{nm})P_{nf}$ and the multiplier is 55 percent.

---

[61] These three beneficiary types are special cases intended to be illustrative only. It seems likely that they will have some relevance to the more complex tax-benefit relationships for working couples whose partners had working careers of varying lengths.

# CHAPTER VII

# Sensitivity to Changes in Earnings and Tax Structure

THE REDISTRIBUTIVE and macroeconomic effects of the payroll tax arise from both "built-in" and policy determinants of its yield. The responsiveness of the tax yield to these stimuli is heavily influenced by the ceiling on taxable earnings, although the statutory rate is uniform. With the ceiling, the earnings distribution determines the effective rate of taxation as well as the degree of regressivity.

The position of the ceiling in the earnings distribution determines the built-in response of the tax yield to changes in aggregate earnings, as well as the response of tax yield to changes in rates and in the ceiling itself. These relationships must be clarified in order to show the impact of the payroll tax structure on cyclical, long-run, and seasonal movements of economic aggregates. Statistical estimates of the general relationship between the tax base and tax yield on the one hand and earnings on the other are presented in this chapter. The generalizations arrived at here are supplemented in Chapter VIII by a more specific appraisal of the role of the tax in postwar economic fluctuations and growth.

The first objective of the estimated relationships outlined is to facilitate an evaluation of the role of the payroll tax in offsetting changes in earnings—its "built-in flexibility." This entails estimation of the extent to which automatic variation of the tax yield (at a given rate and ceiling) tends to offset the indirect effects on incomes of autonomous changes in spending. This facilitates appraisal of the counter-cyclical cushioning of any decline in earnings by a decline in the tax, as well as by the restraint exercised during earnings upswings. Also important is the resistance to long-run growth or decline through automatic variation in the tax yield. It is shown here that payroll taxes have relatively low built-in flexibility, because of low and uniform statutory rates and the dampening effect of the ceiling on taxable earnings.

## Measures of Responsiveness of Taxes to Earnings Changes

The performance of a tax as an automatic stabilizer of real output and prices is measured by the extent to which the presence of the tax reduces a change in real output and prices brought about by a change in autonomous demand.[1] For example, in a time of unemployed resources, an increase in autonomous demand such as military expenditures will generate an increase in production, factor incomes paid out in the course of production, and therefore in consumer demand. Through the multiplier process, this new demand generates further rounds of increases in real output, consumer demand, and prices. Measures of the automatic stabilization power of a tax have been devised to evaluate its dampening impact on these indirect effects of the original autonomous change in demand.

The sensitivity of tax yield to marginal income changes may be best analyzed in terms of two aggregative measures. In the case of the payroll tax, these are the marginal tax rate on earnings in covered employment and the elasticity of the tax with respect to the same earnings base.[2] The first is often taken to be the definition of built-in flexibility; it indicates the absolute change in tax associated with a dollar change in aggregate earnings. The second measures the percentage change in tax associated with a 1 percent change in earnings.

[1] For discussion of this methodological framework, see E. Cary Brown, "The Static Theory of Automatic Fiscal Stabilization," *Journal of Political Economy*, Vol. 63 (October 1955), pp. 427–40.

[2] For many purposes the marginal rate and elasticity may also be measured in relation to a broader base such as the gross national product.

*Marginal Payroll Tax Rate*

The higher the marginal payroll tax rate, the lower the after-tax income generated at each stage of the multiplier process. The tax therefore reduces the effective propensity to consume out of national income, reduces the multiplier, and works toward economic stability. This can be illustrated formally by a linear model of income determination. The aggregate payroll tax $T$ depends on national income $Y$ according to:

$$T = a + mY$$

where $m$ is the marginal tax rate. The consumption function is:

$$C = C_0 + b(Y - a - mY).$$

Private investment and government expenditures are autonomous variables $\bar{I}$ and $\bar{G}$; an accounting identity completes the system:

$$Y = C + \bar{I} + \bar{G}.$$

Combining the second and third equations leads to the equilibrium solution:

$$Y = \frac{C_0 - ab + \bar{I} + \bar{G}}{1 - b(1 - m)}.$$

The multiplier $1/[1 - b(1 - m)]$ shows the role of the marginal payroll tax rate in dampening the ultimate effect on $Y$ of autonomous changes in $\bar{I}$ and $\bar{G}$. The higher the marginal rate $m$, the lower the multiplier. For example, if the marginal propensity to consume out of income after payroll taxes were 0.75, a marginal payroll tax rate of 5 percent would cut the multiplier from 4 to about 3.5; a marginal rate of 10 percent would reduce the effective multiplier to 3.1.[3]

These illustrations are intended to show the direction of the relationship only. However, it should be added that the assumption of a fixed marginal rate $m$ exaggerates the stabilization impact of the payroll tax. Because of the ceiling the tax is regressive, and $m$ is a declining function of aggregate income. As incomes rise, the fraction taxable declines, and the net result is that disposable income and consumption are stabilized even less than they would have been under a fixed marginal rate. Similarly, if incomes fall, the ensuing increase in the mar-

---

[3] In this illustration the marginal propensity to consume is put at a rather low level to reflect the impact of other taxes, in addition to savings.

ginal rate also counteracts part of the decline in taxes resulting from the lower earnings base.

The marginal rate criterion for appraising stabilization properties has one advantage over the relative response measure represented by the tax elasticity. The marginal rate is a direct indicator of the absolute size of the tax offset and is a better basis for comparison of the stabilizing power of different taxes, particularly if measured with respect to an aggregate such as the gross national product (GNP) or national income.[4] However, the marginal rate tells nothing about the mix of real output and price effects, which depends on the degree of slack in the economy at the time of the autonomous change in demand. The greater the slack, the more the stabilizer tends to resist changes in production rather than changes in prices. The elasticity criterion does not separate these components either, but it carries an important implication for the alternative mixes of real and money income changes.

*Elasticity Criterion*

At one extreme, assume an autonomous increase in spending causes no price change, as might be the case in a period of underutilized resources. Any tax elasticity greater than zero would at least partially offset the rise in real income. However, in the case of a spending increase leading to price and money income increases and no rise in real incomes, the elasticity criterion carries a quite different and important message. If the tax elasticity were unity in this case of pure inflation, the yield would rise by the same percentage as incomes and prices, with no change in the tax in real terms. Thus the tax would be neutral with respect to prices, exercising no restraint against inflation. An elasticity greater than unity, as under the progressive individual income tax, would lead to a percentage increase in the tax greater than the increase in incomes and prices. The real value of the tax would increase, depressing real disposable income and exerting a restraining influence on prices; such a tax would assist in price stabilization.

On the other hand, in this pure inflation a tax with elasticity below unity, such as the regressive payroll tax, would rise by a smaller per-

---

[4] A high elasticity does not necessarily mean that the tax is an important stabilizer; a heavy tax with low elasticity may be a stronger stabilizer than a small tax with high elasticity. See Richard Goode, *The Individual Income Tax* (Brookings Institution, 1964), pp. 287–88.

centage than incomes and prices, thereby falling in real terms. The resulting rise in disposable income and consumption would further aggravate the problem of price instability. In this sense such a tax would have a destabilizing impact on prices and would promote further inflation.[5]

Since it will be shown that the payroll tax has an elasticity less than unity, this latter case is of special importance. Although the inflation of the 1960s has been accompanied by some increases in real output, there have been periods in which the inflation was virtually pure. For example, the GNP deflator rose about 4 percent between the first and fourth quarters of 1969, while real GNP advanced less than 1 percent. In a situation like this, it is apparent that the structure of the regressive payroll tax may be aggravating the inflation problem.

To facilitate empirical evaluation of the stabilizing and destabilizing impact of the payroll tax, marginal rates and elasticities are analyzed by means of earnings distribution data and a time series regression model, respectively.

## Tax Yield and Earnings Distribution

### Derivation of the Yield-Earnings Relationship[6]

One approach to analysis of the automatic response of tax yields to income changes is to relate yearly changes in yield to yearly changes in income. However, relationships thus obtained vary with the size of the finite increments and mix the effects of changes in numbers of incomes and the tax structure with the net effect of income change— the primary objective of the inquiry. One way to isolate the effect of income change (and to determine the ceteris paribus response) is to analyze the impact of a very small income change of a fixed percentage

---

[5] It may seem surprising that a tax that increases in money value as spending rises can in any sense be viewed as a destabilizer. However, in the special context discussed, disposable income in money terms rises by a greater percentage than the autonomous spending increase, and this could not be true without the tax. In practice, any destabilizer is likely to be swamped by increases in rates or ceiling, but a further qualification should be mentioned. Insofar as the wage rate rises faster than the price level, as it sometimes does in the U.S. case, a tax with elasticity less than unity could be a stabilizer. even in the context discussed.

[6] This subsection reports derivation of the theoretical relationship between yield and the earnings distribution in the presence of a ceiling. It may be omitted by readers more interested in the findings than in their analytical basis.

on a given income distribution under a given rate structure. For the special case of the payroll tax, relationships are derived here yielding unique marginal response ratios that are virtually exact (subject only to errors in the data).[7]

The role of the ceiling and shape of the earnings distribution in determining the tax base and yield are considered first in formal terms.

Let

$w$ = level of individual earnings

$F(w)$ = number of earners with earnings less than $w$

$F_c$ = number of earners with earnings below the ceiling

$F_n$ = total number of earners

$w_c$ = ceiling on individual taxable earnings.

Consider also the following components of total earnings:

$A_c$ = aggregate earnings of earners below the ceiling

$A_h$ = taxable earnings of earners above the ceiling

$A_u$ = nontaxable earnings of earners above the ceiling

$A_n = A_c + A_h + A_u$ = total earnings

$A_t = A_c + A_h$ = taxable earnings.

The initial "less-than" cumulative frequency distribution function may be represented by the solid curve in Figure 7-1. The number of individuals with annual earnings below the ceiling $w_c$ is $F_c$. The cumulative aggregate earnings received by these earners is represented by the area $A_c$.[8] However, aggregate taxable earnings $A_t$ is given by the sum of the area $A_c$ and the area of the rectangle above it: $A_h = (F_n - F_c)w_c$. The area labeled $A_u$ represents aggregate nontaxable earnings.

Analysis of the yield, stabilization, and fiscal drag properties of the tax requires estimation of relationships between two aggregates—the tax base or taxable earnings $A_t$ and total earnings $A_n$ (the sum of $A_c$, $A_h$, and $A_u$). In addition to the fraction taxable $A_t/A_n$, the rela-

---

[7] The practical validity of these uniquely determined marginal rates and elasticities depends, of course, on the reality of the assumption that all incomes change at the same rate.

[8] Expressed analytically, aggregate earnings of this group is given by:

$$A_c = \int_0^{w_c} w\,dF.$$

## FIGURE 7-1. Effect on Tax Base of Increase in Average Earnings[a]

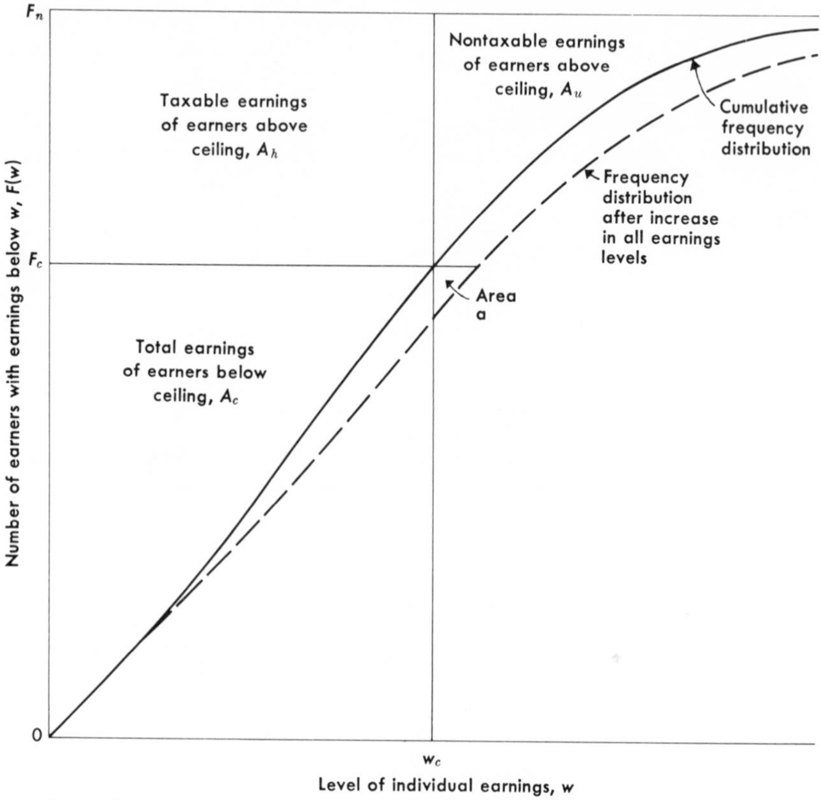

Area labels in figure:

$F_n$

Number of earners with earnings below $w$, $F(w)$

$F_c$

Nontaxable earnings
of earners above
ceiling, $A_u$

Taxable earnings
of earners above
ceiling, $A_h$

Cumulative
frequency
distribution

Frequency
distribution
after increase
in all earnings
levels

Area
$a$

Total earnings
of earners below
ceiling, $A_c$

0

$w_c$

Level of individual earnings, $w$

[a] See text for explanation of symbols.

tionships needed are "built-in flexibility" of the tax base defined as $\partial A_t / \partial A_n$,[9] and the elasticity of $A_t$ with respect to $A_n$ designated $EA_t / EA_n$. If equal percentage changes at all income levels are assumed,[10] these may be derived exactly from the published distributions.

Let all individual earnings levels increase by the same fraction $r$; the new cumulative frequency distribution may be represented by the

[9] Since the tax is at a flat rate applied to the base $A_t$, the built-in flexibility of the tax itself is $t\partial A_t / \partial A_n$, where $t$ is the statutory rate. The elasticity of the tax is the same as for the tax base.

[10] The stability of the inequality measures over time demonstrated in Chapter IV supports the validity of this assumption.

broken curve in Figure 7-1. It can be shown that built-in flexibility is given by:

(7-1) $\quad \dfrac{\partial A_t}{\partial A_n} = \dfrac{A_c}{A_n} = \dfrac{\text{earnings of earners below ceiling}}{\text{total earnings.}}$

This definition is obtained as a limit of the appropriate ratio as the specified rate of earnings increase $r$ approaches zero.[11] The elasticity of taxable earnings with respect to total earnings is then obtainable by definition:

(7-2) $\quad \dfrac{EA_t}{EA_n} = \dfrac{\partial A_t}{\partial A_n} \Big/ \dfrac{A_t}{A_n} = \dfrac{A_c}{A_t} = \dfrac{\text{earnings of earners below ceiling}}{\text{taxable earnings}}.$

Thus all three measures (elasticity, marginal rate, and fraction taxable) of the ceteris paribus marginal response of the tax base to income changes are related by the definition of elasticity and can be derived precisely and uniquely from earnings distribution data.

### *Response Relationships: Empirical Results*

Unpublished old-age, survivors, disability, and health insurance (OASDHI) earnings data supplied by the Social Security Administration (SSA) were used to derive the relationships for 1964 and 1969 presented in Table 7-1. Data for these two years are given to demonstrate the effect on yield responsiveness of an increase in the ceiling relative to mean earnings. The estimates in the table demonstrate the

---

[11] The increase in taxable income $\Delta A_t$ may be approximated by $rA_c$, since the ceiling is unchanged. However, this is an overestimate by the amount represented by the area $a$ in Figure 7-1. Therefore,

$$\frac{\Delta A_t}{\Delta A_n} = \frac{rA_c - a}{rA_n}.$$

The first partial derivative is defined by

$$\frac{\partial A_t}{\partial A_n} = r \xrightarrow{\lim} 0 \, \frac{rA_c - a}{rA_n} = r \xrightarrow{\lim} 0 \, \frac{A_c - \dfrac{a}{r}}{A_n}.$$

The quantity $a$ may be approximated by the area of a triangle:

$$a \cong \frac{rw_c[F(w_c + rw_c) - F(w_c)]}{2}.$$

On the basis of this approximation, $a/r$ approaches zero as $r$ approaches zero, and $\partial A_t / \partial A_n = A_c / A_n$.

**TABLE 7-1. Marginal Response of Taxable Earnings under Social Security to Changes in Total Earnings under Various Hypothetical Ceilings, 1964 and 1969**

| Hypothetical ceiling (dollars) | Nontaxable earnings (billions of dollars) | Earnings of earners below ceiling (billions of dollars) | Fraction taxable, $\dfrac{A_t}{A_n}$ | Marginal rate, $\dfrac{\partial A_t}{\partial A_n} = \dfrac{A_c}{A_n}$ | Elasticity, $\dfrac{EA_t}{EA_n} = \dfrac{A_c}{A_t}$ |
|---|---|---|---|---|---|
| | | | 1964 | | |
| 0 | 325.17[a] | 0.00 | 0.000 | 0.000 | 0.000 |
| 3,000 | 155.52 | 45.18 | 0.522 | 0.139 | 0.266 |
| 3,600 | 132.31 | 62.97 | 0.593 | 0.194 | 0.326 |
| 4,200 | 112.19 | 81.94 | 0.655 | 0.252 | 0.385 |
| 4,800[b] | 94.86 | 102.05 | 0.708 | 0.314 | 0.443 |
| 6,600 | 57.67 | 168.10 | 0.823 | 0.517 | 0.628 |
| 7,800 | 42.97 | 205.14 | 0.868 | 0.631 | 0.727 |
| 9,000 | 33.19 | 231.86 | 0.898 | 0.713 | 0.794 |
| 12,000 | 19.72 | 269.93 | 0.939 | 0.830 | 0.884 |
| 15,000 | 13.26 | 288.36 | 0.959 | 0.887 | 0.924 |
| None | 0.00 | 325.17 | 1.000 | 1.000 | 1.000 |
| | | | 1969 | | |
| 0 | 502.64[a] | 0.00 | 0.000 | 0.000 | 0.000 |
| 3,000 | 288.45 | 45.11 | 0.426 | 0.090 | 0.211 |
| 3,600 | 256.21 | 61.75 | 0.490 | 0.123 | 0.251 |
| 4,200 | 227.00 | 81.35 | 0.548 | 0.162 | 0.295 |
| 4,800 | 200.73 | 102.76 | 0.601 | 0.204 | 0.340 |
| 6,600 | 137.64 | 172.28 | 0.726 | 0.343 | 0.472 |
| 7,800[b] | 106.89 | 221.81 | 0.787 | 0.441 | 0.560 |
| 9,000 | 84.19 | 276.07 | 0.832 | 0.549 | 0.660 |
| 12,000 | 52.22 | 366.42 | 0.896 | 0.729 | 0.814 |
| 15,000 | 36.82 | 410.02 | 0.927 | 0.816 | 0.880 |
| None | 0.00 | 502.64 | 1.000 | 1.000 | 1.000 |

Source: The first three columns are derived from unpublished data supplied by the Social Security Administration, April 1971; see previous subsection for derivation of the other columns.
[a] Aggregate earnings.
[b] Actual ceiling.

extent to which the existence of a relatively low ceiling blunts the impact of earnings changes on the tax base, and therefore on the tax yield. The three measures of tax base response approach zero (by definition) as the relative ceiling approaches zero, and they approach unity asymptotically as the ceiling increases without bound.[12] At the $4,800 ceiling prevailing in 1964, about 71 percent of covered earnings

---

[12] Plots of the three measures against the relative ceiling are virtually the same for each year, indicating a high degree of stability in the shape of the distribution of earnings.

were taxable, but the measures usually stressed in analysis of the response of taxes to income changes were much lower. The estimate of the marginal rate or built-in flexibility of taxable income obtained from relation (7-1) indicates that the earnings tax base would have changed only about $314 million with any $1 billion across-the-board change in aggregate 1964 earnings. (This interpretation depends on the continuing assumption that earnings at all levels experience a uniform relative change.) The elasticity criterion, derived from relation (7-2), indicates a 0.44 percent change in the tax base associated with a 1 percent change in earnings. The marginal rate and elasticity for the OASDHI tax base in 1969 were higher at 0.441 and 0.560 respectively due to the increase in the relative ceiling, $w_c/w$, from 1.14 to 1.44. However, they remained far below the response ratios of the taxable base under the individual income tax.[13]

The depressing effect of a lagging ceiling on the responsiveness of the tax base to income changes is strikingly illustrated by the case of the unemployment insurance (UI) tax ceiling, which remained fixed at $3,000 in most states from 1939 through 1971.[14] By 1969 this ceiling had dropped relatively to about 55 percent of mean earnings ($5,416). On the crude assumption that the relative distribution of income covered under UI is the same as that of OASDHI incomes, Table 7-1 suggests that the UI tax base of 1969 would have changed by only about 9 cents for each dollar change in income covered by UI; the corresponding elasticity was about 21 percent in 1969. The 9 percent figure is strong evidence of the feebleness of the UI tax as a stabilizer.[15]

In the case of OASDHI, the ceiling has tended to keep up with earnings growth in the postwar period, despite temporary lags, and no pronounced trend in the response ratios is evident since 1950. On the other hand those for UI have declined steadily under the fixed ceiling. These patterns are illustrated in Table 7-2. Both tax bases were at their peak sensitivity in 1938 when the $3,000 ceiling for each tax yielded a relative ceiling never to be equaled again. Since 1951 the built-in flexibility measures for the OASDHI tax base have fluc-

[13] Earlier estimates of the response ratios for the income tax base have been close to unity. Due to the progressive rate structure the response ratios for the income tax yield are considerably higher. This comparison is made in greater detail later in this chapter.

[14] In 1972 this ceiling was increased to $4,200 in most states, thereby increasing the response ratios.

[15] This conclusion pertains only to the tax side; UI benefits undoubtedly have a significant counter-cyclical effect.

tuated between 0.30 and 0.45,[16] while elasticity hovered between 0.41 and 0.56. The rough UI estimates show a steady decline in the built-in flexibility measure from the prewar figure of 0.85 to 0.09 in 1969 and a corresponding decline in elasticity. These figures underscore the close dependence of flexibility in the tax on the position of the ceiling in the earnings distribution.

*Flexibility of the Tax Yield*

Probably the most generally useful measure of the degree of automatic stabilization is the built-in flexibility of the tax yield itself—the marginal rate of taxation with respect to covered earnings or with respect to some broader income variant such as the GNP.[17] Estimates of marginal rates with respect to covered earnings were obtained as the product of marginal rates of tax base response in Table 7-2 and statutory tax rates weighted by the wages and salaries and self-employed components.[18] The results (Table 7-3) show low sensitivity of the tax yield to income changes due to low rates as well as the ceiling. The sensitivity of the OASDHI tax to earnings increases climbed after 1950 each time that statutory rates rose; the responsiveness of the UI tax declined as the relative ceiling fell under relatively stable rates on taxable earnings. The built-in flexibility of the taxes in combination rose from 1.79 percent in 1951 to 4.25 percent in 1969 with some minor fluctuations in between.

The elasticities of the tax yield are identical to those for the tax base in Table 7-2. While the UI tax elasticity declined steadily to a low of 21 percent in 1969, the OASDHI elasticity neared its postwar high that year at 55 percent. However, as indicated at the beginning of this chapter, with an elasticity still well below unity the OASDHI tax remains subject to the criticism that it would encourage price increases in a period of nearly pure inflation.

[16] It is interesting to compare these estimates with those based on first differences. The ratios of the change in taxable earnings to the change in total earnings $\Delta A_t / \Delta A_n$ for 1959–63 were 0.46, 0.62, 0.50, 0.49, 0.52, respectively, in those five years of a fixed ceiling, a period in which the marginal rate of taxable earnings fell from 0.42 to 0.34. The widening gap between the two estimates was apparently due to the changing population covered. It could be explained by relatively low incomes for newcomers compared to those already covered or leaving coverage.

[17] Estimates are presented for built-in flexibility only, since the elasticities of the tax base and tax yield are identical under a uniform tax rate.

[18] The response to changes in GNP is discussed later in this chapter.

**TABLE 7-2. Responsiveness of Taxable Earnings under Social Security and Unemployment Insurance to Total Earnings under Statutory Ceiling, 1938 and 1951–69**

| Year | Statutory ceiling (dollars) | Ratio of ceiling to mean earnings | Social security payroll tax | | | Unemployment insurance tax[a] | | |
|---|---|---|---|---|---|---|---|---|
| | | | Fraction taxable | Marginal rate | Elasticity | Fraction taxable | Marginal rate | Elasticity |
| 1938 | 3,000 | 3.282 | 0.955 | 0.854 | 0.894 | 0.955 | 0.854 | 0.894 |
| 1951 | 3,600 | 1.400 | 0.811 | 0.453 | 0.558 | 0.727 | 0.332 | 0.457 |
| 1952 | 3,600 | 1.327 | 0.800 | 0.413 | 0.516 | 0.711 | 0.299 | 0.421 |
| 1953 | 3,600 | 1.251 | 0.781 | 0.371 | 0.475 | 0.687 | 0.266 | 0.388 |
| 1954 | 3,600 | 1.235 | 0.775 | 0.365 | 0.471 | 0.681 | 0.262 | 0.384 |
| 1955 | 4,200 | 1.412 | 0.818 | 0.439 | 0.536 | 0.667 | 0.247 | 0.371 |
| 1956 | 4,200 | 1.301 | 0.786 | 0.396 | 0.504 | 0.633 | 0.222 | 0.351 |
| 1957 | 4,200 | 1.271 | 0.778 | 0.381 | 0.489 | 0.623 | 0.215 | 0.344 |
| 1958 | 4,200 | 1.244 | 0.767 | 0.368 | 0.480 | 0.612 | 0.208 | 0.340 |
| 1959 | 4,800 | 1.349 | 0.793 | 0.415 | 0.523 | 0.589 | 0.186 | 0.316 |
| 1960 | 4,800 | 1.309 | 0.780 | 0.393 | 0.504 | 0.575 | 0.177 | 0.309 |
| 1961 | 4,800 | 1.288 | 0.777 | 0.380 | 0.490 | 0.569 | 0.174 | 0.305 |
| 1962 | 4,800 | 1.230 | 0.760 | 0.354 | 0.466 | 0.551 | 0.161 | 0.293 |
| 1963 | 4,800 | 1.194 | 0.747 | 0.336 | 0.450 | 0.538 | 0.152 | 0.282 |
| 1964 | 4,800 | 1.144 | 0.732 | 0.314 | 0.428 | 0.522 | 0.139 | 0.266 |
| 1965 | 4,800 | 1.113 | 0.722 | 0.295 | 0.409 | 0.509 | 0.130 | 0.255 |
| 1966 | 6,600 | 1.423 | 0.796 | 0.434 | 0.545 | 0.479 | 0.118 | 0.246 |
| 1967 | 6,600 | 1.364 | 0.783 | 0.411 | 0.525 | 0.464 | 0.109 | 0.235 |
| 1968 | 7,800 | 1.519 | 0.818 | 0.425[b] | 0.519[b] | 0.444 | 0.098 | 0.221 |
| 1969 | 7,800 | 1.440 | 0.804 | 0.441 | 0.549 | 0.426 | 0.090 | 0.211 |

Sources: Ceiling, relevant statutes; other figures derived from unpublished data supplied by the Social Security Administration, April 1971.

a. These are rough estimates, which assume a fixed ceiling of $3,000 and the same earnings distribution as that under OASDHI. Official estimates (available for the fraction taxable only) indicate that the present rough method is remarkably accurate.

b. These estimates are suspect, because it was to be expected that the postwar high in the relative ceiling reached in 1968 would produce peaks in these estimates as well. A review of the data supplied by the Social Security Administration indicates a small error in the data for 1968; the estimates for that year are therefore, less reliable.

**TABLE 7-3. Long-run Marginal Rates of Payroll Tax Yields with Respect to Covered Earnings, 1938 and 1951–69**

*(In percent)*

| Year | Social security payroll tax | Unemployment insurance tax | Both taxes |
|------|------|------|------|
| 1938 | 1.71 | n.a. | n.a. |
| 1951 | 1.36 | 0.53 | 1.79 |
| 1952 | 1.21 | 0.43 | 1.56 |
| 1953 | 1.09 | 0.35 | 1.37 |
| 1954 | 1.40 | 0.29 | 1.63 |
| 1955 | 1.72 | 0.30 | 1.97 |
| 1956 | 1.54 | 0.29 | 1.78 |
| 1957 | 1.65 | 0.28 | 1.87 |
| 1958 | 1.61 | 0.27 | 1.82 |
| 1959 | 2.00 | 0.32 | 2.25 |
| 1960 | 2.26 | 0.39 | 2.53 |
| 1961 | 2.22 | 0.37 | 2.51 |
| 1962 | 2.15 | 0.34 | 2.46 |
| 1963 | 2.35 | 0.35 | 2.63 |
| 1964 | 2.22 | 0 31 | 2.47 |
| 1965 | 2.09 | 0.27 | 2.30 |
| 1966 | 3.51 | 0.22 | 3.68 |
| 1967 | 3.51 | 0.17 | 3.64 |
| 1968 | 3.64 | 0.15 | 3.76 |
| 1969 | 4.15 | 0.13 | 4.25 |

Sources: Social security tax estimate is product of marginal rate in Table 7-2 and weighted average of wages and salaries and self-employed statutory rates; unemployment insurance (UI) tax estimate is the product of the marginal rate in Table 7-2 and the average rate of tax on taxable earnings (see Appendix C). The measure for both taxes is the sum of the social security marginal rate and the UI rate, adjusted for a lower degree of coverage by UI. The combined rate of response of the two taxes is measured with respect to the larger earnings base—that for social security.

n.a. Not available.

## Application of a Tax Yield Function

In the last section (tax yield and earnings distribution) the emphasis was on the marginal response of payroll tax yield to specified changes in earnings and the tax structure. The approach was applicable to any given tabulated earnings distribution. It is useful also to generalize these relationships by means of a time series regression model. Such a model goes further than the marginal analysis of the earlier approach. It can provide estimates of the response of the tax yield to large, extra-marginal changes in earnings and the tax structure. Thus it is used in Chapter VIII to estimate yield increases resulting from changes in the tax structure. Such a tax function is useful for the revenue estimation required for evaluation of the economic impact of any given budget. A tax equation can also be used to separate built-in and discretionary changes in taxes and to compare the long-run restraint of alternative taxes on aggregate demand. The fitted model can be used within large econometric systems to simulate the effects of policy instruments. Finally, a payroll tax equation will provide a check on estimated marginal rates and elasticities of the preceding section.[19]

The approach to be taken here is aggregative.[20] It utilizes annual data and depends for its validity on adequate stability of the shape of the earnings distribution over time. This requirement appears to be well satisfied on the basis of the estimates in Chapter IV, which attest to substantial stability of the degree of inequality since World War II. Although the slight pretax upward trend in inequality was shown to be statistically significant, the inequality measures were relatively stable in absolute terms.

## OASDHI Tax Functions

The primary variables to be related in the tax function and the official data sources—U.S. Office of Business Economics (OBE) and Social Security Administration (SSA)[21]—are:

$OA$ = total payroll tax for OASDHI (OBE)

$R_{OA}$ = weighted average statutory tax rate (SSA)

$W$ = total earnings of wage and salary earners and self-employed (OBE)

$W_{OA}$ = total earnings in covered employment (SSA)

$W_t$ = total taxable earnings (SSA)

$E_{OA}$ = number of taxed earners (SSA)

---

[19] The analysis of the preceding section is given general support by the detailed alternative analysis of this section; however, the material in this section may be omitted without loss of continuity by readers interested only in the general findings.

[20] Data for wage earners and self-employed are combined; although separate relations were estimated for the two groups at earlier stages, not enough information was added to merit separating them. The unemployment insurance tax was not analyzed because it is relatively small and (because of its low ceiling) far less sensitive to earnings changes. A more complex model would be needed to analyze the feedback to tax rates through experience rating, under which the employer's tax varies with his employment record.

[21] The data sources are listed in Appendix F.

$w_c$ = ceiling on individual taxable earnings (SSA)

$f_c = W_{OA}/W$ = fraction of earnings covered

$f_t = W_t/W_{OA}$ = fraction of covered earnings taxable.

The models may be derived from an approximate identity:

(7-3)                               $$OA = R_{OA} f_t f_c W.$$

Starting from the right end of this expression, the chain of multiplications leads successively from total earnings (OBE) to covered earnings to taxable earnings to the tax rate to the tax. It is not an exact identity for several reasons. First, the amount of the annual tax as reported by OBE is not precisely consistent with SSA data.[22] Second, the weighted average tax rate, which is based on statutory rates, would not necessarily provide an exact link between taxable earnings and the actual tax, even if the latter were the SSA variant. Finally, for the measured fraction taxable, $f_t$, a functional approximation will be substituted to permit isolation of the role of the ceiling.

The earnings variables and $f_t$ require further clarification. For any given year the tax data for wages and salaries in the OBE series are on a current basis, but the tax on self-employed incomes is lagged one year. Since the OBE tax series represents a hybrid summation of these current and lagged series, the tax rate $R_{OA}$ was constructed to partially allow for this.[23] The fraction taxable $f_t$ was assumed to depend on the ratio of the ceiling $w_c$ to average earnings in covered employment ($\bar{w} = W_{OA}/E_{OA}$). The fraction taxable is zero when the ceiling is zero, and it increases at a decreasing rate with $w_c/\bar{w}$, approaching unity asymptotically. A logarithmic transformation facilitates incorporation of the relationship into equation (7-3). Suppose that a quadratic relationship is adequate in the range of observations:

(7-4)          $\log f_t = c + d_1 \log w_c/\bar{w} + d_2 (\log w_c/\bar{w})^2 + u.$

[22] The OBE tax $OA$ and total earnings base $W$, rather than SSA data, were used in the model to facilitate potential simulation within large models using OBE data. (If revenue estimation were the primary objective, it might be better to explain SSA tax receipts, and there would be no reason to represent $W_{OA}$ by $f_c W$ in the approximate identity.) The OBE tax differs slightly from the SSA figure, mainly because the former is primarily on an accrual basis rather than on a payments basis.

[23] The combined tax rate $R_{OA}$ is a weighted average of the current and lagged statutory rates of the two sectors, the weights being covered current wages and salaries and covered lagged self-employment income, respectively. This only partially removes the inconsistencies, however. The model uses the current ceiling in explaining the total tax, even though the self-employed portion of the tax is lagged. This difficulty is avoided in the last model to be discussed, where only SSA data are used.

By introducing a multiplicative coefficient, exponential coefficients for all variables in equation (7-3) except $f_t$, and the logarithmic transformation, we derive the linear model:

(7-5) $\quad \log OA = a + b_1 \log R_{OA} + b_2 \log f_t + b_3 \log f_c + b_4 \log W + v.$

Combining equations (7-4) and (7-5) leads to a linear model in which the role of the ceiling is made explicit:

(7-6) $\quad \log OA = (a + b_2c) + b_1 \log R_{OA} + b_2d_1 \log w_c/\bar{w} + b_2d_2(\log w_c/\bar{w})^2$
$$+ b_3 \log f_c + b_4 \log W + (u + v).$$

Since the model is linear in the logarithms, the coefficient for each variable is the estimated tax elasticity with respect to that variable. Estimates of the coefficients $b_1$ and $b_4$ are expected to be close to unity, but for pragmatic reasons they are not constrained to that level. The first objective is to link the OBE payroll tax and OBE total wage variables. Coefficients $b_1$ and $b_4$ are allowed to depart from unity in order to accommodate the inconsistencies between the SSA and OBE variables they link.

The coefficients $d_1$ and $d_2$ are of special interest because they provide the best estimate of the slope and curvature of the $f_t$ function within the framework of the overall tax function. Coefficients $d_1$ and $d_2$ are expected to be positive and negative, respectively, in conformity with the slope and curvature of the $f_t$ function previously sketched.

The coefficient of the variable $f_c$ (the fraction of earnings covered) depends on the earnings level and distribution of newly covered earners relative to the earnings structure of those already covered. For example, a coefficient (tax elasticity) of less than unity would indicate that new contributors in the program tended to have earnings higher than those of long-time contributors. This interpretation of the model presumes that the relative ceiling $w_c/\bar{w}$, along with other variables, is held constant. If the tax yield rises by a smaller percentage than the fraction of all wages and salaries in covered employment, this rise must be due to higher average incomes among the new arrivals and therefore a greater fraction of earnings shielded by the ceiling.[24]

[24] The structure of the regression model is not completely satisfactory in this respect. For example, a *relative* ceiling held constant in the context of the entry of high earners implies an upward adjustment of the ceiling and increased taxation of previously covered earners. Even so, a tax elasticity below unity with respect to the fraction covered would clearly mean that the high fraction of the newly covered income shielded by the ceiling more than offsets the increased tax on other incomes.

Three variants of equation (7-6) were also estimated. First, the tax function was placed on an SSA earnings base by substituting $W_{OA}$ for variables $f_c$ and $W$. Second, an alternative revision of equation (7-6) partially finessed the inconsistency between the OBE tax data and SSA earnings data; the link by means of the average tax rate between the taxable earnings base and the OBE tax was eliminated in favor of a model explaining the taxable earnings base itself. Finally, this model explaining SSA taxable earnings was itself placed on an SSA earnings base by replacing $f_c$ and $W$ by $W_{OA}$ and relying on SSA data alone. These three variants of equation (7-6) can be stated in terms of their revision of the latter:

(7-7)                           $f_c$ and $W$ replaced by $W_{OA}$;

(7-8)                           $R_{OA}$ removed and $OA$ replaced by $W_t$;

(7-9)   $R_{OA}$ removed and $OA$ replaced by $W_t$; $f_c$ and $W$ replaced by $W_{OA}$.

Equations (7-6) to (7-9) offer two closely related explanations of the tax yield, as well as two explanations of taxable earnings. They depict the impact on $OA$ and $W_t$ of changes in the direct policy instruments —tax rate, ceiling, and fraction taxable—as well as the impact of changes in earnings.

### Statistical Estimates

The models were estimated by ordinary least squares, based on annual data for 1937–66. Separate fits were also obtained for 1952–66, when the relative ceiling moved in a narrower range. It was assumed that the relationships for the later fifteen-year period would be more reliable for estimation of present and future yields, despite the smaller number of observations.[25]

The regression estimates are recorded in Table 7-4. The very high values of the coefficient of determination $\bar{R}^2$—all greater than 0.9997— are in part due to mutual trends in the variables. The absence of such complications as exemptions and deductions makes payroll tax revenue estimation a relatively simple task. Basically, the payroll tax function has only two explanatory tasks beyond what are essentially identities. It must reconcile OBE and SSA data and explain changes in the

---

[25] The quadratic form of the fraction taxable function appears strained by the high prewar relative ceilings but entirely adequate in the shorter range. The model is also less subject to bias due to any long-run shifts in the size distribution of earnings

**TABLE 7-4. Regression Results for Payroll Tax and Taxable Earnings Variables**[a]

| Dependent variable, model, and regression period | Constant term | Weighted average statutory tax rate, $R_{OA}$ | Ratio of ceiling to mean earnings $w_c/\bar{w}$ | $(w_c/\bar{w})^2$ | Fraction of earnings covered, $f_c$ | Earnings in covered employment, $W_{OA}$ | Total earnings, W | Coefficient of determination, $\bar{R}^2$ | Durbin-Watson statistic | Standard error of estimate |
|---|---|---|---|---|---|---|---|---|---|---|
| **Payroll tax (OA)** | | | | | | | | | | |
| (7-6) 1937–66 | 0.8531 (0.0472) | 0.9734 (0.0186) | 0.5218 (0.0384) | −0.5934 (0.0913) | 1.0103 (0.0242) | — | 1.0022 (0.0237) | 0.99995 | 1.577 | 0.0033 |
| 1952–66 | 0.7491 (0.0709) | 0.9745 (0.0159) | 0.7703 (0.1736) | −1.5272 (0.7654) | 0.8988 (0.0422) | — | 1.0333 (0.0285) | 0.99993 | 2.424 | 0.0015 |
| (7-7) 1937–66 | 0.8441 (0.0307) | 0.9721 (0.0174) | 0.5174 (0.0335) | −0.5788 (0.0700) | — | 1.0062 (0.0175) | — | 0.99995 | 1.516 | 0.0033 |
| 1952–66 | 0.8856 (0.0443) | 0.9841 (0.0181) | 0.5095 (0.1540) | −0.3816 (0.6804) | — | 0.9845 (0.0222) | — | 0.99991 | 1.832 | 0.0019 |
| **Taxable earnings ($W_t$)** | | | | | | | | | | |
| (7-8) 1937–66 | −0.0565 (0.0256) | — | 0.4857 (0.0293) | −0.6066 (0.0510) | 0.9858 (0.0180) | — | 0.9584 (0.0097) | 0.99990 | 1.554 | 0.0029 |
| 1952–66 | −0.1017 (0.0465) | — | 0.5846 (0.1492) | −0.8045 (0.6552) | 0.9209 (0.0367) | — | 0.9707 (0.0149) | 0.99975 | 2.543 | 0.0014 |
| (7-9) 1937–66 | −0.0799 (0.0126) | — | 0.4740 (0.0271) | −0.5716 (0.0386) | — | 0.9674 (0.0046) | — | 0.99990 | 1.326 | 0.0029 |
| 1952–66 | −0.0587 (0.0161) | — | 0.4898 (0.1125) | −0.3904 (0.4967) | — | 0.9568 (0.0049) | — | 0.99976 | 2.377 | 0.0014 |

Source: Derived from models (7-6) through (7-9) discussed in the text, based on annual data as described in Appendix F.
a. All variables are in logarithms. The figures in parentheses are the standard errors of the coefficients.

fraction of taxable earnings. However, the $\bar{R}^2$ values and the standard error of estimate (SEE) figures show that the model performs these tasks exceedingly well. Multiplication of the standard errors of estimate by 2.3 expresses them as relative errors in relation to the original dependent variable before the logarithmic transformation.[26] Thus the SEE for the 1937–66 tax functions is equivalent to 0.8 percent error in the tax yield; the corresponding figure for the taxable earnings function is about 0.7 percent. Under normal distribution of the residuals, about two-thirds would be as small as this or smaller. The SEE of the models fitted to the shorter period is lower—about 0.4 percent. These SEE figures, indicating a typical error of less than 1 percent in estimation of the tax yield, testify to the closeness of the fit in these models; they also offer a more realistic picture than the very high $\bar{R}^2$ values.

The coefficients for the tax rate variable fall slightly below the expected value of one. Although not significantly lower, they have not been constrained to equal unity; it may be assumed that they contribute to reconciliation of the OBE and SSA data. The two terms containing the relative ceiling $w_c/\bar{w}$ explain variations in the fraction taxable. Their coefficients are highly significant in the thirty-year regressions. The square terms are not statistically significant in the fifteen-year fits, which produced very high standard errors. However, the coefficients carry the expected signs and are of the same order of magnitude as those estimated for the entire thirty years; the square terms for the shorter period were retained, despite the inaccuracy of the estimate of their coefficients, to allow for the known curvature of the $f_t$ function.

The variable representing the covered fraction of total earnings has coefficients significantly less than unity in the fifteen-year fits. This was a period in which self-employed workers, with relatively high incomes

---

[26] Let $p$ = the relative error in the original dependent variable, denoting the observed values of $OA$ and the regression estimates by 0 and $e$, respectively:

$$OA_0 = (1 + p)OA_e.$$

The residuals after the logarithmic transformation are then given by

$$\log OA_0 - \log OA_e = \log(1 + p).$$

Equating the standard error of estimate (SEE) with the first term in the Taylor's explanation of $\log(1 + p)$ yields

$$p = 2.3 \text{ SEE}.$$

on the average, entered the program. The low coefficient suggests that, because of the protection of the ceiling, their tax and taxable earnings showed a less than proportional response to the increased coverage. In general the coefficients obtained in these models appear plausible, the Durbin-Watson statistics cast no significant doubt on the results, and the specified relationships are extremely close.

## Tests of the Models

As a further test of the reliability of these models, their "forecasting" performance for years beyond the period of fit was examined; the results are summarized in Table 7-5.[27] The hypothetical projections were compared to the actual levels of the tax and taxable earnings and to a naïve forecast (same change as the previous year). The forecasts of the aggregate tax in 1967 and 1968 by equations (7-6) and (7-7) are accurate no matter which previous period of fit was used. Most of the errors are about 1 percent in the first year and 0.6 percent in the second. The 1968 errors by equations (7-6) and (7-7) were slightly greater than the naïve model's performance, but the latter was outclassed in 1967 when it was off about 15 percent. The naïve model was tricked by the large 1965–66 increase in the tax due to a rise in the ceiling, which was not repeated in the 1966–67 interval; it was fortunate in 1968 that the ceiling increase produced an extra large tax increase about equal to that caused by a rate increase in 1967. The regression models, on the other hand, reacted to these income and statutory rate changes with excellent forecasts in both years.

The regression model forecasts of taxable earnings in 1967 were also within about 1 percent or less, while the naïve model was again too high by over 10 percent. The 1968 results for taxable earnings are not as good, with the regression models off by 1.7 to 2.5 percent; however, this performance was still better than the 7 percent error in the naïve model.

For comparisons with official projections, model (7-9) was also used to project taxable earnings under OASDHI for 1971, 1973, 1975, and 1980 under several assumed ceilings. In these projections, official projections of total earnings in covered employment and the number

---

[27] Beginning in 1967 the tax on nonfarm self-employed was collected currently on a quarterly basis, removing most of the lag. Thus these forecasts and later projections use the current tax rate and earnings of the self-employed in estimating the weighted average effective rate $R_{OA}$.

## TABLE 7-5. Forecasts of the Social Security Payroll Tax and Taxable Earnings for 1967 and 1968, Based on 1937–66 and 1952–66 Regressions

(In billions of dollars)

| Model | Regression period | 1967 | | | | 1968 | | | |
|---|---|---|---|---|---|---|---|---|---|
| | | Actual | Forecast | Regression error | Naïve error[a] | Actual | Forecast | Regression error | Naïve error[a] |
| | | *Payroll tax* | | | | | | | |
| (7-6) | 1937–66 | 28.6 | 28.3 | −0.3 | +4.3 | 32.0 | 32.1 | +0.2 | −0.1 |
| | 1952–66 | 28.6 | 28.6 | −0.1 | +4.3 | 32.0 | 32.3 | +0.3 | −0.1 |
| (7-7) | 1937–66 | 28.6 | 28.3 | −0.3 | +4.3 | 32.0 | 32.2 | +0.2 | −0.1 |
| | 1952–66 | 28.6 | 28.2 | −0.4 | +4.3 | 32.0 | 32.2 | +0.2 | −0.1 |
| | | *Taxable earnings* | | | | | | | |
| (7-8) | 1937–66 | 329.4 | 325.9 | −3.5 | +36.3 | 376.2 | 366.7 | −9.5 | −26.4 |
| | 1952–66 | 329.4 | 327.5 | −1.9 | +36.3 | 376.2 | 369.9 | −6.3 | −26.4 |
| (7-9) | 1937–66 | 329.4 | 326.6 | −2.8 | +36.3 | 376.2 | 367.8 | −8.4 | −26.4 |
| | 1952–66 | 329.4 | 326.2 | −3.2 | +36.3 | 376.2 | 369.8 | −6.4 | −26.4 |

Sources: Same as Table 7-4; in addition, for 1967–68 actual payroll tax and taxable earnings, U.S. Social Security Administration, Social Security Bulletin, Annual Statistical Supplement, 1967, Table 25, p. 33, and Social Security Bulletin, Annual Statistical Supplement, 1968, Table 34, p. 51; and U.S. Department of Commerce, Survey of Current Business, Vol. 49 (July 1969), pp. 26 32, 39. Computations are based on unrounded data.

a. The naïve forecast assumed a one-year change equal to that of the previous year.

of earners were used. In Table 7-6 the results based on model (7-9) are compared with official projections of taxable earnings. Those for later years do not agree as well with SSA projections as the earlier forecasts agreed with the actual data. Projection by the 1952–66 fit agrees somewhat more closely with SSA figures than with those of the 1937–66 regression. However, it departs from SSA by 1 to 4 percent in 1971 and 1973, and 3 to 5 percent in 1975; oddly, the agreement is excellent in 1980, with a maximum discrepancy of just over 1 percent in the projections for the four different ceilings. There is no way of judging the SSA projections against those made by using equation (7-9). However, the agreement seems very good for future years when projected taxable earnings will be as much as double the current levels.

The hypothetical forecasts in Table 7-5 and the projections in Table 7-6 suggest that, given a stable earnings distribution, a single equation model is adequate for explanation of substantial changes in the tax yield and taxable earnings. It is also possible to derive *marginal* responses in taxable earnings from these equations. As a check on the estimates in Table 7-1, equation (7-9) is especially appropriate since

**TABLE 7-6. Projections of Taxable Earnings by Model (7-9) Compared with Official Social Security Administration Projections, Various Ceilings, 1971, 1973, 1975, and 1980**

(In billions of dollars)

| Ceiling (dollars) | 1971 Model (7-9)[a] | 1971 SSA | 1973 Model (7-9)[a] | 1973 SSA | 1975 Model (7-9)[a] | 1975 SSA | 1980 Model (7-9)[a] | 1980 SSA |
|---|---|---|---|---|---|---|---|---|
| 7,800 | 433.0 | 442.9 | 471.3 | 481.3 | 514.4 | 524.2 | 630.7 | 615.1 |
|  | 429.1 | | 464.4 | | 504.6 | | 614.9 | |
| 9,000 | 452.8 | 469.1 | 495.6 | 512.6 | 544.2 | 561.8 | 677.2 | 667.8 |
|  | 452.9 | | 492.2 | | 537.0 | | 661.1 | |
| 12,000 | 480.1 | 506.6 | 531.9 | 560.3 | 591.0 | 620.8 | 757.8 | 758.0 |
|  | 494.5 | | 541.8 | | 596.0 | | 748.8 | |
| 15,600 | 488.7 | 527.8 | 547.3 | 588.4 | 614.7 | 657.3 | 810.0 | 817.3 |
|  | 522.8 | | 577.1 | | 639.5 | | 818.6 | |

Sources: SSA data from unpublished tabulation of the Social Security Administration, Office of Research and Statistics, Dec. 15, 1969; this also included projections of total earnings and number of earners used in the projections by model (7-9). For other data sources relating to model (7-9), see Table 7-4.

[a] The first figure in each set is the projection on the basis of a 1937–66 regression period; the second figure in each set is based on a 1952–66 period.

it is based on SSA data only. A self-contained restatement of that model is:

$$(7\text{-}9) \quad \log W_t = \alpha + \beta \log w_c/\bar{w} + \gamma(\log w_c/\bar{w})^2 + \delta \log W_{OA} + \epsilon.$$

The marginal responses of $W_t$ with respect to changes in $W_{OA}$ are not directly obtainable from this expression, because $W_{OA}$ is embodied in the term $w_c/\bar{w}$. Replacement of $\bar{w}$ by $W_{OA}/E_{OA}$ and further manipulations lead to an estimate of the elasticity of the regression estimate of taxable earnings $W_t$ with respect to total covered earnings $W_{OA}$:

$$(7\text{-}10) \qquad \frac{E\hat{W}_t}{EW_{OA}} = \frac{\partial \log \hat{W}_t}{\partial \log W_{OA}} = -\beta + \delta - 2\gamma \log w_c/\bar{w}.$$

The estimated fraction taxable is directly attainable as $\hat{W}_t/W_{OA}$, and the product of this fraction and the elasticity gives the marginal rate of response of taxable earnings $\partial \hat{W}_t/\partial W_{OA}$.

The elasticity estimate in equation (7-10), derived from (7-9), is a linear function of the logarithm of the relative ceiling. Clearly, it can give a good approximation of the elasticity curve for only a short range; a plot of the estimates in Table 7-1 against $w_c/\bar{w}$ suggests that the elasticity curve starts at zero, exhibits an inflection point, and approaches unity asymptotically. The estimated response ratios based on these time series models are compared in Table 7-7 to those based on the one-year earnings distribution for 1964. The 1937–66 and 1952–66 time series regressions confirm rather well the static estimates based on one year's data. This is especially the case for the regression estimates of the fraction taxable; these all fall within about 0.05 of the one-year estimates. The discrepancies are greater for elasticities and marginal rates, but even these are less than 0.10 in almost all cases. In short, the results of two completely independent estimating techniques—based on time series and a static earnings distribution, respectively—are close enough to suggest that the reliability of both approaches is adequate. The indicated validity of models such as (7-6) to (7-9) is especially advantageous, since these can be used to forecast generally and accurately the response of the tax and the tax base to policy instruments as well as economic variables.[28]

---

[28] An alternative approach would be to base tax yield estimates on the Brookings Institution's samples of individual federal income tax returns for various years. However, only selected years are available, and the tax return earnings variant departs substantially from the social security tax base.

**TABLE 7-7. Alternative Estimates of the Marginal Response of Social Security Taxable Earnings to Earnings Change, 1964**

*(In percent)*

| Hypothetical ceiling (dollars) | Type of estimate | Fraction taxable | Marginal rate | Elasticity |
|---|---|---|---|---|
| 3,000 | Time series, 1937–66 | 0.575 | 0.188 | 0.327 |
|  | Time series, 1952–66 | 0.566 | 0.200 | 0.353 |
|  | One year, 1964 | 0.522 | 0.139 | 0.266 |
| 3,600 | Time series, 1937–66 | 0.637 | 0.266 | 0.417 |
|  | Time series, 1952–66 | 0.629 | 0.261 | 0.415 |
|  | One year, 1964 | 0.593 | 0.194 | 0.326 |
| 4,200 | Time series, 1937–66 | 0.689 | 0.340 | 0.494 |
|  | Time series, 1952–66 | 0.681 | 0.318 | 0.467 |
|  | One year, 1964 | 0.655 | 0.252 | 0.385 |
| 4,800 | Time series, 1937–66 | 0.731 | 0.410 | 0.560 |
|  | Time series, 1952–66 | 0.724 | 0.371 | 0.513 |
|  | One year, 1964 | 0.708 | 0.314 | 0.443 |
| 6,600 | Time series, 1937–66 | 0.812 | 0.583 | 0.718 |
|  | Time series, 1952–66 | 0.820 | 0.509 | 0.621 |
|  | One year, 1964 | 0.823 | 0.517 | 0.628 |
| 9,000 | Time series, 1937–66 | 0.856 | 0.747 | 0.872 |
|  | Time series, 1952–66 | 0.896 | 0.650 | 0.726 |
|  | One year, 1964 | 0.898 | 0.713 | 0.794 |

Sources: Time series estimates, model (7-10), discussed in the text; one-year estimates, Table 7-1, above.

# Conclusions on Responsiveness of Payroll Tax to Earnings Changes

## Comparison with Other Taxes

The sensitivity of payroll taxes to income change can best be compared with that of other taxes by measuring the response of each tax to a change in a common income base such as the GNP. The built-in flexibility of the payroll tax $OA$ with respect to GNP through associated changes in total earnings $W$ may be derived from two components by the identity:

$$\frac{\partial OA}{\partial \text{GNP}} \cong \frac{\partial OA}{\partial W} \cdot \frac{\partial W}{\partial \text{GNP}}.$$

Various estimates of $\partial OA/\partial W$ have already been presented. For some rough and not altogether compatible comparisons, earlier time series regression estimates by William Waldorf will be relied on.[29] Since he found annual changes in total earnings only slightly less than proportional to changes in GNP, his estimates of $\partial W/\partial GNP$ approximate the ratio of total earnings to GNP. His estimates of this coefficient for OASDI and UI covered earnings were 0.578 and 0.530, respectively. The corresponding built-in flexibility measures for 1965 are summarized in Table 7-8, where $Y$ denotes covered incomes and $T$ the tax receipts. Also included are the independent estimates from Table 7-3 above, which are based on earnings distribution data. The latter are about 20 percent lower than Waldorf's time series estimates for OASDI and substantially lower in the case of the smaller UI response ratios. Still, Waldorf's regression results, like those in this study, agree fairly well with the presumably more reliable direct estimates of Table 7-3, which are based on the earnings distribution for 1965.[30]

The estimate in Table 7-8 of the combined built-in flexibility of the OASDI and UI taxes with respect to GNP in 1965 is about 1.35 percent, based on Waldorf's results for $\partial Y/\partial GNP$ and the results in Table 7-3. Although this is substantially short of Waldorf's result of 1.9 percent, both estimates strongly confirm the conclusion that the OASDI and UI payroll tax add up to a weak stabilizer. They fall far short of Waldorf's estimate of 12 percent for the personal income tax, and they also trail the corporation income tax and indirect business taxes in stabilizing power.

The weak showing relative to the income tax was not due simply to the smaller size of the payroll tax. Although the yield of the latter was about 40 percent of the personal income tax yield in 1965, according to the estimate in Table 7-8 its built-in flexibility was only about 11

[29] William H. Waldorf, "Long-Run Federal Tax Functions: A Statistical Analysis," Staff Working Paper in Economics and Statistics, No. 15 (U.S. Department of Commerce, Office of Business Economics, 1968; processed). For an earlier analysis of automatic stabilization in the postwar period, see Wilfred Lewis, Jr., *Federal Fiscal Policy in the Postwar Recessions* (Brookings Institution, 1962). See also Wayne G. Vroman, "The Macroeconomic Effects of Social Insurance" (Ph.D. dissertation, University of Michigan, 1964).

[30] The agreement in the case of OASDI is close. Although the estimates for UI in Table 7-3 are crude, there is reason to favor them over Waldorf's results, which were based on a model that excluded the ceiling as statistically insignificant. If the ceiling had been measured in *relative* terms, the regression models might have confirmed the results of this study—showing flexibility declining with the fall in the relative ceiling.

**TABLE 7-8.** Long-run Marginal Rates of Various Federal Tax Receipts (T), with Respect to Covered Income (Y) and Gross National Product, 1965

*(In percent)*

| Type of tax | $\partial Y/\partial GNP$, Waldorf | Marginal rates | | | |
|---|---|---|---|---|---|
| | | $\partial T/\partial Y$ | | $\partial T/\partial GNP$ | |
| | | Waldorf | Table 7-3 | Waldorf | Table 7-3[a] |
| Total tax receipts | — | — | — | 0.210 | — |
| Personal taxes[b] | 0.790 | 0.145 | — | 0.122 | — |
| Corporate profits tax accruals | 0.103 | 0.397 | — | 0.041 | — |
| Indirect business taxes[b] | — | — | — | 0.024 | — |
| Social insurance tax receipts, total | — | — | — | 0.023 | — |
| Old-age, survivors, and disability insurance | 0.578 | 0.026 | 0.0209 | 0.015 | 0.0121 |
| State and federal unemployment insurance | 0.530 | 0.008 | 0.0027 | 0.004 | 0.0014 |
| Railroad retirement insurance | 0.001 | 0.076 | — | —[c] | — |
| Railroad unemployment insurance | 0.001 | 0.019 | — | —[c] | — |
| Federal civilian employee retirement system | 0.022 | 0.187 | — | 0.004 | — |

Sources: William H. Waldorf, "Long-Run Federal Tax Functions: A Statistical Analysis," Staff Working Paper in Economics and Statistics, No. 15 (Department of Commerce, Office of Business Economics, 1968; processed), p. 9a; Table 7-3 above.

[a] Derived from Table 7-3 and Waldorf's ratio of income to GNP.

[b] Includes nontax receipts.

[c] Less than 0.0005.

percent of that exhibited by the income tax. Thus, even making allowance for the overall magnitude of the payroll tax, it had only about one-fourth of the stabilizing power of the income tax.[31] The same comparison can be made more directly in terms of the elasticities of the tax yield that essentially abstract from the size of the tax. Table 7-2 shows 1965 elasticities of 0.41 for the OASDI tax (and taxable earnings) and 0.26 for the UI tax—far short of Waldorf's 1.55 elasticity for the individual income tax.[32] It should be added (in line with the discussion at the beginning of this chapter) that, in the special context

[31] Similarly the corporation income tax, though not much larger than the payroll tax in 1965, shows a stabilization coefficient about three times as great as the estimate in Table 7-8 for the payroll tax.

[32] William H. Waldorf, "The Responsiveness of Federal Personal Income Taxes to Income Change," *Survey of Current Business*, Vol. 47 (December 1967), p. 44.

of a rise in money incomes accompanied by no change in output, these elasticities below unity stamp the payroll taxes as destabilizing offsets to the positive stabilizing contribution of the individual income tax.

The time series of payroll tax marginal rates presented in Table 7-3 may also be compared to Waldorf's annual results for 1955–65. Table 7-9 records response ratios for various taxes, including *total* contributions for social insurance and the estimates in Table 7-8 for OASDI and UI taxes alone (the latter accounting for about 88 percent of total contributions for social insurance). Waldorf's estimates for the more recent years fall well above the marginal rate estimates in this study, in part because of the greater coverage of total social insurance contributions. It is again apparent that his regression findings do not adequately reflect changes in the relative ceiling (particularly the UI ceiling) in this period. Nevertheless, the agreement between Waldorf's estimates and those of this study is sufficient for a general conclusion. Despite the upward trend exhibited by both estimates of the built-in flexibility of social security taxes between 1955 and 1965, it remains clear that by 1965 the latter were far from catching up with the other three major taxes. Further growth of social security taxes (mainly due to ceiling increases) by 1969 closed the gap somewhat; however, it remains true that these taxes are weak stabilizers, primarily due to the inhibiting effects of the ceilings.

*Qualifications of the Analysis*

At this point it is in order to outline certain qualifications of the statistical work reported in this chapter. The basing of the estimates on annual data qualifies their meaning in at least two respects. First, an income change would not necessarily have the indicated impact on the tax yield in the short run. Changes in tax receipts have lagged slightly behind earnings changes, because a small portion of the tax, such as that paid by the self-employed, is not collected on a withholding basis. The quarterly tax collections from nonfarm self-employed beginning in 1967 have not significantly alleviated this problem in recent years. More important, the seasonal pattern of collections affects the responsiveness at any given time of year. The built-in flexibility of the tax base and the elasticity are close to unity in the month of January when the ceiling spares few incomes—only those above $93,600 a year under the 1968–70 ceiling. The one-month response ratios decline over the year, approaching in December those derived

TABLE 7-9. Long-run Marginal Rates of Various Federal Taxes with Respect to Gross National Product, 1955–65 and 1969

(In percent)

| Year | Total taxes | Personal taxes[a] | Corporate profits tax accruals | Indirect business taxes[a] | Social insurance tax receipts | | | |
|---|---|---|---|---|---|---|---|---|
| | | | | | Total | Social security | Unemployment insurance | Combined social security and unemployment insurance |
| 1955 | 0.202 | 0.118 | 0.047 | 0.025 | 0.012 | 0.010 | 0.002 | 0.012 |
| 1956 | 0.192 | 0.122 | 0.044 | 0.014 | 0.012 | 0.009 | 0.002 | 0.011 |
| 1957 | 0.192 | 0.123 | 0.044 | 0.012 | 0.013 | 0.010 | 0.001 | 0.011 |
| 1958 | 0.163 | 0.121 | 0.041 | 0.016 | 0.017 | 0.009 | 0.001 | 0.010 |
| 1959 | 0.212 | 0.122 | 0.046 | 0.025 | 0.019 | 0.012 | 0.002 | 0.014 |
| 1960 | 0.209 | 0.124 | 0.043 | 0.020 | 0.022 | 0.013 | 0.002 | 0.015 |
| 1961 | 0.210 | 0.123 | 0.042 | 0.022 | 0.023 | 0.013 | 0.002 | 0.015 |
| 1962 | 0.221 | 0.125 | 0.045 | 0.028 | 0.023 | 0.012 | 0.002 | 0.014 |
| 1963 | 0.218 | 0.126 | 0.043 | 0.025 | 0.024 | 0.014 | 0.002 | 0.016 |
| 1964 | 0.213 | 0.115 | 0.042 | 0.026 | 0.024 | 0.013 | 0.002 | 0.015 |
| 1965 | 0.210 | 0.122 | 0.041 | 0.024 | 0.023 | 0.012 | 0.001 | 0.013 |
| 1969 | — | — | — | — | — | 0.024 | 0.001 | 0.025 |

Sources: Waldorf, "Long-Run Federal Tax Functions," p. 10a; for OASDI and UI, Table 7-3 above converted to GNP base by Waldorf's coefficients for the income-GNP rates (ibid., p. 9a).
[a] Includes nontax receipts.

on an annual basis.[33] However, the marginal rates and elasticity in December *with respect to a whole year of income growth* may even be negative. The tax responses may be negative in the sense that the tax base and yield may be lower in December after one year of growth than in the absence of earnings growth.[34]

A second qualification of the one-year measures is that tax offsets operate through the multiplier process to go beyond their initial impact. The multiplier $1/[1 - b(1 - m)]$ derived in the first section of this chapter from a linear model may be used for illustration. For example, for the marginal rate $m$ to reduce the pretax multiplier by one, the model implies $m = (1/b - 1)^2$. In the case of a multiplier of 0.75, the model implies that a marginal rate of 0.111 would cut the multiplier from four to three.

The previous qualification does not disturb the conclusion that the payroll tax is a very weak stabilizer relative to the other major taxes. The large increase in the OASDHI ceiling in 1968 raised the built-in flexibility (combined marginal tax rate with respect to GNP) to about 2.5 percent in 1969—still dwarfed by Waldorf's latest figure of 12 percent for the income tax. Despite the extraordinary postwar growth of the payroll tax—a rise of the combined OASDHI and UI tax from $2.9 billion in 1949 to $41.0 billion in 1969—it remains of minimal importance as an automatic stabilizer or drag on long-run growth. Since the social security system is already running a large surplus, there is no reason to expect the very large increases in rates and ceiling that would be needed to put the payroll tax in the same category with the income tax as an automatic stabilizer. However, such "discretionary" increases in the payroll tax structure as those producing the current surplus could themselves produce a significant fiscal drag. The automatic and discretionary effects of the tax are considered in Chapter VIII, with more specific reference to growth as well as to seasonal and long-term fluctuations.

[33] The discussion here refers to tax accruals. Because of lags in collections, the seasonal pattern of that variant is somewhat different.

[34] Consider earners who (in the absence of growth) would have reached the taxable ceiling some time during the December earning period and others whose annual earnings fell just short of the ceiling. Earlier growth would reduce to some extent the amount of their earnings otherwise taxable in December—or might even swamp the growth of the tax base of earners lower in the scale. This shows why the marginal rate can be very low for the year as a whole even though it begins near unity in January.

# CHAPTER VIII

# Impact on Economic Stability

CHAPTER VII DEALT in general terms on the basis of annual data with the built-in responsiveness of payroll tax yields to income changes. The sluggish reaction of these yields combines with the relative stability of labor income to ensure that the typical payroll tax must be a very weak automatic stabilizer, especially in comparison with the progressive income tax. It is appropriate to consider next the impact of payroll taxes on stability in the context of the actual economic experience. The effects of discretionary changes are considered, as well as the built-in responses.

## Arbitrary Timing of Variations in Tax Structure

*Statutory Rate and Ceiling Increases*

Changes in the payroll tax structure in the United States have usually been scheduled far in advance and have rarely been postponed. Generally moving in the direction of higher tax yields, these revisions have been designed to finance ultimately higher benefits, but in each case the tax has been increased without equal benefit increases and without adequate regard for the state of the economy at the time.[1]

---

[1] Scheduled tax increases have sometimes been adjusted downward to take into account benefit projections rather than to stimulate the economy. It should be reemphasized that the discussion here refers only to tax changes and not to the net impact of social

Before 1965 payroll tax increases were sometimes imposed on a sluggish economy. In recent years the frequent boosts in social security taxes have probably placed a fortuitous restraint on inflation. Increases in the payroll tax rate or ceiling or both went into effect in all four years during the period 1966–69, raising the maximum annual old-age, survivors, disability, and health insurance (OASDHI) tax per employee from $348 to $749 between 1965 and 1969. The broader category—federal contributions for social insurance—is more useful in the analysis of cyclical effects, because the data are available quarterly on a seasonally adjusted basis; this flow rose from $25.8 billion to $48.0 billion at an annual rate between the last quarters of 1965 and of 1969—an increase of 86 percent.[2] A substantial part of this increase was due to an increase in covered earnings subject to tax, but about 40 percent was due to the largely discretionary increase in the overall ratio of contributions to earnings from about 6 percent to over 8 percent—an increase in this ratio of about 33 percent.

The rise in payroll tax rate and taxable ceiling, combined with earnings growth, yielded contributions well in excess of benefit payments in the 1966–69 period. The surplus in federal social insurance funds averaged $6.7 billion a year in that interval, reaching $8.2 billion in 1969, and the surplus in state and local funds averaged $4.7 billion a year in the same period. It is apparent that the steady rise in the payroll tax rate and ceiling, producing yield increases well in excess of benefit increases, was a fortunate offset to the strong inflationary pressures at work from 1965 on, after the sharp escalation of the Vietnam war. Social insurance programs were cutting sharply into disposable income long before the surtax on the individual income tax went into effect in 1968. The combined surplus of $13.9 billion in federal, state, and local social insurance trust funds substantially exceeded the proceeds of the surtax in 1969, its peak year.[3]

---

security receipts and outlays. During some years benefit increases alleviated tax increases that had been imposed on a slow economy. More generally, the discussion does not imply that perverse effects of tax increases cannot be offset by other public policies. Although monetary policy can alleviate the results of poorly timed tax increases, it seems more efficient to eliminate such increases.

[2] The statistics given here and in the following discussion are derived from the national income accounts, primarily from *Survey of Current Business*, Vol. 51 (July 1971), and *U.S. National Income and Product Accounts, 1964–67* (a *Survey of Current Business* reprint, 1971).

[3] On a cash receipts basis, the effective surtax rate was about 12.5 percent in 1969, because the tax for the second quarter of 1968 was not withheld and not collected until 1969.

The surplus in the unemployment insurance (UI) fund, running over $1 billion in some years, was a normal "built-in" reaction to low unemployment. However, most of the social security fund surplus was the incidental outcome of the perennial congressional intent to keep social security on a "sound actuarial basis" by expanding the trust funds. Whatever the merit of this policy, it certainly placed a substantial check on the growth rate of gross national product (GNP) at a time when a faster growth rate would have reflected mainly price increases rather than real growth. In the absence of these surpluses, the four-year price rise would undoubtedly have substantially exceeded the 16 percent indicated by the GNP deflator over the 1965–69 interval.

The original policy of trust fund accumulation has gradually given ground to pay-as-you-go financing over the years, but enough of the old outlook persisted to produce incidental anti-inflationary tax increases during the late 1960s. Although this steady growth of payroll taxation proved fortuitous in that period of continuing economic expansion and prosperity, this has not always been the case. On a number of occasions statutory tax increases have acted as perverse fiscal policies because they have become effective during or shortly before a business slump.

The first social security tax at a 2 percent rate became effective January 1, 1937, along with a railroad retirement tax and a substantial increase in UI taxes. Although a marked recovery from the depth of the Great Depression had already occurred, a great deal of slack remained in the economy. The official unemployment rate was still very high, averaging 14 percent in 1937. It was hardly a propitious time to reduce spending power, with new payroll taxes amounting to about $1 billion and not significantly offset by benefits. The sharp economic contraction of 1937–38 began in May 1937—only four or five months after this new tax was initiated.[4] The new cut into purchasing power stirred sharp criticism that it was aggravating an already bleak economic situation.[5] Not only was the tax installed in total disregard of the current economic climate, but it undoubtedly also helped to bring on the ensuing economic contraction and to intensify the pace and extent of the decline.

[4] The business cycle reference dates referred to in this chapter are those specified by the National Bureau of Economic Research.

[5] For discussion of this controversy, see Kenneth D. Roose, *The Economics of Recession and Revival: An Interpretation of 1937–38* (Archon Books, 1969).

Another perverse statutory rate increase went into effect at the beginning of 1954—a time when the nation's economy was in the midst of the second recession after World War II. The tax rate was raised by one-third (from 3 to 4 percent), despite a seasonally adjusted unemployment rate of 4.9 percent in January 1954 and a business contraction that had clearly been under way for some months. This tax increase of about $1.28 billion a year was concentrated in the early part of the year because of the ceiling on taxable earnings that causes collections to decline over the year. The tax increase may have been a factor in making this recession the longest of the postwar period: thirteen months, from July 1953 to August 1954.

Although not perverse when they took effect, the statutory rate increases of 1957 and 1960 may well have contributed to the onset— or at least to the intensity—of recessions shortly thereafter. The 1957 increase of one-half a percentage point amounted to a $0.87 billion increase in tax revenue in 1957, while the 1960 increase of one full point raised tax collections by about $2.0 billion, with both annual totals most pronounced in the early part of the year. The ceiling and rate increases in 1959 also significantly affected the rate of change of GNP as late as the 1960–61 recession, owing to lags in their economic impact. The combined effect of the 1959 and 1960 changes increased the 1960 OASDI tax by $3.9 billion.[6] Recessions began in July 1957 and May 1960, shortly after the tax increases of 1957 and 1959–60, respectively. These arbitrarily scheduled increases undoubtedly aggravated the subsequent recessions and may even have helped to precipitate them. The probable economic impact of these rate increases in a dynamic context is considered quantitatively later. Although only the perverse cases are considered, it should be noted that not all changes in the payroll tax structure have been perverse. For example, the 1971 postponement of a scheduled ceiling increase came during an economic slowdown.

*Arbitrary Seasonality in Collections*

While not usually considered a discretionary adjustment of the tax yield, the seasonal pattern of collections is subject to control, and the present pattern is arbitrary. The seasonal variation is due primarily to the practice of collecting the tax at a fixed rate until the ceiling is

---

[6] This allows for both ceiling and rate changes and was estimated by equation (7-6) in the last chapter.

reached for each individual. In the first month every covered person is paying social security taxes and the average tax per person is at its peak on an accrual basis;[7] at year's end only 65 to 75 percent are still subject to the OASDHI tax, and the average tax per capita is at its minimum. Since the ceiling for the UI tax is lower than the OASDHI ceiling—$3,000 in most states until 1972, then $4,200—the percentage for whom this tax is still accruing at the end of the year is far smaller. With the increased ceiling, the seasonality will be even greater. The pattern of seasonality for all types of contributions for social insurance on a quarterly basis is somewhat less pronounced; since data on this basis are conveniently available, they are summarized for two years in Table 8-1.[8] A large increase in collections occurs seasonally in the first quarter of each year, when earners who had previously passed the ceiling begin to pay again. In the first quarter of 1970 the actual increase (the one-quarter total) amounted to $4.9 billion, of which $4.8 billion may be interpreted as seasonal.[9] There was a further seasonal rise of $0.6 billion in the second quarter, making a two-quarter total of $5.4 billion.[10]

The $4.8 billion first-quarter seasonal rise in the federal collection of contributions in 1970 may be compared to the $19.4 billion seasonal decline in GNP in the first quarter, implied by the figures in

[7] Because of various factors such as lags in collections, the seasonal peak in actual collections does not occur at the very beginning of the year (as is explained later).

[8] For a more detailed description of seasonality based on OASDHI payments only, see Joseph M. Bonin, *Some Economic Effects of Seasonality in OASDHI Tax Payments,* U.S. Social Security Administration, Office of Research and Statistics, Research Report 20 (1967).

[9] The table implies that $4.8 billion of the observed increase was seasonal, since the seasonally adjusted series rose by only $0.1 billion. No changes in rate or ceiling occurred between 1969 and 1970, and these estimates should be relatively free of the bias believed to be inherent in the seasonal adjustment procedure during years when the ceiling has changed.

[10] A seasonal decline might be expected in the second quarter as some earners pass the ceiling. However, such a tendency is apparently overwhelmed by at least three factors: (1) because of a lag in federal collections, some fraction of low-tax fourth-quarter accruals are collected in the first quarter, while about the same fraction of high-tax first-quarter accruals are collected in the second quarter (since the employee portion of the tax is withheld on a current basis, there is no corresponding lag in the impact of this tax on disposable income); (2) despite recent efforts to put them on a quarterly basis, most collections from the self-employed are on an annual basis and are probably concentrated in the second quarter if paid just before the deadline in April of the following year; and (3) a seasonal rise in employment and earnings in the second quarter makes for higher collections in that period.

**TABLE 8-1. Seasonality in Quarterly Federal Contributions for Social Insurance and in Gross National Product, 1969 and 1970**

*(In billions of dollars)*

| Year and quarter | Contributions for social insurance | | | Gross national product | | |
|---|---|---|---|---|---|---|
| | Not adjusted | Seasonally adjusted | Implied index | Not adjusted | Seasonally adjusted | Implied index |
| 1969:1 | 13.0 | 11.3 | 115 | 216.9 | 226.6 | 96 |
| 2 | 13.6 | 11.6 | 117 | 232.4 | 230.4 | 101 |
| 3 | 11.0 | 11.8 | 93 | 233.0 | 235.0 | 99 |
| 4 | 9.1 | 12.0 | 76 | 246.7 | 237.0 | 104 |
| 1970:1 | 14.0 | 12.1 | 116 | 229.3 | 239.0 | 96 |
| 2 | 14.8 | 12.3 | 120 | 244.2 | 242.1 | 101 |
| 3 | 11.6 | 12.5 | 93 | 242.6 | 245.9 | 99 |
| 4 | 9.0 | 12.5 | 72 | 258.0 | 247.1 | 104 |

Source: U.S. Department of Commerce, *Survey of Current Business*, Vol. 51 (July 1971), pp. 13, 20, 26, 27. The seasonally adjusted quarterly estimates were obtained by dividing the official quarterly estimates at annual rates by four.

Table 8-1, and to the $15.9 billion seasonal decline in consumption implied elsewhere in the national income accounts.[11] The seasonal rise in collections is clearly a perverse policy result in this context. At a time of year when economic activity is temporarily depressed, owing to the post-Christmas slowdown, winter weather, income tax liabilities, and other factors, the situation is regularly aggravated by a large increase in taxes biting into disposable income. In 1969–70 the first-quarter tax increase clearly augmented by a substantial amount the "normal" seasonal decline in disposable income.[12] This extra drag on disposable income is fairly large relative to the seasonal decline in consumption, and it undoubtedly explained a significant part of the decline. The fourth-quarter situation is also perverse because GNP and consumption are then at their seasonal peaks and payroll taxes cut less deeply into disposable income than in any other quarter. In short, these taxes aggravate overall seasonality at the beginning and end of each year.

[11] It should be stressed again that these are quarterly totals, not annual rates.

[12] The effect on the change in disposable income was less than $4.8 billion, because the rise in accrued employer contributions does not affect disposable income; on the other hand, the rise in employee tax withheld was higher than indicated because of the lag in collections of the latter.

Since the seasonal pattern of collections is essentially autonomous and controllable by public policy, this opens to question the wisdom of a collections practice that aggravates an already pronounced seasonal pattern of income and spending. Although seasonal declines in disposable income and economic activity are brief and undoubtedly less serious than long-run swings, they cause difficulties for families unable or unwilling to budget for them and account for some wasted industrial capacity.[13] In particular, many families may find that when bills for holiday spending come due an automatic tax increase reduces their capacity to pay them. These perversities alone seem sufficient to justify alteration of the collection pattern.[14]

# Effect of Poorly Timed Statutory Changes

The direction of the economic impact of various discretionary changes in payroll tax yields has been summarized above. It seems worthwhile to indicate next, at least roughly, the likely order of magnitude of these effects. (This discussion is presented separately because of the speculative nature of the method and findings.) Here an attempt is made to abstract from seasonality by stressing seasonally adjusted data, so that the impact of the taxes on cycles of a greater duration may be considered. For illustration, the OASDHI statutory changes mentioned above are considered here, as well as possible perverse behavior of the UI tax under experience rating.

## Application of a Multiplier Model[15]

The objective is to indicate the effect of changes in payroll taxes on quarterly GNP; this requires a model of income determination that provides for a "multiplier" effect embodying lagged adjustments. A simple six-equation model applied by Okun to an analysis of the im-

---

[13] The effect on individual incomes is undoubtedly more significant than the waste of capacity, since most of the latter is probably avoided by a rational inventory policy on the part of producers.

[14] The expected effects of this seasonality are undoubtedly offset to some extent by Federal Reserve monetary policy, but reduction of the seasonal fluctuations would offer a more direct approach to the problem.

[15] This subsection outlines a multiplier model and its application to the problem of isolating the effects of tax changes. It may be omitted by readers more interested in the subsequent findings.

pact of the 1964–65 cut in individual income tax rates seems adequate for this exercise.[16]

The model provides for induced investment as well as pure consumption effects. The six equations are (1) GNP identity summing consumption, fixed investment, and inventory investment, and conventional functions explaining (2) consumption; (3) disposable income; (4) fixed investment; (5) inventory investment; and (6) corporate cash flow. The six fitted equations constitute a difference equation system portraying lagged responses. In this analysis the system was solved simultaneously, so that estimated successive quarterly GNP effects of a $1 change in personal taxes, and therefore in disposable income, could be traced onward from the quarter in which the change occurred. The path was traced through only ten quarters, because the asymptotic convergence to the steady-state multiplier appeared adequate at that point for illustrative purposes.

The fitted difference equation system indicates that a $1 cut in individual taxes (meaning a rise in disposable income) in a quarter tends to add $0.42 to GNP in that quarter through increased consumption and induced investment. As the $1 cut is maintained, additional spending out of the enhanced incomes produces a hypothetical net GNP gain of $0.84 in the second quarter. Net effects indicated in the third through the tenth quarters are $1.23, $1.57, $1.85, $2.06, $2.20, $2.30, $2.34, and $2.36, respectively.[17] In the empirical exercises discussed here, the full multiplier effect of the tax change on GNP is assumed to be attained by the tenth quarter. This path of theoretical increments to GNP is used in two types of evaluation of the impact of tax changes. The first is an estimate of the effects of poorly timed statutory rate changes on the quarterly path of the GNP. The second (reported in the next section) compares the effects of income and payroll tax changes on economic stability following World

[16] The objective was derivation of a quarterly GNP multiplier path on the assumption of a change in a single autonomous variable—personal tax rates. For this purpose a small macroeconomic system seemed as reliable as a large detailed model. For details of the model used, see Arthur M. Okun, "Measuring the Impact of the 1964 Tax Reduction," in Walter W. Heller (ed.), *Perspectives on Economic Growth* (Random House, 1968).

[17] This series is approaching a level somewhat below the steady state multiplier of $2.59 cited in the Okun study (*ibid.*, p. 45) because the small dividend effects were ignored for simplicity in the application of the model here. The doubling of the GNP effect in the second quarter, before the increments began to diminish, results from the estimated lags in consumer and investor response.

War II. As the methods adopted for these two exercises are admittedly very abstract, they are outlined briefly below.

The most speculative aspect of a statistical appraisal of this type is the estimation of the ceteris paribus impact of the tax change. Given an acceptable multiplier model, the computation is straightforward. However, the personal tax multiplier model applied in both problems considered here is an oversimplified structure; for example, no distinction is made between the effect on consumption of different types of personal tax cuts. The analysis of the impact of a tax change in abstraction from possible changes in other exogenous factors, such as the benefit structure and monetary policy, may seem even more artificial. No monetary explanatory variables are included in the investment equations of the model from which the quarterly multipliers are derived. To simulate the impact of the tax change in isolation, it is assumed that monetary policy accommodates to changes in demand for financial assets and for loans, so that credit conditions are neither tightened nor relaxed and interest rates are not affected.[18]

Another assumption involved in this isolation of tax effects is that government spending and private spending propensities (out of disposable income) are not affected by tax changes. It should be reiterated that such an assumption is only a device relied upon for hypothetical isolation of the tax effects. Furthermore, this application of the multiplier series takes no account of the effect on the tax base of the tax-induced impact on GNP.[19] These second-order effects were assumed to be of minor importance in analysis of the impact of a tax change on GNP over the following ten quarters.

Finally, the analytical method used here does not permit any generalizations about the relative size of the price and real components of

---

[18] This is not to say that monetary policy plays no role in this simulation; without its "accommodation" the results would be different, and in that sense the impact of the tax change is not completely or purely isolated. In any case, this formulation is not put forward as necessarily the best definition of a "neutral" monetary policy. The point is that it seems to make more sense to ask the result of a tax change with the price and availability of credit unchanged rather than in the context of, say, a fixed money supply. For a criticism of Okun's original analysis by Friedman, see his "Has Fiscal Policy Been Oversold?" in Milton Friedman and Walter W. Heller, *Monetary vs. Fiscal Policy* (Norton, 1969), pp. 55–57. For a comment, see Arthur M. Okun, *The Political Economy of Prosperity* (Brookings Institution, 1970), pp. 53–59.

[19] For example, a tax increase in a given quarter is assumed to depress the GNP in the current and subsequent quarters as indicated by the model; no further adjustment is made to allow for subsequent tax decreases due to the decline of GNP.

changes in GNP. This depends on the degree of slack in the economy (or the slope of the Phillips curve) at the time of the tax change. However, in the analysis of effects on recessions to be considered, it may be safely presumed that most of the depressing effect on the economy is in real terms.

In sum, the simple model applied here is probably adequate to simulate the short-run, ceteris paribus, real effects of small statutory tax increases.

*Impact of Statutory Increases before and during Recessions*

The analysis reported below concentrates on times when social security tax legislation has had perverse effects.[20] As indicated at the beginning of this chapter, payroll tax increases have at times performed positively in restraint of economic fluctuations, particularly since 1965. It seems appropriate, however, to discuss here the type of fiscal behavior that calls for correction. Furthermore, the multiplier model used in the analysis is most meaningful with respect to the perverse fiscal policies sometimes followed before and during recessions. With increasing slack in the economy, the GNP effects estimated by the multiplier model are predominantly real and not simply a reflection of price increases.[21]

Rate and/or ceiling increases in the OASDI tax were imposed during or shortly before the beginning of three of the four postwar recessions. Table 8-2 assesses the extent to which these tax increases aggravated each of the three economic slowdowns.[22] The first perverse postwar increase occurred in 1954, when the OASDI tax was increased from 3 to 4 percent in the middle of the 1953–54 recession. This second postwar recession had been under way since the third quarter of 1953. The rate change raised the OASDI tax by about $1.28 billion in the

[20] For a more general analysis of postwar fiscal policies and instruments affecting the recessions after World War II, see Wilfred Lewis, Jr., *Federal Fiscal Policy in the Postwar Recessions* (Brookings Institution, 1962).

[21] This stress on the recession experience does not imply that the multiplier model and fiscal tools are inapplicable in an inflationary situation. The point is that in the latter case the primary impact of fiscal measures is on prices rather than on output and employment.

[22] Only previous tax increases not more than ten quarters earlier were analyzed. The objective was to isolate effects on quarterly changes rather than on levels. Lagged effects were assumed to be fully worked out by ten quarters, so that there would be no further effects on rates of change in GNP. Another qualification of the method adopted is that it assumes the impact of both employer and employee taxes on disposable income is felt immediately.

## TABLE 8-2. Impact on Gross National Product of OASDI Tax Rate and Ceiling Increases before and during Three Postwar Recessions

*(In billions of dollars at seasonally adjusted annual rates)*

| Year and quarter | Turning point[a] | Gross national product | Amount of tax increase[b] | Estimated cut in GNP[c] | Hypothetical GNP[d] |
|---|---|---|---|---|---|
| 1953:3 | Peak | 365.8 | — | — | 365.8 |
| 4 | | 360.8 | — | — | 360.8 |
| 1954:1 | | 360.7 | 1.28 | 0.54 | 361.2 |
| 2 | | 360.4 | 1.27 | 1.08 | 361.5 |
| 3 | Trough | 364.7 | 1.28 | 1.57 | 366.3 |
| 4 | | 373.4 | 1.30 | 2.01 | 375.4 |
| 1957:1 | | 436.9 | 0.87 | 0.37 | 437.3 |
| 2 | | 439.9 | 0.87 | 0.73 | 440.6 |
| 3 | Peak | 446.3 | 0.89 | 1.08 | 447.4 |
| 4 | | 441.5 | 0.87 | 1.38 | 442.9 |
| 1958:1 | | 434.7 | 0.87 | 1.62 | 436.3 |
| 2 | Trough | 438.3 | 0.86 | 1.79 | 440.1 |
| 3 | | 451.4 | 0.89 | 1.93 | 453.3 |
| 4 | | 464.4 | 0.89 | 2.02 | 466.4 |
| 1959:1 | | 474.0 | 1.79 | 0.75 | 474.8 |
| 2 | | 486.9 | 1.84 | 1.53 | 488.4 |
| 3 | | 484.0 | 1.86 | 2.25 | 486.3 |
| 4 | | 490.5 | 1.86 | 2.89 | 493.4 |
| 1960:1 | | 503.0 | 3.85 | 4.25 | 507.3 |
| 2 | Peak | 504.7 | 3.88 | 5.50 | 510.2 |
| 3 | | 504.2 | 3.90 | 6.56 | 510.8 |
| 4 | | 503.3 | 3.94 | 7.46 | 510.8 |
| 1961:1 | Trough | 503.6 | —[e] | 8.14 | 511.7 |
| 2 | | 514.9 | —[e] | 8.62 | 523.5 |

Source: U.S. Department of Commerce, Office of Business Economics, *The National Income and Product Accounts of the United States, 1929–1965: Statistical* Tables (1966), pp. 2–3, 52–53.

[a] Business cycle turning dates as specified by the National Bureau of Economic Research.

[b] Estimated on an annual basis and distributed in a quarterly pattern in proportion to the pattern exhibited by seasonally adjusted contributions for social security. The term "increase" refers to the amount by which the tax is higher in the given quarter than it would have been without the tax increase; thus it is not a quarterly first difference, except in the case of the first quarter (when the tax increase first went into effect). The annual tax increases in the first two periods were derived on the basis of the relative change in rates and the actual level of the OASDI tax (OA$_w$ and OA$_{s-1}$ variables; see Appendix F). For the last period involving both rate and ceiling increases, the tax change was estimated on the basis of the change in predicted yields indicated by equation (7-6).

[c] Derived by application of multiplier path deduced from Okun model. See Arthur M. Okun, "Measuring the Impact of the 1964 Tax Reduction," in Walter W. Heller (ed.), *Perspectives on Economic Growth* (Random House, 1968). The multiplied GNP effect was primarily the lagged impact of the initial tax increase occurring in the first quarter; however, the multiplied effect of the small changes within the year is also included.

[d] Actual GNP plus estimated cut in GNP due to specified tax increases only. The cumulative effect of earlier increases is not included, because the objective is to isolate tax-induced changes in GNP. Tax increases ten quarters or more before the period in question are assumed to have no first difference effects this much later.

[e] Small additional changes in tax, in the absence of rate change, were ignored in computations for the first two quarters of 1961.

calendar year 1954. The estimated seasonally adjusted quarterly increases on an annual basis are shown in Table 8-2. Application of the multiplier model indicates that the tax increase depressed GNP, on an annual basis, by $0.5 billion in the first quarter of 1954 and by $1.1 billion and $1.6 billion in the second and third quarters.[23] The model indicates that without the tax increase GNP would have risen by $0.5 billion instead of falling by $1.1 billion between the peak and trough quarters. Although this depression of GNP by the tax in this interval amounts to slightly less than 0.5 percent, a tax-induced GNP cut of $1.6 billion in the middle of a perceived economic slowdown can scarcely be defended. Scheduled payroll tax increases have been postponed at other times, and this one clearly should have been.

The half-point rate increase in 1957 went into effect before the beginning of the recession that year. Although it amounted to less than $1 billion a year, the model indicates that it had depressed GNP by about $1.8 billion by the time of the trough of the 1957–58 recession, with about $0.71 billion of this contraction occurring after the peak. While these amounts are again rather small, they aggravated somewhat a severe recession that produced an $8 billion decline in GNP, aided in part by this tax increase. While the recession may not have been foreseeable, a rollback of the recent tax increase might have been considered as soon as the reality of the recession became clear. It is true that rollbacks of a tax increase have lagged effects and may only help fuel the next inflation, but such a risk should not prevent considering a rollback of a tax increase that may have helped precipitate a recession and is continuing to aggravate it.

The 1960–61 recession was preceded by substantial payroll tax increases at the start of both 1959 and 1960, and the slow rate of recovery in 1962 and 1963 may have been partly due to tax rate increases in those years. Increases in both rate and ceiling in 1959 raised the tax that year by about $1.8 billion, and a further increase added $3.9 billion more in 1960. According to the model, these two increases had restrained GNP by about $8 billion by the first quarter of 1961—the trough of the recession. While much of the rise in taxes occurred before the recession, the GNP was depressed by about $2.6 billion between peak and trough. The estimates indicate that instead of a $1.1 billion decline in GNP during the recession, there would have been a

[23] All quarterly estimates to be discussed here are seasonally adjusted and at annual rates.

$1.5 billion rise without the tax increase. While these magnitudes are also rather small, the tax continues to rise in relative terms year after year, and some consideration should be given to the state of the economy when tax changes are contemplated.

## Initial Imposition of the Social Security Tax

Perhaps the most striking example of a payroll tax increase at the wrong moment—and the largest in relative terms—involved the first imposition of the social security tax in 1937. Although this tax increase was not perverse in the usual sense, since the economy was in an expansion phase until May 1937, the Great Depression was not really over. Although unemployment was going down, the official rate was still on the order of 15 percent. The "expansion" did not appear altogether robust. Certainly it does not now appear to have been a suitable time to impose a 2 percent, no-exemption social security tax on payrolls, plus a railroad retirement tax, and a large increase in the UI tax. This is especially true since the new tax was not to be significantly offset by benefits. However, the "insurance principle" dictated that the only way to start the program was to begin the accumulation of large reserves, whatever the state of the economy. The fact that benefits could have commenced at once, financed on a current basis, was apprently given little consideration. The insurance principle had a life of its own and apparently was more important to many than economic reality.[24]

The 2 percent social security tax added $576 million to tax receipts in 1937, and the railroad and UI increases brought the payroll tax increase to about $1.1 billion that year. Built-in reactions reduced the social security and railroad taxes slightly in 1938, but expanded coverage by the UI tax increased its yield by $205 million. The net result was an increase of about $1.25 billion in those three taxes between 1936 and 1938. Although the drag imposed by the new tax on the stagnant economy of 1937 cannot be accurately estimated, it must have been substantial. Quarterly data are not available, but the postwar multiplier model suggests that the GNP change may have been depressed by about $1.8 billion, or about 2 percent of 1937 GNP,

[24] The conventional wisdom of today that reacts negatively to a large tax increase in a period of 15 percent unemployment was less prevalent in 1936. Some may have thought of the social security surpluses as contributing toward a balanced budget; this may also deserve some of the credit for the perverse policy.

between the peak and trough of the recession.[25] Although the actual $6 billion GNP decline in this severe recession can be only partially explained by the $1.25 billion tax increase between 1936 and 1938, it is likely that it carried some of the blame. Looking back, it seems extraordinary that a tax increase of this magnitude, raising federal receipts by about 25 percent, was allowed to go into effect with the unemployment rate near 15 percent. While not the equal of some perverse fiscal and monetary policies pursued in the early thirties, this victory of the insurance principle is nonetheless memorable.[26] Such arbitrary timing of statutory payroll tax increases as this one and others in the postwar period supplement the poor showing of the tax because of its inherent weakness as a built-in stabilizer.[27]

## Relative Postwar Stabilizing Effects of Income and Payroll Taxes

The statistical approach used in this study for analysis of the tax impact on GNP was outlined at the beginning of the preceding section, where the problem entailed a short-run appraisal of the ceteris paribus effects of statutory changes. The question considered here is the overall effect on stability of observed changes in yield resulting from built-in as well as statutory changes. The relative magnitude of fluctuations in the GNP with and without a tax involves a long-run evaluation, and the method is even more speculative. However, the impact of the tax can be considered cycle by cycle. In this case, even if the effect of the taxes in absolute terms cannot be reliably estimated, the relative impact of the two taxes on economic stability may be compared with confidence.

The evaluation of stabilizing impact requires the measurement of economic fluctuations. One way to approach this question is to compare variations in actual GNP with variations in hypothetical GNP

[25] This rough estimate assumes equal quarterly GNP and tax receipts during 1937 and 1938, respectively. The recession was dated from May 1937 to June 1938.

[26] It could be argued that the attractiveness of the new social program was responsible for this perverse tax increase. However, no such immediate tax increase would have been called for without acceptance of the insurance principle.

[27] Not all of the $1.25 billion increase was statutory; there were minor built-in changes, and the large UI tax increase may have been partly due to experience rating. In a sense the latter rate structure is not statutory, although the rates did change according to plan.

without the tax, as suggested in a formal analysis by Friedman, who assumed for simplicity a stationary state and adopted the variance as the measure of fluctuations in the level of economic activity.[28] In the long-run evaluation here, covering data for more than twenty years, the variance of the relative departures was measured from an estimated exponential trend line. This part of the overall variance of GNP is an appropriate measure of the short-run fluctuations to be compared, with and without each tax. Since the actual and hypothetical trend lines are different, the variance of each series was measured around its own trend line. The measure of the stabilizing performance of a tax was then defined as the ratio of this variance in the hypothetical absence of the tax to the actual variance.[29] A ratio greater (less) than unity indicates the tax was a net stabilizer (destabilizer) in the period studied.

The decision to measure relative variation around trend rather than to rely on the ordinary variance around the mean called for a trend model. The assumption adopted—a linear semilogarithmic trend—had two advantages. First, no departure from trend linearity was apparent in the semilogarithmic plot of postwar GNP or of the hypothetical GNP series. Second, equal residuals in the regression of transformed GNP against time represented equal relative variations in the original variables.[30]

[28] Milton Friedman, "The Effects of a Full-Employment Policy on Economic Stability: A Formal Analysis," in Milton Friedman, *Essays in Positive Economics* (University of Chicago Press, 1953). The present empirical application of this approach parallels in some respects that used in an interesting exercise by Neil A. Palomba in "Unemployment Compensation Program: Stabilizing or Destabilizing?" *Journal of Political Economy*, Vol. 76 (January–February 1968), pp. 91–100. Multipliers derived from the Okun model were also used there, but the GNP variance was not measured around a trend line as in the exercise here. The method by which the multiplier models were used to estimate hypothetical GNP was not explained in the article nor in the Ph.D. dissertation underlying it, entitled, "A Measure of the Stabilizing Effect of the Unemployment Compensation Program—With Emphasis on the Experience Rating Controversy (University of Minnesota, 1966).

[29] Estimation of the hypothetical GNP allowed for the lags indicated by the model. In this case the full multiplied effect of a tax was assumed to be reached in the tenth quarter following its imposition. The hypothetical GNP—that is, the GNP in the absence of a tax—for any given quarter is estimated by adding to the actual GNP the multiplied impact of the level of the tax ten quarters earlier, plus the multiplied impacts of subsequent changes in the tax through the quarter in question.

[30] It seemed appropriate to compare the *relative* variation of actual and hypothetical GNP from their respective trend lines; this also insured comparability of the results for two different points in time.

The two quarterly seasonally adjusted tax series used were "personal tax and nontax receipts" and "contributions for social insurance" from the national income accounts. For convenience, these are designated hereafter as income tax (IT) and payroll tax (PT), even though the series used are somewhat broader in coverage than the usual income and payroll tax concepts.[31] Hypothetical GNP, in the absence of income tax on the one hand and payroll tax on the other (GNP$_{IT}$ and GNP$_{PT}$, respectively), was estimated as explained above.

*Empirical Findings for Postwar Period by Cycle*

Measures of variation around the least squares exponential GNP trend lines are presented in Table 8-3. The fit for the entire period of eighty-seven quarters studied points to a degree of stabilization by the income tax but not by the payroll tax. The variance of residuals from the trend of the hypothetical GNP was 13 percent above that for the actual GNP. Expressed in terms of the relative residuals (original units), the hypothetical standard error of estimate is 4.5 percent, as against 4.2 percent in the actual series. While there is no way of testing the significance of this difference, the contrast between it and the slight degree of destabilization indicated for the payroll tax is about what might be expected.[32] The ratios for the four separate peak-to-peak cycles are also inconclusive. The income tax appears to have been a destabilizer in the third cycle, but it should be noted that this could be largely a result of the lag in the collection of capital gains. Large accruals of liabilities in 1959 first came due during the recession that began in 1960.

The income tax is shown to be a substantial stabilizer only in the last cycle, where the statistical result is fairly convincing, but the last cycle is incomplete, since no peak had been specified at the time the data was analyzed. The test covered a long period—thirty-nine quarters—and the hypothetical GNP no-tax residuals exceeded the residuals in the actual GNP in twenty-eight of those; the standard error of estimate measured as a percentage of the original units is 1.5 per-

---

[31] These data were adopted for this analysis because the narrower variants were not available on a quarterly, seasonally adjusted basis. The inclusion of nontaxes and estate and gift taxes caused the series used to exceed the income tax by about 4 percent in the period beginning in 1960. Federal "contributions for social insurance" exceeded OASDHI plus UI taxes by about 12 percent in the same period.

[32] The F test is not strictly applicable, but it does suggest that the 1.13 ratio is probably not significantly different from unity at the 5 percent level.

**TABLE 8-3. Postwar Variation of Gross National Product and Hypothetical GNP without Income and Payroll Taxes around Semilogarithmic Trend Lines, and Variance Ratios**

| | Variation around trend[a] | | | Variance ratios[b] | |
|---|---|---|---|---|---|
| | | Hypothetical GNP | | | |
| Period (year and quarter) | GNP | Without income tax, $GNP_{IT}$ | Without payroll tax, $GNP_{PT}$ | $\dfrac{V(GNP_{IT})}{V(GNP)}$ | $\dfrac{V(GNP_{PT})}{V(GNP)}$ |
| 1948:2–1969:4 | 0.0180 (4.2) | 0.0191 (4.5) | 0.0179 (4.2) | 1.13 | 0.98 |
| 1948:2–1953:2 | 0.0150 (3.5) | 0.0155 (3.6) | 0.0149 (3.5) | 1.06 | 0.98 |
| 1953:3–1957:2 | 0.0068 (1.6) | 0.0068 (1.6) | 0.0067 (1.6) | 1.00 | 0.98 |
| 1957:3–1960:1 | 0.0081 (1.9) | 0.0069 (1.6) | 0.0077 (1.8) | 0.74 | 0.92 |
| 1960:2–1969:4 | 0.0066 (1.5) | 0.0085 (2.0) | 0.0070 (1.6) | 1.67 | 1.12 |

Sources: Based on seasonally adjusted quarterly data for gross national product, personal tax and nontax receipts, and contributions for social insurance from Department of Commerce, Office of Business Economics, *The National Income and Product Accounts of the United States, 1929–1965: Statistical Tables* (1966), and *Survey of Current Business*, various issues. See text for methodology.

[a] Figures without parentheses are standard errors of estimate. Figures in parentheses are standard errors of estimate with the units transformed from logarithmic residuals to percentage deviations in the original variable.

[b] The figures given refer to ratios of the variances around the fitted trend lines. They measure the stabilizing performance of the tax. A ratio greater (less) than unity indicates that the tax is a net stabilizer (destabilizer) for the period indicated.

cent for the actual GNP and 2.0 percent for the hypothetical GNP. According to this multiplier model, the income tax appreciably stabilized the GNP on a smooth growth path in that interval. Although the departures from unity of the variance ratios may not be significant in the case of the income tax, when viewed collectively they seem substantially larger than in the case of the smaller payroll tax; this is in line with earlier discussion in which the payroll tax was shown to exhibit sluggish built-in response to income changes and to have undergone perverse statutory changes.

It would be tempting to infer that the results for the period 1948–69 in Table 8-3 show that the income tax is a substantial stabilizer while the payroll tax is about neutral—that is, has no effect on cyclical fluctuations. However, such an inference would have to be heavily qualified. First, it should be repeated that this analysis does not separate built-in and discretionary tax changes; since the latter are included, the results do not describe inherent characteristics of either type of tax.[33] Second, the statistical support for this proposition concerning stabilization properties is itself inadequate. The main reason for presenting the estimates is to suggest that the postwar payroll tax has had no significant or consistent effect on economic stability. Even the behavior of the income tax was unimpressive, except in the last cycle. Neither tax appears to be a significant stabilizer over complete cycles. Although each presumably has a healthy restraining influence in times of vigorous expansion, the lagged stimulus of either in recessions is often too little or too late.

The lack of stabilization in practice of the large, progressive income tax is probably due to the substantial lags in the effects of tax changes as well as to statutory changes that have perverse effects shortly afterwards. The desired built-in response takes place during the recession, but the effects of earlier tax increases may live on to swamp the counter-cyclical forces. However, substantial lags between tax accruals and collections may also bear some responsibility. As mentioned above, the volatile capital gains component can lead to large collections at an inappropriate time. In the particular case of recessions only three or four quarters in duration (see Table 8-2), it is not surprising that the stabilizing impact appears nominal. According to the multiplier model, the first and second quarter effects of a one-dollar cut in taxes are expansion of GNP by only 42 cents and 84 cents, respectively. By the fifth or sixth quarters, when the multiplied impact has become substantial, it is no longer needed because the recession is already over.

*Effects during Postwar Recessions*

The effects of income and payroll taxes in 1948–61 during recessions only are compared in Table 8-4.[34] The income tax is shown as a fairly strong stabilizer in 1948–49. The actual fall in GNP of $8.9 billion compares favorably with the hypothetical (no-tax) decline of $14.1 billion from peak to trough; according to the model, net de-

[33] Built-in flexibility is considered in Chapter VII; the preceding section of this chapter deals with statutory changes only, while the net postwar effects of both are summarized here.

[34] Although only recessions are considered here, payroll tax increases have undoubtedly produced a fortuitous stabilizing impact on occasion, as during the major Vietnam buildup beginning in 1965.

**TABLE 8-4. Effects of Income Taxes and Payroll Taxes on Gross National Product in Postwar Recessions**

*(In billions of dollars at seasonally adjusted annual rates)*

| | | Hypothetical GNP | | | |
| | | Without income tax, $GNP_{IT}$ | | Without payroll tax, $GNP_{PT}$ | |
| Recession dates (year and quarter) | Change in GNP | Change | Effect | Change | Effect |
|---|---|---|---|---|---|
| 1948:4–1949:4 | −8.9 | −14.1 | 5.2 | −8.6 | −0.3 |
| 1953:3–1954:3 | −1.1 | −3.8 | 2.7 | −0.3 | −0.8 |
| 1957:3–1958:2 | −8.0 | −6.8 | −1.2 | −6.6 | −1.4 |
| 1960:2–1961:1 | −1.1 | 4.1 | −5.2 | 2.5 | −3.6 |

Sources: Same as Table 8-3.

clines in the income tax had a $5.2 billion positive effect on GNP, checking its decline by that amount. However, much of this result was fortuitous. Income-splitting produced substantial income tax cuts in 1948, before the recession, strongly supplementing later built-in responses in producing a favorable impact on GNP. The income tax performed well in the 1953–54 recession without benefit of statutory assistance. However, the income tax was a destabilizer in the 1957–58 and 1960–61 recessions. In 1960–61 it appears to have turned a potential gain of $4.1 billion into a decline of $1.1 billion; apparently, this was due to a steady built-in rise in the tax of $6.1 billion during the eighteen months before the recession began, as well as to further increases during it. On balance, over these four recessions, the income tax appears to have contributed little to economic stability. Evidently, lagged reactions did as much damage in the last recession as they accomplished on the positive side in the first.

The performance of payroll taxes during these recessions was consistently negative and became steadily more so. The steady built-in growth of contributions for social insurance before each recession combined with the untimely statutory changes discussed earlier to produce a destabilizing impact in each recession. This culminated in an estimated $3.6 billion depression of GNP change between peak and trough of the 1960–61 recession—a result consistent with the $2.6 billion restraint due to the 1959 and 1960 OASDI statutory increases analyzed in Table 8-2. In sum, payroll taxes appear to have exerted a consistent and growing destabilizing influence during these four recessions. On balance, payroll taxes compare unfavorably with the income tax, which exerted a net counter-cyclical impact in two of the four recessions. The negative performance of payroll taxes during recessions contrasts with its roughly neutral overall performance (see Table 8-3). Apparently, its restraining influence during expansions roughly offsets the depressing effect during recessions of lagged responses to earlier tax increases.

An apologetic caveat is in order at this point. The numerical "estimates" discussed in the two preceding sections should not camouflage the speculative character of the methods used to produce them. The simplified structure of the model and the many simplifying assumptions adopted, as outlined earlier, attest to the shaky foundation of this exercise. Perhaps the best that can be said for the results reported here is that the crucial lags were derived from a fitted model with conventional structural equations. Application of these lags to the problem of estimating tax effects on GNP at least seems superior to sheer guesswork and perhaps not much different from simulations within a detailed econometric model.[35]

A further qualification of the finding that payroll and income taxes have low stabilizing power is also in order. The immediate built-in impact of withheld taxes on disposable income is clearly counter-cyclical. When incomes fall, withheld taxes also fall and the income tax declines substantially. Certainly, the tax structure operates to reduce the immediate decline in disposable income, except when offset by collection lags, as in the case of capital gains. The speculative results reported here do not dispute this. They simply suggest that lags in consumer and investor response may be sufficient on occasion to nullify the desired effect of the tax system on disposable incomes. They suggest also that collection lags inherent in the present tax system, especially in the volatile capital gains component, may produce destabilizing effects.

### The Special Case of the Unemployment Insurance Tax

No special analysis of the stabilizing properties of the unemployment insurance tax has been attempted here. However, this tax is of

---

[35] For simulations of the impact of social security within the framework of a large econometric model, see Wayne G. Vroman, "The Macroeconomic Effects of Social Insurance" (Ph.D. dissertation, University of Michigan, 1967).

special interest because of the "experience-rating" provisions which suggest that the tax may be inherently destabilizing. Every state has such a provision, under which the tax rate of each firm tends to vary directly with its unemployment experience.[36] The objective is to provide an incentive to employers to maintain a low record of unemployment, insofar as this is within the control of the firm. However, it may be assumed that most fluctuations in unemployment are caused by factors external to the firm. In such cases, a fall in the aggregate demand, causing a rise in unemployment, tends to raise UI tax rates (due to the experience-rating provision), and it is apparent that this may be a perverse and possibly destabilizing property of the UI tax. It tends to reinforce in a formalized way the ad hoc tendency of states to raise tax rates as their reserves decline with the payment of benefits.

It was shown in Chapter VII that, because of the low ceiling, the UI tax is a very weak built-in stabilizer. The possibility arises, therefore, that the tax is a destabilizer on balance, owing both to experience rating and to the natural tendency to raise taxes when unemployment increases. This question was considered by Neil Palomba,[37] who compared actual GNP variance with hypothetical GNP variance in the absence of UI collections. Since the postwar ratio of the latter to the former was about 1.03, he concluded that the tax was not destabilizing.[38] Palomba obtained results consistently of this order for five different experience-rating systems and for different postwar cycles. He also tested a hypothetical fixed tax rate of 2.7 percent, obtaining ratios about the same or slightly lower, which suggested that experience rating did not worsen the cyclical performance of the tax.

All of Palomba's results are consistent with the conclusion that the UI tax is not destabilizing, with or without experience rating. Since this finding may seem out of line with a priori expectations, reasons for it should be considered. With the possible exception of his fixed 2.7 percent rate test, Palomba's findings do not necessarily indicate that the experience rating itself is not a destabilizing factor. It

[36] For a description of the postwar UI tax rate experience, see Richard A. Lester, *The Economics of Unemployment Compensation* (Princeton University, Department of Economics, Industrial Relations Section, 1962), pp. 68–73.

[37] "Unemployment Compensation Program." See this article for a discussion of the different types of experience-rating formulas.

[38] The excess of this ratio over unity is certainly not sufficient to establish the converse proposition—that the tax *is* a stabilizer.

could have been offset by whatever small degree of built-in flexibility still exists or by counter-cyclical statutory changes, if any; or it could be so small as to be statistically undetectable. Furthermore, most of the variance measured by Palomba (around the mean) is due to trend, and it would be difficult for any cyclical variable to make itself visible in the ratio. These factors seem sufficient to conceal any possible pro-cyclical result of experience rating. On the other hand, the usual lags of a year or so in rate adjustment make it unlikely that there would consistently be perverse effects. Rate increases caused by postwar re-cessions, for example, generally became effective after the recessions were over, and still further time was required before the economic effects worked themselves out. While Palomba's findings do not give the final answer on experience rating itself, his case against the exis-tence of generally perverse effects seems plausible.

## The Postwar Impact of Payroll Tax Seasonality

The response of seasonally adjusted GNP to changes in seasonally adjusted taxes has been considered above. The analysis of stabiliza-tion effects abstracted from changes caused by seasonality in tax col-lections. The direction of the impact of tax yield seasonality on other economic aggregates was discussed early in this chapter. It would also be useful to estimate empirically the magnitude of the effect of this seasonality on other variables.

Seasonality in collections can be expected to affect within-the-year variations in consumption. No estimate of this relationship has been carried out in this study, but a brief reference to an earlier study by Joseph M. Bonin is in order.[39] His study attempted to isolate the effect on consumption of seasonality in OASDHI employee tax payments.[40] Regression models were used in his study to explain "seasonals" in aggregate consumption and its components.[41] These seasonals were regressed on seasonals for (1) OASDHI employee tax payments, (2)

[39] *Some Economic Effects of Seasonality in OASDHI Tax Payments.*

[40] The employer tax was not considered. Even if borne by labor in the long run, sea-sonal variations in the employer tax clearly have no seasonal impact on disposable income.

[41] A "seasonal" in a quarterly observation was defined as the "absolute seasonal ad-justment value" (*Some Economic Effects*, p. 14) or the unadjusted value less the sea-sonally adjusted value (*ibid.*, p. 8). Thus a positive "seasonal," such as that in the first quarter, implies an above-average level of the tax.

personal income tax, (3) installment credit, (4) noninstallment credit, and (5) current receipts before OASDHI withholding, plus quarterly dummies designed to explain some of the seasonality in consumption not explained by the five behavioral variables. Both current dollar and deflated values were used, but the latter were stressed.

Regression results for the OASDHI tax as one of the explanatory variables in each of Bonin's regressions are given in Table 8-5. Although questionable in some respects, the findings are of interest. These statistics suggest a consistent pattern of the expected negative association between spending and the tax, except in the case of nondurables. The tax variable is generally significant in the regression models in competition with four other behavioral variables and the quarterly dummies. According to the partial correlation coefficients, the durable goods category and its three subgroups are most responsive to seasonal changes in the OASDHI tax. The partial correlation coefficient for all durables indicates that the tax variable explains an impressive 42 percent of the variance not explained by all of the other variables in the model. Bonin's finding of a high degree of sensitivity to seasonal tax changes on the part of durable goods consumption only is in accord with a priori expectations. It is generally assumed that spending on durables is much more income elastic than spending on nondurables and services. Consumption in the latter categories is less postponable and flexible, and the low partial correlations obtained in Bonin's study support this hypothesis.

Unfortunately, the large size of the regression coefficients obtained in the Bonin study weaken its message. For example, one re-

**TABLE 8-5. Estimated Response of Deflated Absolute Consumption Seasonals to OASDHI Tax Seasonals, 1952–64**

| Consumption variable | Partial correlation | Regression coefficient | Standard error |
|---|---|---|---|
| Personal consumption | −0.47 | −3.05 | 0.87 |
| Total durables | −0.65 | −2.77 | 0.49 |
|   Automobiles and parts | −0.47 | −1.37 | 0.40 |
|   Furnishings and household equipment | −0.57 | −0.90 | 0.20 |
|   Other durables | −0.58 | −0.68 | 0.15 |
| Nondurables | 0.01 | 0.03 | 0.67 |
| Services | −0.26 | −0.51 | 0.29 |

Source: Joseph M. Bonin, *Some Economic Effects of Seasonality in OASDHI Tax Payments*, U.S. Social Security Administration, Office of Research and Statistics, Research Report 20 (1967), pp. 32–33.

gression implies that a one-dollar seasonal decrease in the tax toward the end of the calendar year tends to increase consumption of durables by $2.77, a spending increase significantly greater than the plausible upper limit of one dollar. This unacceptably large coefficient may suggest to some that the results merely reflect (noncausal) coincidences such as the traditional rise in fourth-quarter spending at a time when the payroll tax happens to be falling. However, the dummy variables offer some defense against this criticism, since they act as proxies for all seasonal factors not accounted for by the behavioral variables in the model. If the regression procedure is successful, the dummies should prevent the tax and other behavioral variables from absorbing much of the effects of habit and tradition, in which case the coefficients for the behavioral variables should indicate association over and above the obviously coincidental relationships. The regressions indicate that, after the dummies have explained all of the "orthodox" consumption seasonality they can, seasonality in the OASDHI tax can explain a significant proportion of the residual variance.

Whatever the success of the dummy variable technique, the fact remains that the coefficients for total consumption and durable goods are implausibly large. It seems likely that the importance of the tax variable is being exaggerated in the regressions, because it is acting as a proxy for some behavioral variable not included. For example, unemployment seasonality (not included in the model) is also negatively correlated with consumption, rising early in the year and falling at the end. The income effects of unemployment changes could affect consumption and probably should have been included in the model.[42] Since seasonality in the payroll tax and unemployment are positively correlated, exclusion of the latter may have resulted in the exaggerated explanatory credit given to the former.

Clearly the Bonin findings are meaningful only with respect to the direction of the association and the indicated concentration of the tax impact on the consumption of durable goods. They offer some support for the proposition that the seasonal collection pattern of the OASDHI tax should be modified to prevent its stimulation of undesirable seasonality in the economy.

---

[42] Alternatively, the positive correlation between personal income seasonality and consumption could be taken into account directly, although the implied personal income seasonals are not available.

## Conclusions

Statutory increases in the payroll tax structure appear to have contributed significantly to the intensity of recessions when imposed during the slack period of the 1930s, and before and during three recessions after World War II. Arbitrary and preventable seasonal patterns in collections have also aggravated the inherent tendency of the economy to sag in the winter and soar in the fall.

A rough quantitative evaluation of the stabilizing effect of built-in and statutory changes in income and payroll taxes was not very complimentary to either. An overall postwar test, plus separate tests for the four peak-to-peak cycles, suggested only modest counter-cyclical pressure by the income tax, and the payroll tax appeared neutral at best. Separate analyses of the four recessions following World War II suggest that in that context the income tax was on balance neutral and that the payroll tax aggravated the recessions to an increasing extent over time. While the lag structure applied in these rough tests of the GNP impact of tax changes is of unknown validity, the results appear plausible. If the lag pattern is anything like that indicated, it is not surprising that built-in and statutory tax increases before a recession, and even perverse increases later, may have lagged effects offsetting or swamping any built-in tax cuts during the recession itself. However, until the method of forecasting is improved and policy makers begin to act on the basis of forecasts, not much can be done about this.[43]

---

[43] Several qualifications of these highly tentative findings should be repeated. First, they are partially the outcome of discretionary tax changes (sometimes perverse), not the result of built-in changes alone. Second, the immediate built-in effects of withholding on disposable income are clearly in the desired direction; lags in spending response appear to have blunted the stabilization impact of these taxes. In the case of the income tax, the lag in capital gains collections may also prove destabilizing. Finally, in the case of the payroll tax, it should be reiterated that tax changes alone are being considered. Changes in benefits and monetary policy which often go hand-in-hand with the latter can and often have contributed to stabilization.

# CHAPTER IX

# Allocative and Growth Effects

THIS STUDY has dodged for the most part any reference to allocative and growth effects of the payroll tax—two issues usually considered in economic studies of a particular type of tax. Some reasons for this omission and brief comments on the two issues are presented in this chapter.

## Resource Allocation and Economic Efficiency

The impact of a tax on the allocation of resources among industries, firms, and regions is a standard candidate for investigation in a study such as this one. The question usually raised is the extent to which a tax causes distortions, inefficiency, and economic waste. Techniques have been devised to approximate the economic losses that may occur due to the disturbance of the free market equilibrium by a tax. However, in the case of the old-age, survivors, disability, and health insurance (OASDHI) and unemployment insurance (UI) payroll taxes, the allocative effects were considered of secondary importance for a number of reasons.

### Discrimination between Labor and Capital

It might be presumed that a major allocative impact of the payroll tax would result from its discriminatory imposition on a single factor

—in this case, labor. If the tax should increase the cost of labor, it might appear that employers would be encouraged to substitute capital for the taxed factor. However, persuasive theoretical discussion has already suggested that this is not so, since the cost of capital would also be increased. This aggregative argument, of course, does not deny allocative effects of rate differentials.[1] In any case, the analysis in Chapters II and III suggests that the entire burden of a tax tied to the use of labor falls on the income share of labor itself. If this is correct, the payroll tax does not increase the aggregate cost of labor to employers, and the issue of overall substitution of capital for labor does not even arise. This leaves only the minor rate differentials within the payroll tax itself as a potential source of allocative effects.

## Tax Coverage and Statutory Rate Differentials

For this study, the choice was made at the outset to concentrate on taxes of very general coverage, such as the typical payroll taxes of the era following World War II. A tax with uniform rates applied rather generally to all industries, firms, and regions is not expected to reallocate resources within these categories. The degree of labor and capital mobility between the very small and economically atypical sector covered by neither social security nor government employee retirement programs, on the one hand, and the covered sector, on the other hand, is undoubtedly very slight. Even though the coverage of the UI system is less general, the same must be true under that program; for example, it does not seem likely that the UI tax in covered industries will drive labor or capital to uncovered sectors, such as academic institutions.

In short, any allocative effect resulting from incomplete coverage of the major U.S. payroll taxes is probably trivial. However, the effect is greater in the case of recently introduced payroll taxes which discriminate sharply in favor of uncovered sectors that are competing

---

[1] For discussion of this point, see Carl S. Shoup, *Public Finance* (Aldine, 1969), p. 412; E. J. Mishan, "The Emperor's New Clothes: The Payroll Tax Stripped Bare," *Bankers' Magazine*, Vol. 192 (July 1961), pp. 17–22; Paul A. Samuelson, "A New Theorem on Nonsubstitution," in Joseph E. Stiglitz (ed.), *The Collected Scientific Papers of Paul A. Samuelson* (M.I.T. Press, 1966), Vol. 1, pp. 520–36; Martin Norr and Pierre Kerlan (correspondent), *Taxation in France*, World Tax Series, Harvard Law School (Commerce Clearing House, 1966), pp. 206–07; "Taxes on Wages or Employment and Family Allowances in European Countries," in United Nations, Economic Commission for Europe, *Economic Bulletin for Europe*, Vol. 4 (August 1952), pp. 48–49.

with the taxed sectors for labor and capital. These include such taxes as the British selective employment tax (SET) scheme, which taxes services and subsidizes manufacturing; urban earnings taxes, which favor suburban economic activity; and earnings taxes on commuters. While these more recent payroll taxes are growing in importance, they are mainly beyond the scope of this book.[2]

In addition to the attention given the contrast between covered and noncovered sectors, considerable study has been made in the past of two types of tax rate differentials among covered economic units: (1) a system of mainly statutory differentials under the UI program, and (2) a pattern of effective rate differentials in both the OASDHI and UI taxes. The statutory differentials arising from disparate state UI programs and those caused by the "experience-rating" structure can be expected to produce some price and allocative effects.[3] It has also been argued that such differentials tend to frustrate attempts by the employer to shift the tax.[4] Several points should be made in response to these arguments. First, the mobility of labor and capital may be sufficient to produce some direct allocative response to an earnings tax differential of 2 or 3 percentage points, but it is unlikely to be substantial. With respect to the potential reallocation of capital in particular, this tax differential seems a small stimulus compared to the cost of moving a firm to another state or substituting capital for labor.[5]

It is more likely that employers will respond initially to these small

[2] As pointed out in Chapter I, some work has already been done on these taxes, including a particularly interesting though inconclusive study of the SET. See W. B. Reddaway, *Effects of the Selective Employment Tax: First Report on the Distributive Trades* (London: Her Majesty's Stationery Office, 1970). This report suggests tentatively that the tax appears to have achieved a shift of labor from services to manufacturing and an increase in productivity in the former sector sufficient to recoup a substantial portion of the tax (see especially pp. 123–24). It should be recalled from Chapter II, however, that relative price and labor allocation effects due to such a selective tax are not inconsistent with the key proposition that labor bears the entire payroll tax.

[3] Such effects would only be totally absent under special conditions, such as complete inelasticity of individual labor supply.

[4] Richard A. Lester, *The Economics of Unemployment Compensation* (Princeton University, Department of Economics, Industrial Relations Section, 1962), pp. 60–68.

[5] It is not clear that even such an enormous tax differential as that between the corporate and noncorporate sectors has had substantial allocative effects. Actually, the effective differential may not be as great as it appears because of the role of the corporate structure as an individual income tax shelter. For an analysis of allocative effects of the corporation income tax, see Arnold C. Harberger, "Efficiency Effects of Taxes on Income From Capital," in Marian Krzyzaniak (ed.), *Effects of Corporation Income Tax* (Wayne State University Press, 1966).

tax differentials with price adjustments and wage restraint, which may in turn produce some reallocation of capital and labor. As Lester has pointed out, price competition may be sufficient to restrain forward shifting of the tax differential by the more highly taxed employers.[6] Price increases should at least result in some contraction of sales and output. With or without price increases, the employer can be expected to restrain the growth of wage rates. Such wage restraint would be a natural response to any newly imposed tax differential that would otherwise raise his labor costs without a validating change in labor productivity. This in turn would produce a wage differential to which workers might tend to react according to their mobility. In the particular case of intrastate wage differentials among firms, such as those resulting from experience rating, the earner might need only to change jobs within a town to erase the differential.

The primary purpose here is not to answer the question of which potential allocative or price effect of these rate differentials is likely to be the most substantial. Probably there has been some effect from a number of factors: wage restraint, movement of labor, price increases (leading to lower volume), and even a move of labor and firms from state to state. Indeed, the two-sector competitive model outlined in Chapter II portrays exactly this set of adjustments to the imposition of an employer tax on labor in one sector. Whether the taxed sector reacts by cutting wages, raising prices, or both, the new equilibrium solution reveals in the taxed sector a lower wage rate, lower employment, a higher product price, and a lower output, as well as the full burden of the tax on labor's share. However, these logical results from the formal model do not deny that any reallocation and waste resulting from the small UI rate differentials are probably relatively trivial —certainly less important than the effect of the tax on factor shares.[7]

---

[6] Lester, *Economics of Unemployment Compensation*, pp. 60–64.

[7] This is not to say that even small allocative effects are totally unimportant with respect to efficiency. Some distortions and waste may result from these rate differentials, but the likely allocative distortions did not seem quantitatively significant enough to justify a statistical evaluation similar to that pioneered by Harberger. Such an analysis is in order in the case of a large differential, like the one between the corporate and noncorporate sector. See Arnold C. Harberger, "The Corporation Income Tax: An Empirical Appraisal," in *Tax Revision Compendium*, Compendium of Papers on Broadening the Tax Base, submitted to the House Committee on Ways and Means (1959), Vol. 1, pp. 231–50. A differential of at most 2 or 3 percentage points in the payroll tax did not appear to merit this type of analysis. However, for a brief analysis of welfare costs, see Ronald F. Hoffman, "Welfare Cost Calculations and the Payroll Tax" (unpublished paper, no date).

With respect to potential reallocation, it is essential to repeat an important point. Even if the allocative effect of OASDHI or UI taxes, such as a movement of labor to a low-tax sector, is found to be more substantial than is surmised here, this finding is still not inconsistent with the proposition that labor bears the tax. As shown in Chapter II, even substantial reallocation of labor is not necessarily inconsistent with this incidence proposition, which is highly significant for most problems considered in this study.

### Other Effective Rate Differentials

The second type of tax rate differential to attract attention over the years is the pattern of effective rate variation that is present even in the case of the OASDHI tax, despite its uniform nominal rates. The rate of tax on a single factor (labor), measured as a percentage of value added, varies by firm, industry, and region for two reasons. First, this effective tax rate is highest for labor-intensive economic and geographical units. Second, due to the ceiling on taxable earnings, the effective rate on total wages and salaries (and also on value added) is lower, the greater the portion that is exempt by the ceiling. Roughly speaking, the higher the average earnings are in a firm, the lower is the effective tax rate. To some this has indicated an incentive to use more overtime labor and skilled labor. However, some points can be made to suggest that these tax rate variations lack behavioral significance.

Various efforts have been made to appraise the presumed inequities and allocative effects due to these differentials.[8] No such evaluation was undertaken in this study, however, because a priori reasoning suggests that these differentials have even less impact on price and allocative behavior than do statutory differentials in the UI tax. They are likely to have little impact on employer behavior and no direct effect at all on the motivation of labor. Reasons for this judgment are outlined below.

For illustration, consider industry differentials due to contrasting

---

[8] In the mid-thirties social security proponents found it necessary to ward off attacks by business on these alleged inequities. See, for example, a detailed prewar analysis of these differentials measured in endless ways: H. P. Mulford, *Incidence and Effects of the Pay-Roll Tax*, Preliminary Report, Prepared for the Bureau of Research and Statistics of the Social Security Board (Oct. 1, 1936; processed). For a postwar study asserting substantial distortions, see Elizabeth Deran, "Industry Variations in the Social Security Tax: Effects on Equity and Resource Allocation," *Quarterly Review of Economics and Business*, Vol. 7 (Autumn 1967), pp. 7–17.

labor intensity. For 1963 Deran[9] shows the highest employer tax rate on value added to be 2.0 percent in the wage-intensive leather and leather products industry and the lowest to be 0.4 percent in oil and gas extraction.[10] Presumably the firms in each industry have already attempted to shift the tax by means of price increases and/or wage restraint. Such actions may have had allocative effects on some leather employers, for example, if their *competitors* in the product and labor market faced lower tax rates against which to react. The low-tax competitors with low labor intensity may have captured some of the market and labor from those with larger price and wage reactions, thereby tending to equalize labor intensity among firms.[11] However, if all firms in the leather industry faced the same tax rate on value added, they would have shifted the entire real tax to labor through some combination of price and wage adjustment, according to the analysis in Chapters II and III. Capital would not have fled, because the rate of return would have remained unchanged. The price increases and wage decreases in the oil industry would have been smaller because of the 1.6 percent differential in their favor; however, this differential would directly produce allocative effects only to the extent to which the leather industry had lost labor to the oil industry. Since labor mobility between such diverse industries is probably relatively low, labor reallocation due to such differentials should be even less than that between competing firms with rate differentials.

Undoubtedly, in the case of competing industries such as steel and aluminum, there could be some direct short-run allocative effects on each if their labor intensity differed.[12] However, the cases of competing industries and firms with markedly different labor intensity seem likely to produce allocative effects which are second order at best compared to those due to the statutory UI differentials among competitors. The degree of competition determines the allocative effect of either type of differential, but the opinion expressed here

[9] "Industry Variations in the Social Security Tax," p. 13.

[10] A small part of this discrepancy was due to the ceiling, but the initial concern here is with the main factor—differing labor intensity.

[11] This movement of labor is not due to any direct effect of the tax differential. The effective rate on value added is irrelevant to labor. Any move by labor is due to pressure on the basic wage as the employer tries to shift his tax differential.

[12] This would not be true in the long run when tax-induced increases in labor costs would be reflected also in the cost of capital equipment. For references to discussions of this question, see note 1 above.

merely assumes that (1) the effect will only be important where competition is strong and direct, and (2) that in such confrontations among firms (generally those engaged in the same activity) the effect of variation of labor intensity will not be great.

A further point remains to be made. It has been assumed that the employer tax is completely shifted to labor. It might be supposed that a high rate of tax on value added in one industry would drive labor to an industry where the effective rate of tax is low. This does not follow, because what is relevant to the worker is the tax rate on earnings, not value added. Under OASDHI this is the same in all industries whatever the rate on value added, except for a minor complication introduced by the ceiling. If the worker does move, it will be because employer pressure on wages has reduced the basic wage below what he can get elsewhere, not because the new employer pays a lower tax rate on value added.

The other aspect of the effective cross-section variation in the OASDHI rate is the relatively high tax rate on low-wage labor. This differential is different in its likely effect from the others. In the case of a statutory differential between employers, for example, the high-tax employer can expect to lose labor to his competitors as the result of his more substantial price increases and/or wage cuts in reaction to the tax. However, the employer with low-wage, high-tax labor need not expect wage cuts to drive labor to competitors with low tax rates. There are two reasons for this. First, unlike the other differentials, the high tax rate goes *with* the worker, and he is not competitive until his wage-plus-tax per unit of productivity falls to the level paid to high-wage, low-tax workers. Second, the low-wage labor may not be mobile or readily able to be substituted for the high-wage labor in other firms. In any case, after the tax is imposed, the new equilibrium requires equal wage-plus-tax per unit of productivity. This can only be achieved by the low-wage worker's absorbing the tax differential that is operating against him.

The new equilibrium involving this wage adjustment can come about through pressures on high-tax wages due to price increases leading to sales contraction, direct wage restraint imposed by employers, and/or competition from low-tax labor. Although the mixture by which the wage adjustment is achieved may be complex, it is doubtful that much reallocation of labor among firms will ultimately take place. On the assumption that the tax is borne by labor, the high-tax worker must eventually accept a relatively low basic wage per unit of productivity or lose his job. Nothing is to be gained by his trying to move to another industry, as he would be forced to do if the employer shifted the tax by means of price increases rather than wage restraint.

This discussion has suggested the directions of the likely reactions to the sudden imposition of a substantial tax rate differential due to the ceiling. Actually, the differentials are extremely small, and it is unlikely that they would elicit any significant competitive interaction among economic units.[13] What is more likely is that the tax will be absorbed by both high-wage and low-wage labor through wage restraint over time. The higher tax on the low-wage worker must be absorbed, because he cannot escape it by moving as can workers in firms with high statutory rates.

An important point should be reemphasized here. The fear has been expressed that the high tax rate on low-wage labor will encourage substitution of skilled for unskilled labor. However, if the analysis in this study is correct, the tax will be borne by labor and there will be no incentive for substitution. Since unskilled workers are not displaced, this outcome simply reaffirms that the payroll tax is regressive and bears most heavily on them. (The tax does, of course, offer some incentive to workers to become more skilled and/or to work longer hours in order to reduce their effective tax rates.)

Finally, however the minor allocative effects work themselves out, the effective tax rate on earnings alone will still be lower, the higher the earner's wage above the ceiling. This might suggest a special incentive for the worker to try to break into a higher wage industry. It is true that the only way the worker can reduce his tax rate is to find a job in which he earns a greater excess above the current taxable ceiling. However, workers earning above the ceiling pay a lump-sum tax which has no impact on economic behavior. Achievement of a lower effective tax rate would bring no tax saving in absolute terms, and the tax differential therefore adds nothing to the always-present incentive to find a job with better pay.[14] As in the case of rate differen-

---

[13] For 1963 Deran shows a maximum OASDI tax rate on wages and salaries of 3.8 percent for hotels and other lodging places and a minimum rate of 2.5 percent in metal mining ("Industry Variations in the Social Security Tax," p. 13).

[14] For a worker below the ceiling, the tax decreases slightly the incentive to move to a higher-paying job.

tials due to labor intensivity, those due to the ceiling offer no direct incentive for labor to move, even when the entire tax falls on labor. Such an incentive will only be felt if wage restraint due to a relatively high tax rate reduces the *basic* wage below that attainable elsewhere.

*Summary of Coverage, Rate Differentials, and Allocation*

To sum up, the direction of the price and allocative effects of the degree of coverage and statutory rate differentials in the payroll tax is predictable with some confidence, but the magnitudes are unknown. The small size of these differentials discourages any detailed analysis of their impact on prices, resource use, and efficiency. Moreover, for the reasons just outlined, the impact of effective rate differentials due to variations in labor intensity and average earnings are assumed to be even more trivial.

The preoccupation of neoclassical economics with the optimum allocation of scarce resources to unlimited demands was shaken by the depression. The subsequent shift of emphasis from the problems of allocation and efficiency to the determinants of aggregate output and its distribution may have now gone too far. One may concede this in general terms without feeling compelled to assess the allocative, distortion, and waste effects of any given public policy. In the case of the OASDHI and UI taxes, a detailed exploration of this question would itself be an inefficient allocation of resources.[15]

# The Long-run Rate of Growth

There is no ready-made apology for failure to evaluate the impact of payroll taxes on the rate of growth; it cannot be claimed that the impact is trivial. The main deterrent to such an evaluation is that the analysis of the long-run impact of changes in a single exogenous variable like the payroll tax (with others such as monetary policy and benefits held constant, or specified in some arbitrary way) would be an even more speculative effort than the short-run analysis of Chapter VIII. The most that can be offered is speculation about the extent to which the payroll tax imposes a drag on the economy as compared with its most direct rival, the income tax.

[15] For a formal microeconomic analysis of a tax on a particular factor of production, see Alan Williams, *Public Finance and Budgetary Policy* (Praeger, 1963), pp. 141–47. For an analysis of the costs of distortions produced by the payroll tax, see Hoffman, "Welfare Cost Calculations and the Payroll Tax."

## Resource Allocation

If the payroll tax has such minor allocative effects as suggested in the preceding section, it cannot be accused of significantly slowing growth by promoting inefficient use of resources. It is very doubtful that either capital or labor is driven to any significant extent into less productive uses by the small differentials in this tax across industries and regions. It is more likely that UI differentials favoring industries and firms with low unemployment records would promote efficiency and growth by enticing labor and capital away from the slack sectors. However, these allocative incentives, like others in the payroll tax structure, do not appear quantitatively significant. With respect to allocative efficiency, there is no reason to suspect that this tax on one factor suffers by comparison with the individual income tax, even though the latter is free of such discrimination.

## Work Incentives and Resource Use

The effect of the income and payroll taxes on the aggregate supply of the factors capital and labor is a more debatable question. In particular, it has been suggested that a heavy tax on labor decreases work incentive and increases a preference for leisure. If the payroll tax is assumed to fall on labor, it may be thought that the quantity of labor supplied will tend to be depressed. However, even the direction of the effect on effort is in doubt. There is no way of comparing empirically the contraction of labor supply due to the "substitution effect" with the possible expansion due to the "income effect." Although some workers may substitute leisure for work in reaction to a lower net wage, others may find themselves forced to work more hours in order to make ends meet after their income has fallen. In any case, no evidence has yet appeared disputing the common presumption that aggregate labor supply is highly inelastic with respect to the wage rate.

The ceiling on taxable earnings is relevant to the question of incentives, just as it is to appraising the built-in flexibility of the tax. Covered earners above the ceiling (varying in number from 25 to 35 percent in the 1960–70 decade and paying a lump-sum tax) save no tax by working less. They also are unmoved by ceiling increases, unless the ceiling catches up with their income level. Even rate increases amount to a smaller percentage of their earnings than they do for earners below the ceiling. In short, the work disincentive effect of a given payroll tax on earners above the ceiling is zero, and the effect of ceiling and rate increases is minimal. At the same time, it has not been suggested in the literature that taxes on below-average earners are a serious disincentive to work; it is assumed that the income effect of a tax may even increase their work incentive.

That the payroll tax suffers few demerits as a disincentive to work could place it in contrast with the progressive income tax, which has been charged with discouraging economic growth by penalizing extra effort with ever-higher marginal tax rates.[16] Although a disincentive effect of the income tax has been frequently alleged, there is no empirical evidence that the tax has a strong impact on labor supplied and no agreement on this point in the literature. As in the case of the payroll tax, there is no way of measuring the relative strength of the substitution and income effects of the tax. Even if most employees were inclined to contract the amount of labor offered, rigidities in work habits and commitments would probably block much of this in practice. A recent detailed study concluded that "the loss of annual output due to work disincentives caused by the progressive income tax is of negligible proportions."[17]

It seems safe to conclude that, if there is any difference at all between the taxes, the payroll tax has less disincentive effect on growth than does the income tax, but that any difference is unlikely to be great. While any disincentive effect of the payroll tax must surely be trivial, any substantial work restraint imposed by the income tax also remains to be proved.

### Effect on Personal Saving

The one competition in which the payroll tax scores against the income tax is in its impact on personal saving. Here, the evaluation of relative growth effects depends heavily on the conclusion that the payroll tax is borne entirely by labor. As a regressive tax on the earn-

---

[16] For an unfavorable comparison of the income tax to the payroll tax on this count, see Otto Eckstein, "Financing the System of Social Insurance," in William G. Bowen and others (eds.), *The American System of Social Insurance: Its Philosophy, Impact, and Future Development* (McGraw-Hill, 1968).

[17] Robin Barlow, Harvey E. Brazer, and James N. Morgan, *Economic Behavior of the Affluent* (Brookings Institution, 1966), p. 3; see pp. 129–50 for the authors' evidence for their proposition.

ings of labor, it siphons off income of which only a small portion would have been saved without the tax. Clearly, the payroll tax cuts into personal saving far less than the income tax at high rates on high-income potential savers—that is, for a given total yield of the two taxes, the greater the concentration on payroll taxes, the higher the saving.

The payroll tax achieves its net favorable impact on personal saving—relative to the income tax—by constraining the consumption of low-income families. The price they pay out of current incomes is an involuntary contribution to the greater saving potential of higher income groups who would otherwise be paying higher income taxes. Whether the payroll taxpayers ultimately receive some degree of quid pro quo depends on the extent to which the enhanced saving and investment potential actually generates more rapid growth and ultimately higher consumption.

The achievement through the payroll tax of a higher saving ratio than would exist under the income tax alone is not without risk. Because of the volatility of investment spending, the higher saving ratio increases the instability of the economy, and any slumps due to a shortage of investment offsets to the higher saving would be more severe than otherwise. Nevertheless, the regressive payroll tax is a lesser drag on potential growth than the progressive income tax. A key issue in the comparison of the taxes then becomes the trade-off between greater growth potential under the payroll tax and greater equity and stability under the income tax. The social decision concerns the price to be paid for the growth potential.

The foregoing discussion of personal savings entailed no assumptions about benefit outlays, monetary policy, or other exogenous factors. The effect of the degree of concentration on payroll tax relative to income tax was considered on the assumption that the sum of the two yields is held constant. Other aspects of the saving impact which have been discussed in the literature have tended to mingle the effects of taxes and benefits. It has been suggested that personal saving is reduced by the existence of a social security program, because the anticipation of benefits reduces the amount that individuals feel they must accumulate privately. It is difficult to see how this point can be disputed, but it has nevertheless been argued on the basis of empirical studies that the security provided by the anticipation of benefits appears to lead to even greater private saving in behalf of major new goals.[18] Whatever the merits of these points, it is clear that the empirical studies did not attempt to isolate the effects of the tax on saving. The position of the saving function relating expected saving to disposable income would presumably depend on the expected level of benefits: the greater the expectations, the lower the schedule. However, the effect of the tax would be seen in a move along a given curve rather than in a shift of the curve. (Any actual analysis would have to distinguish the effects of payroll taxes on savings from those of the income tax and other leakages from personal income.)

The payroll tax also plays an ambivalent role in the accumulation of surpluses or deficits by the federal government. However, the surplus or deficit depends on the difference between expenditures under OASDHI, on the one hand, and the sum of payroll taxes and other receipts of the trust fund, on the other. So it is not useful to specify what contribution the payroll tax makes to "government saving," as long as the other factors are variable. It was suggested in Chapter VIII that high surpluses in the trust fund over recent years achieved a fortuitous restraint on inflation, but since the determinants of the trust fund are probably interdependent there is no unique way of isolating the impact of the tax on the surplus in a meaningful way.

Despite the above qualification, any tendency toward chronic surpluses or deficits under the social security system deserves careful attention. For example, the 1972 social security legislation enacted under Public Law 92-366, and signed July 1, 1972, appears certain to generate surpluses. The automatic ceiling adjustment assures that the effective tax rate will be fairly stable. Thus the tax per worker will rise roughly in proportion to average earnings increases. However, benefits per capita will rise only as fast as the consumer price index. Taxes will therefore rise faster than benefits, and this could impose a fiscal

---

[18] That individuals covered by pension plans tend to save more than others certainly offers no proof of this. See Joseph A. Pechman, Henry J. Aaron, and Michael K. Taussig, *Social Security: Perspectives for Reform* (Brookings Institution, 1968), p. 186. For further discussion of the question, see Roger F. Murray, "Economic Aspects of Pensions: A Summary Report," in *Old Age Income Assurance*, Pt. 5: *Financial Aspects of Pension Plans*, A Compendium of Papers on Problems and Policy Issues in the Public and Private Pension System Submitted to the Subcommittee on Fiscal Policy of the Joint Economic Committee, 90 Cong. 1 sess. (1967), pp. 69–78; Phillip Cagan, *The Effect of Pension Plans on Aggregate Saving: Evidence from a Sample Survey*, Occasional Paper 95 (Columbia University Press for National Bureau of Economic Research, 1965); and George Katona, *The Mass Consumption Society* (McGraw-Hill, 1964), pp. 182–202.

drag on the economy unless offset by other spending increases or tax cuts.

## Significance of Allocation and Growth Effects

This chapter has summarized a priori expectations about the effects of the payroll tax on allocative efficiency and growth. Because interest in these problems is evidenced in the literature on taxation, they are considered briefly here despite their apparent insignificance and intractability, respectively.

It is concluded that the imposition of the tax on a single factor does not make for reallocation. Given its wide coverage and incidence on labor's share, the payroll tax creates no incentive to use less labor. Although the direction of most allocative effects can be forecast with some confidence, there is also little reason to expect substantial re-allocation of resources or price effects due to the minor rate differentials inherent in OASDHI and UI—the major U.S. payroll taxes. The impact of statutory differentials should be small, and that of those due to labor intensity and the ceiling even smaller. If these conclusions are correct, the payroll tax is not vulnerable to the charges that it causes wasteful reallocation and that it may aggravate unemployment by stimulating substitution of capital for labor. Nor does there appear to be any basis for the fear that the taxable ceiling causes substitution of skilled for unskilled labor. In short, the main conclusion in this argument is that the payroll tax probably has little effect on resource allocation.

The differential rates under the UI tax may even have a minor favorable impact on efficiency and growth. Insofar as the tax discriminates against firms and regions with high unemployment, it may encourage reallocation of labor from slack to tight labor markets. However, with respect to growth, the one major difference between the impact of the payroll tax and that of the income tax concerns personal saving. A substitution of an income tax increase for an equal decrease in payroll tax yields would clearly depress saving. However, this potential stimulation of growth has its price. It raises the question of the optimum trade-off between the reduced growth potential achieved in this way and the greater equity and stability available through heavier reliance on the income tax.

CHAPTER X

# Evaluation and Policy Conclusions

A RECAPITULATION of the economic effects of payroll taxation, presenting in detail the case for and against it, would be superfluous at this point. However, a brief comparative evaluation of the income and payroll taxes may be useful. The main policy implications of such a comparison can then be reviewed, along with the improved prospects for reform. First, it may be prudent to justify evaluating the payroll tax independently of the benefits for which it is earmarked.

## Conceptual Issues in Evaluating the Payroll Tax

A major problem encountered in the evaluation of the payroll tax is finding the appropriate frame of reference. It is sometimes suggested that the only way to evaluate the effects of the tax is to weigh its net effect and the benefits financed by it. The ever-present constraint imposed by the "insurance principle" against clear thinking on the subject has been stressed throughout this study. As an earmarked tax, this particular revenue device has been shielded from the great weight of criticism that would otherwise have been brought against it. It has been argued here that this heavy tax on the working poor, which also

252

discriminates against middle-income groups, is an extraordinary anachronism existing side by side with massive antipoverty programs and a general consensus in favor of progressive taxation. It has also been contended that a critique of these properties of the tax need not be suspended until the distribution of the proceeds is also analyzed.

In the minds of some of its proponents, the poverty-accentuating and regressive properties of the payroll tax are irrelevant, because the working poor and middle-income groups are simply being required to save for their old age and will eventually get what they have paid for and more. From this point of view, the payroll tax is above suspicion as long as the entire social security package is likely to have a progressive impact. This appears to place critics of the tax in an awkward position, because they must concede that the lifetime benefit-tax structure is indeed progressive. Even though it can be shown that the "insurance principle" is little more than a facade, it is certainly likely that low-income groups will tend to gain a higher lifetime return on their contributions than higher income ranks (see Chapter VI). This leads to the key question: If the social security package is likely to have progressive impact on lifetime incomes, although benefits are not guaranteed, is it artificial to criticize the tax independently of the associated benefit structure? The answer to this lies in (1) the long lag between payments and receipts, and (2) the intergenerational nature of transfers under social security pension programs.

Despite the insurance rhetoric, the essence of social security programs is that they engineer a transfer of income from the working population to retired or other nonearning beneficiaries. On the basis of past experience, the current earner can expect similar transfers in his own behalf in the future. It is also entirely reasonable for both taxpayers and beneficiaries to view this as a cooperative process even though the quid pro quo is far from one-for-one. However, the fact remains that under the present roughly pay-as-you-go system, the earner today is actually contributing to the current support of others.[1] In the case of the OASDHI program, it may be as much as a half-century before the same is done for the earner paying taxes today.

---

[1] He might be doing so privately if there were no public retirement program. The important point, however, is that the current earner is contributing to the support of others rather than simply saving for his own old age. The distinction is important because it suggests that the distribution of tax burdens is not rigidly fixed by any individual actuarial relationships.

From this point of view, it is quite appropriate to evaluate the tax independently. If an earner today is officially classified as living in poverty and/or unable to pay income tax, how can he be judged capable of paying a payroll tax? If equity requires his exemption from one tax, logic requires his exemption from all taxes. The decision to aid nonearners on a current basis does not in any way justify the waiving of the ability-to-pay principle in the case of the payroll tax. Neither the insurance nor the earmarking concept should be allowed to obscure the fact that the working poor are being taxed heavily today to finance current transfers to the nonearning population. It is small consolation for a family being driven deeper into poverty by the payroll tax now to be reminded that the earning population can be expected to support them upon their own retirement in a generation or so.[2]

A related conceptual issue concerns the legitimacy of evaluating the payroll tax independently of other taxes. Critics who point to the payroll tax as a tax charged to persons "without ability to pay" may be said to be unduly selective, because most other taxes are similarly vulnerable. Only under the income tax is a serious, if not totally successful, effort made to avoid this anomaly. However, the inequity of other taxes does not exempt the payroll tax from criticism; indeed, it, more than other regressive taxes, deserves special attention because of its large size and rapid rate of growth. However, for the summary evaluation in the next section, it appears appropriate to compare the payroll tax to the more equitable income tax rather than to other regressive taxes.

It can also be pointed out that price increases and wage cuts have an impact on the working poor just as unfortunate as that of the payroll tax. Such a reduction of the real wage can be chalked up as one of the failures of government economic policy in pursuit of stable growth. However, such failures are subject to criticism of a different order from that merited by the deliberate and direct imposition of a

---

[2] Nothing said here in criticism of *taxation* of the poor is intended to contradict the more general proposition that the net positive or negative tax transfer to individuals should be linked to their economic position. Aside from its taxation of the working poor, the overall social security program is also subject to the criticism that it helps the aged, not all of whom are poor, and burdens others who are poor, rather than simply helping the poor alone, as a negative income tax would do. Modification or elimination of the payroll tax would obviously constitute only a partial move toward equity in the overall transfer picture.

heavy tax on families exempt from the income tax and officially classified as living in poverty.

A final point should be made in defense of evaluation of the payroll tax independently of benefits. It was shown in Chapter VI that
low-income workers may anticipate relatively high real rates of return
on their social security contributions—as high as 7 percent or more.
It has already been pointed out that reference to these ultimate benefits is misleading because the tax is burying the poor deeper in poverty
now. This argument should be elaborated. It may appear to those well
enough off to save that a real rate of return of more than 7 percent on
savings is very attractive—certainly better than that attainable under
available interest rates eroded by the inflation of recent years. However, for families too poor to save, the current tax compounds their
problems and undoubtedly tends to increase their indebtedness if they
are fortunate enough to be able to borrow.

Low-income dissavers tend to resort to consumer loans at rates of
3 percent a month or even higher. (Real rates of interest are, of course,
somewhat lower due to inflation.) Their doing so reveals that they
apply a very high discount rate to future income; it also seems safe to
say that if the poor want all possible spending power right now, this
type of borrowing is more a sign of need than of profligacy. In any
case, whatever the reasons for their borrowing, the likelihood of a 7
percent return in the distant future can scarcely be used to justify a
tax that leads them to pay annual interest rates of 36 percent or more.
Even those who insist on taking into account the prospective benefits
would find it difficult to justify forcing the poor to save at an ultimate
7 percent at the same time that they are borrowing at 36 percent.

## Comparative Evaluation of Payroll and Income Taxes

The best way to sum up and evaluate briefly the role of the payroll
tax in the overall revenue picture is to compare it with the income tax,
which is being increasingly recommended as a more equitable alternative.[3] Underlying such a comparison are certain premises that should
be made explicit. First, the conclusion that the entire burden of the
payroll tax rests on the income share of labor is critical for evaluating

[3] For detailed comparisons of the two taxes, see Joseph A. Pechman, Henry J. Aaron,
and Michael K. Taussig, *Social Security: Perspectives for Reform* (Brookings Institution,
1968), especially Chap. 8.

equity effects and other properties. Second, it is presumed that regressivity in a tax is inequitable. Although there have been defenders of a fixed proportional tax, the value judgment against an inverse relationship between tax rates and ability to pay appears generally held. (This pertains only to the presumed unfairness of such a tax and does not deny that a regressive tax may offer less restraint of savings and growth.)

### Tax Equity

The chief indictment against the payroll tax is its heavy burden on the working poor who are exempt from the income tax under the ability-to-pay criterion. The highest payroll tax rate on wages and salaries is approaching 13 percent, and it is paid by those earning less than the unemployment insurance (UI) ceiling—generally $4,200. At the other end of the spectrum, taxpayers are recognized as capable of paying effective income tax rates as high as 50 or 60 percent, but their effective payroll tax rate is negligible. Although inequities exist in the income tax, because of special preferences, the general progressivity inherent in its rate structure stands out sharply against the inequitable structure of the payroll tax.

The perversity of the payroll tax rate curve is so pronounced that it overshadows the rising slope of the income tax curve in certain ranges. The result is that the combined rate curve for the two dominant direct taxes on individuals is regressive over a substantial interval, so that a two-person family earning $10,800 in 1973 may pay a higher combined tax rate than one earning nearly $23,000. Thus the two taxes together produce a further, though less pronounced, inequity. Middle-income persons with earnings in the vicinity of the social security ceiling are discriminated against compared to others earning more than twice as much. Moreover, these contradictions are becoming more manifest as the payroll tax grows at a faster pace than other taxes. On grounds of equity, the case for turning from payroll tax to income tax is very strong.

### Contribution to Economic Stability

With respect to its contribution toward economic stability, the payroll tax is inferior to the income tax in two minor respects. Its built-in offsetting response to income changes is very weak because of its overall regressivity resulting from the taxable ceiling and its exclusion of property income; on the other hand, the income tax responds strongly to income changes. In practice, the lags in tax collections and in response of the gross national product to tax-induced effects of income change are such that neither tax appears to be an effective automatic stabilizer; even the income tax earns only a slight plus mark on this criterion.

The payroll tax also earns demerits for some perverse and destabilizing tax increases, which have been installed without concern for the condition of the economy. The most important was the original installation of the social security tax in 1937, when payroll taxes raised federal revenues by 25 percent in a setting of 15 percent unemployment, but there have been other perverse tax increases since that time. Furthermore, a seasonal upswing of tax collections in the winter and a decline in the fall aggravate "normal" seasonal swings in aggregate economic activity. On the other hand, changes in income tax rates have been less frequent and better timed. The seasonality in income tax collections is also less pronounced and less perverse. The income tax again earns a small plus mark on these scores, but a more rational policy toward payroll tax rate changes and seasonality could eliminate this difference.

## Efficiency, Incentives, and Growth

The only fundamental difference between the two taxes as they affect efficiency, incentives, and growth was found to be in their relative impact on saving. Evaluation of the taxes on this criterion is the other side of the coin from the equity question. Because the payroll tax is regressive and bears most heavily on low incomes, it can be safely assumed that it cuts less sharply into potential saving than does the income tax. Thus for a given total of the two taxes, the higher the payroll tax, the greater the saving and the greater the potential growth rate. This improved growth prospect is bought at the expense of hardship for low-income groups and the increased instability attending a high saving ratio. Given this trade-off, the optimum mix of the two taxes depends mainly on the value judgment of the population taken collectively, though balance-of-payment and international competitive considerations are also relevant to the choice of an appropriate mix. However, there can be little doubt that the payroll tax allows for greater saving. Whether this is a clear plus in favor of the payroll tax depends on whether the additional saving generated by less reliance on the income tax actually brings forth sufficient real investment to drive the economy forward more rapidly on a high employment growth path.

## Implications of Tax Reform Proposals

The previous evaluation does not point unambiguously to the desirability of a relative shrinkage of the payroll tax. Even if the trappings of the insurance principle can be successfully jettisoned so that the payroll tax can be considered rationally, the case for substituting the income tax for part or all of it depends primarily on equity grounds. This, of course, raises the venerable question of a possible conflict between equity and efficiency. It is generally assumed that, in an economy in which saving is determined by the aggregate of individual decisions, a reduction of income inequality must be paid for by a contraction of saving and of the rate of growth. There is, of course, no objective means of determining the optimum trade-off between the two.

Despite the absence of an objective rationale for the direction of the policy change, several considerations appear to justify the proposals of Chapter V entailing the partial or complete substitution of the income tax for the payroll tax. First, the promotion of a high saving rate by means of the payroll tax does not guarantee an increase in the growth rate sufficient to offset the price paid in greater volatility of the economy. In any case, the saving loss resulting from deemphasis of the payroll tax may not be substantial. Moreover, the reduction in saving could be offset by increased government saving (that is, through higher income tax rates). Second, even if there is great fear of the consequences of a complete phasing out of the payroll tax, a modest first step can be taken through the use of exemptions to end the worst inequities at a very small cost in revenue and potential saving. Finally, the ever-increasing reliance on the payroll tax since World War II may have been due more to convenience than rational policy, and this suggests that procedures for reversing this trend should at least be considered.

Two types of payroll tax reform proposals are set forth in Chapter V. The first type involves internal restructuring of the payroll tax itself. One proposal provides for relief at the bottom of the income distribution by means of exemptions and deductions similar to those under the income tax. It was shown that if these are phased out rapidly for incomes above the exemption levels, the cost could be met by an increase in the income tax yield of as little as 4 percent. This would be an efficient and inexpensive first step, generally eliminating the tax on families in poverty—probably the most indefensible feature of the payroll tax. It could be supplemented by reform at the other end of the earnings distribution. An increase or removal of the ceiling, coupled with a rate reduction, would reduce regressivity without expanding the tax yield. However, as the tax would remain regressive with respect to total income, a move toward the income tax would be more equitable.

The second type of proposal covers more substantial reforms, including the full replacement of the payroll tax by the income tax. It would be difficult to put this through the legislative process in a once-and-for-all proportional adjustment of the current income tax structure, since it would require an increase in income tax yield on the order of 45 percent. However, such a full replacement might be feasible on a step-by-step basis. A more constructive and efficient approach entails a restructuring of the effective income tax rate in order to take over the full burden of the payroll tax in an equitable way. It was shown in Chapter V that this could accomplish several desirable objectives: (1) the combined payroll and income tax on very low incomes could be largely eliminated; (2) the regressivity in the present combined tax rate curve could be eliminated in favor of a smooth progressive rate curve; (3) regressivity at the top of the distribution could be ended; and (4) incomes around the median and below could receive net tax relief at the expense of other income ranges currently favored by inequitable depressions of the rate curve. These are substantial gains in equity; their achievement by coupling elimination of the payroll tax with income tax rate adjustments appears quite feasible.[4]

Details of the alternative mechanisms by which the income tax could be substituted for the payroll tax have not been considered in this study. One such device entails integration of the two taxes. The income tax could absorb the employee payroll tax directly, or the same thing could be accomplished through a credit for employee tax payments against the individual income tax. The burden of the employee tax would be fully removed if cash refunds were paid to those

---

[4] This would, of course, leave untouched the inequities arising from special preferences under the income tax.

whose employee payroll tax exceeded the income tax. Any psychological advantage of the earmarked tax could be retained under either of these devices while in effect the income tax was substituted for the employee tax. There is, of course, no need to restrict integration to the employee tax. The taxpayer could also receive credit for the employer tax paid in his name. Such a credit would be consistent with the conclusion of this study that the employee pays that tax also through restraint of real wage rates.

An alternative to substituting the income tax for the payroll tax is general revenue financing of benefits. This has already been initiated on a small scale to cover part of the cost of Medicare and for social security benefits for persons of seventy-two and over. This would be an improvement on the regressive payroll tax, since the taxes supplying the fund are, on balance, progressive. It would, of course, still entail substantial increases in income tax rates. However, the impact would be less progressive than substitution of the income tax alone.

As long as the payroll tax remains in force, various potential reforms of payroll tax policy should be considered. A greater effort should be made to avoid aggravating recessions by untimely tax increases. The perverse seasonality of collections could be eliminated, or altered so as to work against the inherent seasonality in the economy. At the very least, payroll tax collections should be spread fairly evenly over the year. This would require only that earners above the ceiling be charged one-twelfth of the ceiling each month, with small adjustments at the end of the year to allow for changes in individual earnings.

## Prospects for Payroll Tax Reform

It may seem utopian to contemplate drastic alteration or phasing out of so massive and entrenched a fiscal device as the payroll tax. However, recent developments suggest that such action might be palatable to a majority of the population if the facts were clarified. Most taxpayers complain about the income tax, but their wrath is blunted by the general belief that it is a fair tax overall, despite some inequities. There is little visible wrath against the payroll tax because most of those who pay it do not realize how heavy and inequitable its burden actually is. As taxpayers with middle and lower incomes become more aware of this burden and the inequities discussed in this study, they may prefer to take their chances under an expanded income tax.

Most wage and salary recipients with very low incomes would probably be surprised to learn that they will be paying effective payroll tax rates of about 13 percent in 1973, although they are completely exempt under the income tax. They would also consider this payroll tax rate discriminatory in comparison with the negligible effective rates paid by high-salaried earners. The knowledge that a clear majority of taxpayers are paying higher payroll taxes than income taxes would also have considerable impact. In particular, the knowledge that the 1973 payroll tax will exceed the income tax for families of four earning wages or salaries up to about $12,000 would be impressive to many earners, as would knowing that two-earner families of four earning nearly $15,000 may pay as much payroll tax as income tax. Also striking is the fact that a middle-income family of four persons with a single earner at the scheduled $10,800 ceiling in 1973 will pay a combined income and payroll tax rate higher than that charged those with higher earnings (up to about $20,000 a year). The combined tax rate reaches its first peak at the taxable ceiling, which has tended to move in the vicinity of the median income in recent years. The regression in the *combined* tax rate curve for a substantial range above the ceiling broadens the potential opposition to the payroll tax.

In recent years the payroll tax has become a major burden to a substantial fraction of the population. While this burden on low and middle incomes has been growing, public tolerance of increasing support for antipoverty programs appears to have been ebbing. Even the effort to end penalization of work effort under welfare programs and achieve a modest graduated supplement for low-income earners under the proposed family assistance plan encountered great resistance. No doubt one reason for the inadequate support of such programs is that they help only a minority. A reform of the payroll tax and/or its replacement by the income tax may be more viable, because such a renovation could benefit the majority of the population while ending some substantial inequities.

As it gradually becomes understood, the regressive burden of the payroll tax on low-income and lower-middle-income groups is clearly capable of generating substantial support for a phasing out of the tax. Even the nonearning poor offer a potential base of support for lower payroll taxes, for there could be indirect gains for this group. For example, if welfare regulations were relaxed to reduce the economic penalty attending acceptance of private child support, not only would more such support be forthcoming, but its base would be increased by a cut in the payroll tax. But the swing group may turn out to be the middle-income class. When median earners begin to realize they are paying total direct taxes at a rate higher than earners with as much as twice their income, they too may be moved toward a revolt against the payroll tax. If so, reformist sentiment could become strong enough to alleviate the burden on both low- and middle-income groups and could make up in part for the failure to advance directly on the poverty front, particularly with respect to aid to the working poor.

# Sources and Processing of Data for Analysis of Incidence

THIS APPENDIX gives the statistical sources for the cross-country and U.S. time series data analyzed in Chapter III and describes the criteria for selecting countries and the processing of the data.

## Country Data

The sources used in the cross-country regression analysis in Chapter III are listed below. They are referred to in this appendix by the number preceding the citation in each case.

1. United Nations, Department of Economic and Social Affairs, *The Growth of World Industry, 1938–1961: National Tables*, ST/STAT/SER.P/2 (United Nations, 1963).

2. United Nations, Department of Economic and Social Affairs, *The Growth of World Industry, 1938–1961: International Analyses and Tables*, ST/STAT/SER.P/3 (United Nations, 1965).

3. United Nations, Department of Economic and Social Affairs, *Statistical Yearbook, 1965* (United Nations, 1966).

4. United Nations, Department of Economic and Social Affairs, *Yearbook of National Account Statistics, 1965* (United Nations, 1966).

5. U.S. Bureau of the Census, *Statistical Abstract of the United States, 1958*, and the issues for 1959 and 1960.

6. U.S. Social Security Administration, *Social Security Programs in the United States* (1968).

Virtually all of the census-of-manufactures data on wages and salaries, value added, and employment were taken from source 1. For a few countries information was taken from sources 3 and 4.

The effective employer tax rate $t$ was estimated from statutory rates in source 6. Five types of employer payroll taxes were included; they were earmarked for: (1) old-age, survivors, and disability insurance and related programs, (2) health and maternity insurance, (3) unemployment insurance, (4) family allowance programs, and (5) work injuries insurance. Estimates of effective rates took account of the taxable ceiling in each country. The statutory rate was adjusted on the basis of a graphic relation between percentage of earnings taxable and the ratio of the ceiling to mean earnings, as observed in the United States. In the case of those countries that also specified minimum taxable income, each earner was assumed to earn at least the minimum, and the effective rate was adjusted downward on the basis of the fraction of the total wage bill that was exempt by the minimum.

Four alternative sets of conversion ratios were used—$x_1$, $x_2$, $x_3$, and $x_4$ —to convert currencies into dollars. The estimates $x_1$ and $x_4$ were "purchasing power parity ratios" based on price indexes; they were estimated by the United Nations and reported in source 2, pp. 310–11, and source 4, Table 9B, respectively. These conversion ratios produced generally closer fits than the more arbitrary sets of official exchange rates $x_2$ and $x_3$. These two sets (which differ slightly as a result of alternative treatment of multiple exchange rates) were based on source 5, and on source 4, Table 9A, respectively.

Countries were selected for analysis if data on value added ($V$), wages and salaries ($W$), and employment ($L$) were available for aggregate manufacturing in at least one of the years 1957–59; most of the censuses were for the year 1958. A few additional countries were included for which the census fell just outside the 1957–59 period and for which the "number engaged" was available rather than the number of employees. This yielded data on aggregate manufacturing for sixty-four countries labeled sets A, B, C. After fitting the models to these sixty-four observations, the twenty countries with the smallest total wage bills (set C) were dropped and the models refitted. Finally, countries in set B with data on number engaged only, with surveys outside the 1957–59 period or without data available in the main United Nations source (1) were dropped, leaving thirty observations. This process was an attempt to use more reliable data successively while sacrificing observations. However, results for the three different sets of aggregative data were all consistent with the hypothesis that the overall shifting coefficient equals unity, as shown in Table 3-2.

The industry analysis in Tables 3-4 and 3-5 covers all countries among the original sixty-four for which data were available on an industry basis.

# U.S. Time Series Data

Sources for the five basic variables underlying the industry time series analysis in Chapter III for the years 1947–64 are described below.

$V$ = *value added.* Source: U.S. Department of Commerce, Office of Business Economics, *The National Income and Product Accounts of the United States, 1929–1965: Statistical Tables* (1966), pp. 19–21.

$W$ = *wages and salaries, including private fringe benefits.* Source: *Ibid.*, pp. 91–93, adjusted by subtraction of employers' contributions for social security, from source listed under $T$ below.

$T$ = *employers' contributions for social security.* Source: Special tabulation provided by the U.S. Department of Commerce, Office of Business Economics.

$P$ = *price index for industry output.* Source: U.S. Department of Commerce, Office of Business Economics, "Comparison of Federal Reserve and OBE Measures of Real Manufacturing Output, 1947–64" (OBE, December 1966; processed), Appendix F, implicit price deflators for value added.

$H$ = *total hours paid per week.* Source: *Manpower Report of the President,* Message from the President of the United States, H. Doc. 406, 89 Cong. 2 sess. (1966); product of gross average weekly hours of production for nonsupervisory workers, p. 204, and the annual average number employed, p. 200.

# Additional Regression Results and a Comparison with Earlier Results

CROSS-COUNTRY DATA for twelve two-digit industries underlying an unpublished study of the elasticity of substitution by Y. Murata and K. J. Arrow were used for some additional estimates.[1] There were two objectives for these tests. The first was to check the data-gathering and -processing procedures described in Appendix A, as well as the regression program used, against the work of Murata and Arrow, who relied on some of the same sources. Second, it seemed worthwhile to ascertain whether use of the total compensation variable, including the employer tax, would materially affect the estimates of the elasticity of substitution.

Two-variable regressions relating productivity and the wage rate are reported in Table B-1. The first, third, and sixth numerical columns (including regression slopes and $\bar{R}_2$) check with a high degree of accuracy against the unpublished regression results supplied by Murata and Arrow. A later comparison of the processed data used here with tabulations by Murata and Arrow showed only minor rounding discrepancies and slight differences in interpretation of exchange rates, none of which altered the regression results.

The coefficient for the wage rate log $w$ (without payroll tax) in the first

[1] For a discussion of the results of the unpublished Murata and Arrow study (1965), see Marc Nerlove, "Recent Empirical Studies of the CES and Related Production Functions," in Murray Brown and others, *The Theory and Empirical Analysis of Production*, Studies in Income and Wealth, Vol. 31, by the Conference on Research in Income and Wealth (Columbia University Press for the National Bureau of Economic Research, 1967), pp. 58–72.

**TABLE B-1.** Intercountry Estimates of Elasticities of Substitution and of Their Reciprocals, Using Basic Wage Rates and Total Compensation Rates, Twelve Industries, 1957–59[a]

| Industry | Elasticity of substitution | | Reciprocal of elasticity | | Degrees of freedom | Coefficient of determination | |
|---|---|---|---|---|---|---|---|
| | Regression 1[b] | Regression 2[c] | Regression 3[d] | Regression 4[e] | | Without tax | With tax |
| Food, beverages, and tobacco | 0.725 (0.054) | 0.741 (0.056) | 1.248 (0.093) | 1.219 (0.091) | 19 | 0.906 | 0.903 |
| Textiles | 0.827 (0.069) | 0.849 (0.067) | 1.073 (0.090) | 1.059 (0.084) | 19 | 0.888 | 0.899 |
| Clothing, footwear, etc. | 0.804 (0.043) | 0.819 (0.047) | 1.189 (0.064) | 1.161 (0.066) | 17 | 0.956 | 0.951 |
| Wood and wood products | 0.919 (0.074) | 0.925 (0.076) | 0.976 (0.078) | 0.965 (0.079) | 18 | 0.896 | 0.893 |
| Pulp and paper products | 0.788 (0.061) | 0.803 (0.063) | 1.142 (0.089) | 1.120 (0.089) | 18 | 0.901 | 0.899 |
| Printing and publications | 0.932 (0.065) | 0.939 (0.065) | 0.992 (0.069) | 0.985 (0.068) | 17 | 0.924 | 0.924 |
| Leather and leather products | 0.699 (0.051) | 0.696 (0.058) | 1.313 (0.096) | 1.287 (0.107) | 18 | 0.917 | 0.895 |
| Rubber products | 0.768 (0.106) | 0.782 (0.110) | 0.998 (0.138) | 0.972 (0.136) | 15 | 0.767 | 0.761 |
| Chemicals and chemical products | 0.834 (0.087) | 0.840 (0.091) | 1.011 (0.106) | 0.991 (0.108) | 16 | 0.843 | 0.832 |
| Nonmetallic mineral products | 0.859 (0.051) | 0.867 (0.054) | 1.086 (0.065) | 1.070 (0.067) | 20 | 0.933 | 0.927 |
| Basic metals | 0.873 (0.063) | 0.883 (0.066) | 1.057 (0.077) | 1.040 (0.077) | 17 | 0.922 | 0.919 |
| Metal products | 0.922 (0.070) | 0.927 (0.071) | 0.989 (0.075) | 0.982 (0.075) | 18 | 0.912 | 0.910 |

Source: See Appendix A. The official exchange rate variable $x_2$ discussed in Appendix A was used as the conversion factor in the computations. The numbers in parentheses are standard errors of the coefficients.

[a] The countries used were those used by Y. Murata and K. J. Arrow in a 1965 unpublished study in which elasticities of substitution for two-digit countries were estimated: Australia, Belgium, Canada, Denmark, El Salvador, Finland, India, Iraq, Ireland, Japan, Luxembourg, Mexico, New Zealand, Norway, Pakistan, the Philippines, Portugal, Puerto Rico, Singapore, Sweden, United Arab Republic, United Kingdom, and United States. (Data were not available from all of the countries for any one industry.)

The regression results for wage rates without tax shown in this table (regressions 1 and 3) were compared and found to agree with the results of the Murata-Arrow study.

[b] Productivity, log $V/L$, on basic wage rate without tax, log $w$, where $V$ = value added and $L$ = number of workers.

[c] Productivity, log $V/L$, on total compensation rate, log $w(1 + t)$.

[d] Basic wage rate without tax, log $w(1 + t)$, on productivity, log $V/L$.

[e] Total compensation rate, log $w(1 + t)$, on productivity, log $V/L$.

column has been traditionally interpreted as the direct estimate of the elasticity of substitution.[2] The findings shown in Table B-1 confirm early studies in that all coefficients are less than unity when log $V/L$ (ratio of value added to number of workers) is the dependent variable; nine of them are significantly so at the 5 percent level on the one-tail test. However, because there is no a priori justification for the particular direction of fit specified, log $w$ is also regressed on log $V/L$ to obtain estimates of the reciprocal of the elasticity tabulated in the third numerical column; all coefficients except four are found to be greater than unity, but only three are significantly so at the 5 percent level.

The wage variable in the Murata and Arrow study, like others before it based on manufacturing censuses, excludes employer contributions for social insurance. In this framework, total labor cost per worker would be a more appropriate variable for the production function. The second and fourth columns of Table B-1 record the same type of estimates but include the estimated employer payroll tax. All of the direct estimates remain less than unity, but all except one are appreciably higher than the former esti- mates, and the coefficient for chemicals and chemical products is no longer significantly below unity. The estimates of the reciprocal of the elasticity are correspondingly smaller than before, and five of the twelve are now be- low unity.[3] Clearly, the estimation of the elasticity of substitution by means of the reciprocal substantially raises the first estimates. However, inclusion of the tax casts some further doubt on the proposition that the elasticity is generally well below unity.

[2] This interpretation has been disputed, as discussed in Chapter III. However, the present objective is simply to ask what including the employer tax does to these estimates, rather than to join the methodological controversy.

[3] The effect of inclusion of the tax on the estimated elasticities of substitution is most readily clarified in these reciprocal estimates. It appears that the elasticity of total com- pensation with respect to productivity is less than the elasticity of the basic wage. This suggests that employer contributions are less responsive to productivity increases than the basic wage, which may simply mean that employer contributions are a smaller part of compensation as the productivity of a country becomes higher. Exclusion of the em- ployer tax can, nevertheless, bias the estimates of the elasticity of substitution.

# Sources for Analysis of Effects on Income Distribution

THE SOURCES for the data underlying the discussion of the payroll and income tax structure in Chapter IV are given below.

## Social Security Tax Structure

The statutory old-age, survivors, disability, and health insurance (OASDHI) tax rates applicable to taxable earnings and the taxable ceilings used in Chapter IV are recorded in Table C-1. Also included are average effective state annual unemployment insurance (UI) rates. The state contribution rates in Table C-1 represent the national average as estimated by the U.S. Department of Labor. The standard state contribution rate has been 2.7 percent on taxable earnings, but the "experience rating" applicable in most states has caused the actual average to vary from year to year, mostly going below 2.7 percent. Experience rating seeks to reward employers with good employment records; that is, employers are actually required to pay some rate between zero and 3 percent, instead of the standard 2.7 percent, depending on the number of layoffs.

The average state UI contribution rates in Table C-1 do not include the federal unemployment taxes—an additional 0.3 percent paid by employers up to 1964, 0.4 percent up to 1970, and 0.5 percent thereafter to cover the costs to the federal government of administering the unemployment program. In the tabulations and graphic data underlying Chapter IV, the federal tax rate was included in computing the average state UI tax.

**TABLE C-1.** Social Security (OASDHI) Taxable Ceiling and Rates and Unemployment Insurance Contribution Rates, 1949–69, and Estimates for 1973

| Year | OASDHI taxable ceiling (dollars) | OASDHI statutory rates: employer plus employee (percent) | Average employer state UI contribution rates (percent) |
|------|------|------|------|
| 1949 | 3,000 | 2 | 1.3 |
| 1950 | 3,000 | 3 | 1.5 |
| 1951 | 3,600 | 3 | 1.6 |
| 1952 | 3,600 | 3 | 1.45 |
| 1953 | 3,600 | 3 | 1.3 |
| 1954 | 3,600 | 4 | 1.1 |
| 1955 | 4,200 | 4 | 1.2 |
| 1956 | 4,200 | 4 | 1.3 |
| 1957 | 4,200 | 4.5 | 1.3 |
| 1958 | 4,200 | 4.5 | 1.3 |
| 1959 | 4,800 | 5 | 1.7 |
| 1960 | 4,800 | 6 | 1.9 |
| 1961 | 4,800 | 6 | 2.1 |
| 1962 | 4,800 | 6.25 | 2.4 |
| 1963 | 4,800 | 7.25 | 2.3 |
| 1964 | 4,800 | 7.25 | 2.2 |
| 1965 | 4,800 | 7.25 | 2.1 |
| 1966 | 6,600 | 8.4 | 1.9 |
| 1967 | 6,600 | 8.8 | 1.6 |
| 1968 | 7,800 | 8.8 | 1.5 |
| 1969 | 7,800 | 9.6 | 1.4 |
| 1973 | 10,800[a] | 11.0[a] | 2.0[b] |

Sources: For 1949–69, U.S. Social Security Administration, *Social Security Bulletin, Annual Statistical Supplement, 1967*, Table 21, p. 29, and Table 16, p. 25. For the years not shown in Table 16, the UI rates were obtained from U.S. Department of Labor, Bureau of Employment Security. For 1973, see notes a and b below.
[a] Scheduled under social security legislation enacted by P.L. 92-336, signed July 1, 1972.
[b] Estimated by author.

## Individual Income Tax

The income taxes and tax rates used in Figures 4-1 through 4-7 were computed on the assumption that through 1963 all taxpayers used the standard deduction provision. From 1964 on, either the standard or the minimum standard deduction was assumed, depending on which was greater. Since the primary emphasis in this study is on relatively low incomes, this assumption appears reasonable. However, excluding itemization does exaggerate slightly the tax paid by a typical taxpayer at a given level.

For the figures showing incomes with social security and individual income taxes (Figures 4-1 to 4-5), the income taxes were computed from the specified rate structure rather than read from the optional tables provided by the Internal Revenue Service (IRS). The IRS tables would have yielded cruder estimates, because they show the same tax for a range of incomes. Their use is not mandatory; a taxpayer can request that his taxes be computed individually, but most do not. The method used here yields answers that differ slightly from those found in practice. The main reason for exact computations in this study was to apply the same method for all income levels and to avoid discontinuities.

For 1968 and 1969, the 1967 income tax rates were used, with an upward adjustment of 7.5 percent and 10 percent, respectively, for the surtax.

## Poverty Lines

The 1959–68 data are unpublished estimates by the U.S. Bureau of the Census. For these data and for each family size separately, the poverty line was regressed on the consumer price index (CPI), and the regression equations were then used to estimate the poverty levels for the other years on the basis of the value of the CPI for each year. This method allows the poverty cutoff points to reflect changes in the CPI only. Poverty lines were officially based also on definitions of "minimum requirements" for a family,[1] a concept requiring frequent reevaluation, until 1969, when the official decision was made to follow the CPI only, using the original 1963 poverty lines as a benchmark.[2] The 1963 figures were adjusted forward and backward in proportion to the CPI to obtain the 1959–68 figures.

The regression equations based on the 1959–68 data, which were used here to extend the series to cover 1949 through 1969, were extremely close fits. If the poverty lines had been fitted to the CPI lagged one year, the correlation coefficient would probably have been even closer to unity; however, the regression relationships actually used were so close that such a refinement would probably make little difference.

[1] See, for example, *Economic Report of the President, January 1969*, pp. 151–53.
[2] U.S. Bureau of the Census, *Current Population Reports*, Series P-23, No. 28, "Revision in Poverty Statistics, 1959–1968" (1969).

# Sources and Methods of Simulating Modifications of the Tax Structure

A REPRESENTATIVE SAMPLE of approximately 100,000 individual income tax returns for 1964 was used for Chapter V in order to take advantage of information on exemptions per tax return "family" and the breakdown of income by source.[1] This 1964 sample was used to simulate the impact of various modifications of the tax structure. The 100,000 tax returns were grouped by income classes; from the data on each return, the computer produced estimates of payroll taxes and income taxes under specified structures and summed within each income class. It should be acknowledged at the outset, however, that the tax return sample is an imperfect vehicle for analysis of changes in the old-age, survivors, and disability insurance (OASDI) payroll tax structure. The tax return income base is broader than the social security income base, due mainly to its coverage of the large government and railroad employee groups excluded from OASDI; for this reason estimation of the OASDI tax base from Internal Revenue Service (IRS) data carries an upward bias in the aggregate. On the other hand, there is also an opposing bias since the tax return data do not permit identification of returns with multiple earners; the unavoidable assumption of one applicable ceiling per return understates the tax base. The first step was to investigate the net effect of these biases and provide a basis for approximate adjustment of estimates based on tax returns to consistency with the OASDI tax base. For this purpose estimates of taxable income under various ceilings were obtained from the 1964 sample of tax

[1] The income tax sample applied was the file made available by the U.S. Department of the Treasury, Internal Revenue Service, to the Brookings Institution.

returns and compared with detailed Social Security Administration (SSA) statistics available for the same year.[2]

Figure D-1 presents 1964 comparisons of the estimates based on the tax return sample with the SSA estimates.[3] The upper part of the figure relates aggregate taxable earnings to the ceiling on taxable earnings. The peak points at the extreme right show total covered earnings from the two sources, since no effective ceiling is applied in that case. The tax return sample shows total covered earnings of $364 billion, as against $323 billion from the SSA source.[4] Failure to allow for the separate taxable ceilings of multiple earners in the tax sample plays no role in this discrepancy, since all earnings are taxable. The fact that the SSA figure is 11 percent lower is almost entirely due to the omission of government, railroad, and other workers from social security coverage.[5]

The credibility of the tax sample and the plausibility of the 11 percent discrepancy is also enhanced by a comparison with *Statistics of Income* for 1964. The latter shows wages and salaries at $323.3 billion while the total is $324.1 billion in the blown-up tax sample;[6] this is certainly within the margin to be expected when large samples are drawn from the tax return population. The official figure from the same source for 1964 self-employed earnings is $35.2 billion, which seems statistically consistent with the $39.6 billion figure in the blown-up sample.[7]

---

[2] The total taxable earnings was computed individually for each return. It was taken to be the sum of wages and salaries and self-employed income up to the taxable ceiling, except that self-employed income under $400 was excluded in keeping with 1964 law. The individual quantities were aggregated and blown up to a population basis. The SSA estimates are from Michael Resnick, "Annual Earnings and the Taxable Maximum for OASDHI," *Social Security Bulletin*, Vol. 29 (November 1966), pp. 39–40.

[3] Each SSA curve in Figure D-1 is based on points corresponding to ten specified ceilings, including zero and infinity. The tax return curves are based on eight points. The complete curves were obtained by graphic interpolation.

[4] These figures represent the total for 65.4 million tax returns and 77.7 million social security taxpayers, respectively, in 1964.

[5] The degree of underreporting of earnings may also vary between the two sources, but in general it is to be expected that earnings not reported for income tax are generally excluded from the social security tax base as well.

[6] U.S. Internal Revenue Service, *Statistics of Income—1964: Individual Income Tax Returns* (1967), p. 9.

[7] Results from the tax sample can also be checked against Internal Revenue Service data under assumed ceilings. For example, *Statistics of Income—1964*, Table 7, pp. 22–23, presents the distribution of wages and salaries. For any given ceiling the amount of taxable wages and salaries may be derived as the sum of the total wages and salaries of earners below the ceiling and the covered portion of wages and salaries accruing to earners above the ceiling. This type of derivation from *Statistics of Income* yields a taxable wages and salaries curve which virtually coincides with that obtained from the tax sample. This suggests that the sample is a reliable guide to the distribution of wages and salaries as well as to their aggregate.

**FIGURE D-1. Relationship between Social Security Tax Base and Ceiling on Taxable Earnings, 1964**

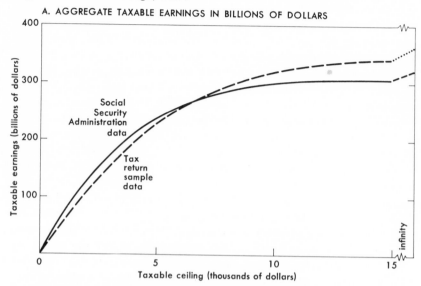

A. AGGREGATE TAXABLE EARNINGS IN BILLIONS OF DOLLARS

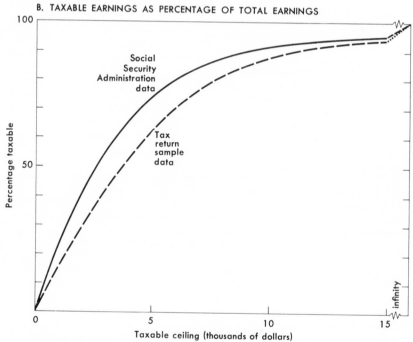

B. TAXABLE EARNINGS AS PERCENTAGE OF TOTAL EARNINGS

Sources: Michael Resnick, "Annual Earnings and the Taxable Maximum for OASDHI," *Social Security Bulletin*, Vol. 29 (November 1966), pp. 39–40; the Brookings Institution's file of approximately 100,000 individual federal income tax returns for 1964.

The lower part of Figure D-1 represents a rough attempt to abstract from that part of the discrepancy between total earnings shown on the tax return sample and those in the SSA data which is due to differences in coverage. Expressing the taxable earnings as a percentage of covered earnings would completely remove the effect of coverage differences if covered and uncovered earnings were in the same ratio throughout the income distribution. This condition holds only approximately, since, for example, government and railroad earnings are relatively high. Still, the discrepancy can probably be ascribed primarily to the higher tax coverage of multiple earners recognized in the social security data. Once an effective ceiling is introduced, the fraction of covered earnings that is taxable becomes higher than is indicated by the single earner assumption underlying the tax return estimates. For example, in 1964 a couple with total earnings of $9,600 could be fully taxable, although the tax return curve recognizes only a single $4,800 ceiling.

The discrepancy between the two curves in the lower part of Figure D-1 is a rough measure of the overall discrimination against multiple earners in comparison with single earner families having the same total income. It shows approximately the extra tax base, over and above what would be the case if multiple earners had the same base as single earners with equal earnings. Under the 1964 ceiling of $4,800, this feature of the payroll tax added about 20 percent to the tax base.

The inability to allow directly for the relatively high tax base of multiple earners of a given sum is the more intractable of the two biases in the tax return sample estimate. As indicated in the upper half of Figure D-1, the excess of tax return earnings over social security earnings dwindles rapidly as the ceiling is reduced; it is actually reversed by the time the hypothetical ceiling of $6,200 is reached. Thus even in the case of the actual $4,800 ceiling in 1964, taxable earnings under social security exceeded the tax return sample estimate by 7 percent, despite the considerably broader earnings coverage of the tax return sample. It is clear that the lower the ceiling, the more multiple earners tend to be taxed on combined earnings above the ceiling for a single earner, and the more severe is the downward bias due to the tax return sample assumption of a single ceiling for total earnings.

In sum, the downward bias of the estimate based on the tax file, caused by ignoring multiple earners, outweighed the upward bias resulting from broader coverage for ceilings up to about $6,200 in 1964. The tax returns contain no data permitting a direct correction for either of these biases in the computation applied to each return. The best that could be done was to adjust the various estimates based on the tax file to achieve consistency with 1964 SSA data. Estimates from the tax file of taxable earnings under any given exemption structure, like those without exemptions, were known to be in error. On the basis of the top part of Figure D-1, it was recognized that these errors could run as high as 20 percent. However, it was presumed that the tax file estimate of the ratio of taxable earnings after exemptions to the level before exemptions was an accurate indicator of the effect of the change. These ratios from the tax file were therefore applied to social security figures on taxable earnings under the given ceiling without exemptions to estimate the effect of exemptions on the actual social security base.[8] This adjustment device appears satisfactory, particularly in the cases of the more modest schemes which show reductions in the tax base of generally under 15 percent. In any case it seems likely that this procedure is far better than no adjustment at all.

A final methodological point concerns the stress on data for the year 1964. This date was chosen as the one affording the most complete reconciliation between the SSA data and the tax return sample data needed for the simulations. If a fairly stable relative earnings distribution is assumed, as demonstrated in Chapter IV, the relationships for 1964 can be generalized and applied to later years. The ceilings and exemption plans applied to the 1964 distribution were revised for later years in proportion to changes in mean earnings. Estimates of percentage of earnings taxable based on these adjusted ceilings and exemptions could then be related to current dollar amounts in the later years.

---

[8] For example, under a $4,800 ceiling, the SSA source shows $236.5 billion, or 73.3 percent taxable, in 1964. A computation based on the tax file shows under exemption plan 700A-5 (see Table 5-1) a new base 92 percent of the original. By multiplication the estimated new social security figures are $217.6 billion, or 67.4 percent taxable.

# Response of Tax Yield to Income Change under Specified Relative Ceilings

THE RESPONSIVENESS of the old-age, survivors, disability, and health insurance (OASDHI) tax yield to changes in income depends on the position of the individual taxable ceiling in the earnings distribution. For this reason, the steady growth of earnings complicates the estimation of the effect of ceiling changes. On the assumption that the relative distribution of earnings remains fairly stable over time, the ratio of the ceiling to mean earnings ($w_c/\overline{w}$) determines the yield response ratios. The schedule in Table E-1 approximates these relationships on the basis of the estimates given in Table 7-1. It is useful for making estimates of the impact of ceiling increases under given or projected levels of mean earnings.

**TABLE E-1. Relationship of Social Security Tax Response Ratios to Relative Ceilings**

| Ratio of ceiling to mean earnings, $w_c/\overline{w}$ | Fraction taxable, $A_t/A_n$ | Elasticity, $EA_t/EA_n$ | Marginal rate, $\partial A_t/\partial A_n$ |
|---|---|---|---|
| 0.0 | 0.00 | 0.00 | 0.00 |
| 0.5 | 0.38 | 0.19 | 0.08 |
| 0.6 | 0.45 | 0.23 | 0.11 |
| 0.7 | 0.51 | 0.26 | 0.14 |
| 0.8 | 0.57 | 0.30 | 0.17 |
| 0.9 | 0.61 | 0.34 | 0.21 |
| 1.0 | 0.65 | 0.38 | 0.25 |
| 1.1 | 0.69 | 0.42 | 0.29 |
| 1.2 | 0.72 | 0.46 | 0.34 |
| 1.3 | 0.75 | 0.50 | 0.38 |
| 1.4 | 0.78 | 0.55 | 0.43 |
| 1.5 | 0.80 | 0.59 | 0.47 |
| 1.6 | 0.82 | 0.64 | 0.52 |
| 1.8 | 0.85 | 0.71 | 0.61 |
| 2.0 | 0.88 | 0.77 | 0.67 |
| 2.5 | 0.92 | 0.86 | 0.78 |
| 3.0 | 0.93 | 0.89 | 0.83 |
| Infinity | 1.00 | 1.00 | 1.00 |

Source: Estimated by graphic interpolation of the estimated relationships for 1969 presented in Table 7-1. The curves for 1964 and 1969 were very close, indicating a high degree of stability of the relative distribution of earnings between those two years. The accuracy of the tabulated relationships for later application depends on continued stability in the shape of the earnings distribution.

# Definitions and Sources for
# Tax Yield Functions

LISTED BELOW are definitions, descriptions, and sources of data to which the tax functions of Chapter VII were fitted.

| Variable | Definition and source |
|---|---|
| $OA_w$ | Employer plus employee contributions (from wages and salaries) for old-age, survivors, and disability insurance (OASDI). Sources: For 1937–63, U.S. Department of Commerce, Office of Business Economics, The National Income and Product Accounts of the United States, 1929–1965: Statistical Tables (1966), Table 3.8, pp. 58–59; for 1964–66, Office of Business Economics, Survey of Current Business, Vol. 47 (July 1967), Table 3.8, p. 27. |
| $OA_{s-1}$ | Self-employed contributions for OASDI, lagged one year. Source: Same as for $OA_w$. |
| $r_w$ | Statutory payroll contribution rates for OASDI (total of employee and employer contribution rates). Source: U.S. Social Security Administration, Social Security Bulletin, Annual Statistical Supplement, 1965, Table 19, p. 24. |
| $r_{s-1}$ | Statutory self-employed contribution rates for OASDI, lagged one year. Source: Same as for $r_w$. |
| $W_{OA_w}$ | Covered earnings of wage and salary earners. Sources: For 1937–50, Social Security Administration, Social Security Bulletin, Annual Statistical Supplement, 1965, Table 22, p. 27; for |

| *Variable* | *Definition and source* |
|---|---|
| | 1951–66, *Social Security Bulletin, Annual Statistical Supplement, 1966*, Table 15, p. 32. |
| $W_{OA_{s-1}}$ | Covered earnings of self-employed, lagged one year. Sources: Same as for $W_{OA_w}$. |
| $R_{OA}$ | Average of $r_w$ and $r_{s-1}$ weighted by $W_{OA_w}$ and $W_{OA_{s-1}}$, respectively. |
| $W_w$ | Total earnings of wage and salary earners (*total U.S. wages and salaries minus "Rest of the world"*). Sources: For 1937–62, Office of Business Economics, *The National Income and Product Accounts of the United States, 1929–1965: Statistical Tables*, Table 6.2, pp. 94–97; for 1963–66, Office of Business Economics, *Survey of Current Business*, Vol. 47 (July 1967), Table 6.2, p. 34. |
| $W_{s-1}$ | Total earnings of self-employed, lagged one year. Source: Office of Business Economics, *The National Income and Product Accounts of the United States, 1929–1965: Statistical Tables*, Table 2.1, pp. 32–33. |
| $W_{tw}$ | Taxable earnings of wage and salary earners. Sources: Same as for $W_{OA_w}$. |
| $W_{ts-1}$ | Taxable earnings of self-employed, lagged one year. Sources: Same as for $W_{OA_w}$. |
| $w_c$ | Ceiling on individual taxable earnings. Source: Same as for $r_w$. |
| $E_{OA_w}$ | Number of wage and salary earners with taxable earnings. Sources: Same as for $W_{OA_w}$. |
| $E_{OA_{s-1}}$ | Number of self-employed with taxable earnings, lagged one year. Source: Table 23, p. 27, of 1951–66 source given for $W_{OA_w}$. |

# Index

Aaron, Henry J., 4$n$, 24$n$, 82$n$, 117$n$, 158, 176, 250$n$, 255$n$
Aaron model, 176–77
Allocative effect: marginal productivity theory, 33–36; of payroll tax, 4–5, 14, 19, 238–46, 251; as qualification of incidence analysis, 47–49; of UI tax, 19, 247. *See also* Price; Wage
Arrow, K. J., 64$n$
Automation: payroll tax effect, 5–6, 41, 240

Balassa, Bela A., 25$n$
Ball, Robert M., 8$n$
Barlow, Robin, 248$n$
Bayo, Francisco, 160$n$, 169$n$, 176$n$
Black, Duncan, 33$n$
BLS. *See* U.S. Bureau of Labor Statistics
Bonin, Joseph M., 234–36
Bowen, William G., 58$n$, 248$n$
Brazer, Harvey E., 248$n$
Bridges, Benjamin, Jr., 156$n$
Brittain, John A., 107$n$
Brown, E. Cary, 185$n$
Brown, Harry Gunnison, 32–33
Buchanan, James M., 154$n$
Business cycle: payroll tax effect, 18–19, 213–16. *See also* Economy

Cagan, Phillip, 250$n$
Campbell, Colin D., 154–55, 178
Campbell, Rosemary, 154$n$

Carroll, J. J., 82$n$
Ceiling on payroll tax base: *1938*, 193; *1964*, 119–20, 123, 126–27, 131–34, 144, 192; *1966*, 95–96; *1969*, 89, 92, 125–29, 193; *1972*, 250–51; *1973*, 88–89, 92, 96, 129, 261; *1974*, 88, 98; and built-in flexibility, 184–85; and business cycle, 18; effects of increases, 98–108, 138; effects on tax yield, 188–96; and reform schemes, 116–29, 149–50, 259; and regressivity, 20, 130, 135, 138–39; tax rate effects, 92–94
CES. *See* Constant elasticity of substitution
Chase, Samuel B., Jr., 161$n$
Cobb-Douglas production function, 33
Cohen, Wilbur J., 7, 22$n$
Colbert, Jean Baptiste, 2$n$
Collective bargaining: employer tax effect, 6, 80; and incidence, 25; payroll tax effect, 16; and private pensions, 28
Commuter tax, 4, 6; migration effect, 19, 240
Constant elasticity of substitution (CES) function: in cross-country regression, 64–65, 67; in time series analysis, 74
Consumption: and incidence concept, 53; payroll tax effect, 24, 186–88, 218–19, 234–36, 249; study assumption, 53; tax transfer effect, 50–52
Cook, L. D., 82$n$
Corporation income tax, 5, 38, 208
Cross-section regression: CES function,

281